REAR
WINDOW

REAR WINDOW

The Making of a Hitchcock Masterpiece in the Hollywood Golden Age

JENNIFER O'CALLAGHAN

CITADEL PRESS
Kensington Publishing Corp.
kensingtonbooks.com

To Vlad, with love.

CONTENTS

MEET THE CAST

Alfred Hitchcock—The Auteur Who Pulled the Strings
Jimmy Stewart—The Everyman with the Camera Lens
Grace Kelly—The Glacial Blonde Who Seduced America
Raymond Burr—The Suspicious Neighbor across the Courtyard
Thelma Ritter—The Insurance Nurse Who Lightened the Mood
Cornell Woolrich—The Pulp Fiction Writer with the Idea
John Michael Hayes—The Wordsmith Who Pulled It All Together

SUPPORTING PLAYERS

Edith Head, Wendell Corey, Georgine Darcy, Ingrid Bergman, Alma Hitchcock, Prince Rainier III, Gloria Hatrick McLean, François Truffaut, Anita Colby, Sheldon Abend, David O. Selznick

Just a Little Neighborhood Murder

HOLLYWOOD'S POSTWAR GOLDEN AGE WAS SOMEWHAT OF A DOUBLE-EDGED sword. In one sense, it was like a dream you didn't want to wake from. Legendary stars were born, and no, they weren't just like us (at least, not according to the publicity machine that pumped them out). Gene Kelly joyfully hoofed his way through the rain with astonishing athleticism, while Bette Davis radiated a brand of self-assurance that mere mortals could only dream of attaining. After the horror and trauma of World War II, American cinema was a welcome delight that helped everyone wipe recent difficulties from their memory. On the other hand, it clearly wasn't a time synonymous with unfiltered self-expression. The experimental French New Wave and New Hollywood eras of the sixties and seventies were a long way off, and film studios were playing it safe budget-wise as they competed with the increasing popularity of television.

One of the biggest threats to cinematic creativity was the Hays Code, a set of strict guidelines implemented by the film industry in 1934 that prohibited profanity, nudity, sex, and graphic violence. Consequently, it became an arduous undertaking to produce a remotely true-to-life film. Not only that, the strained atmosphere in Hollywood was burdensome, as U.S. senator Joseph McCarthy initiated a communist witch hunt that divided the film community. Some of the top creative talents in Hollywood were blacklisted from the industry, and a sense of doom lurked in the air.

In 1953, legendary producer Joshua Logan sent a film treatment to Alfred Hitchcock for an experimental mainstream film that no one had yet attempted. In spite of the rigid rules of postwar Hollywood, Hitchcock knew this envelope-pushing movie had to be made. Being a voyeuristic tale, it was appropriately titled *Rear Window*. To his surprise, or perhaps as he had predicted, it would go on to become one of the most highly acclaimed films in American history for its authentic portrayal of human behavior.

Rear Window's plot was unexpectedly ordinary. Adapted from mystery writer Cornell Woolrich's short story "It Had to Be Murder," an action photographer with a broken leg is holed up in his New York apartment. From his wheelchair, with a bird's-eye view into neighbors' windows across the courtyard, he witnesses a gruesome murder . . . or does he? Aided by the mobility of his loving girlfriend (whom he fails to appreciate) and his plucky nurse (who serves as his voice of reason), he gradually learns the truth about his neighbor Lars Thorwald (the man across the courtyard who might be a stone-cold murderer).

When Hitchcock presented the premise to Paramount, *Rear Window* seemed very un-Hollywood on paper. With the limited setting, mostly filmed in a shabby, dark room of the protagonist's apartment, studio executives weren't sure what to make of it. It was also possible during such a conservative time in history, audiences could morally object to its voyeuristic nature, but Hitchcock played on his skills of persuasion and convinced the studio to support his vision.

Once *Rear Window* was greenlit, it would need a script that breathed humanity into a noir short story that lacked warmth and romance. Added to the pressure, Hitchcock had the impossible task of casting an actress who held her own opposite Jimmy Stewart—a woman with strength of conviction, who was also the picture of femininity. In a film this special, the actress would have to be ethereal, almost not of this world. In the days of pinups and girls next door, where would he find such an actress?

With all the creative challenges *Rear Window* presented, it's a wonder that Hitchcock moved forward with it. In an era of lighthearted musicals and happily-ever-after romances, this Peeping Tom tale didn't sound like it would have crowds lining up at the box office. Though the story was simple and limited to one dingy location, Hitchcock and his key players dug into its universal themes of human suffering and loneliness. If the writing and sequences were tight enough, the risk might pay off.

One of the biggest gambles of all was the lead character, L. B. "Jeff" Jefferies. He wasn't a cookie-cutter hero or a moralist do-gooder. He spent his days spying on neighbors across the courtyard and passing judgment without understanding their life circumstances. How would the audience empathize enough to invest in him for 112 whole minutes? Where would a loving romance fit in with such a morbid crime? Most alarmingly, with the moral code in place, how would Hitchcock get away with conveying a murder where a man actually *disposes* parts of his wife in the flower bed and the East River? But *Rear Window* was not your average murder mystery, and Hitchcock's secret weapons of subtlety and symbolism (sharpened by the silent era) were ultimately the backbone of the film.

In the fifties, a woman's place was at home in the kitchen, but *Rear Window* would flip these gender stereotypes with a courageous, career-driven woman and a cynical, invalid man capable of change. Thanks to the eventual casting of Grace Kelly and Jimmy Stewart, this unlikely dynamic would come alive on-screen and even offer movie-goers a new perspective on relationships. For the first time, a commercially successful film would force its audience to examine their inner life and the way they regarded others. *Rear Window* held a mirror to society without preaching. It simply presented the universal facts of human behavior.

With all that was working against him in the early fifties, how did Hitchcock manage to pull off an accessible film that still retained its art house appeal? And how did he eventually discover America's soon-to-be dream girl, Grace Kelly? This book is about this special group of people and the history they made with *Rear Window* in the glorious, turbulent Golden Age.

REAR
WINDOW

CHAPTER ONE

Juggling Wolves in Hollywood

GREENWICH VILLAGE GOES TO LA-LA LAND

ALFRED HITCHCOCK SETTLED HIS HEAVY FRAME INTO HIS DIRECTOR'S chair and peered up at the most magnificent indoor set Hollywood had ever created. He exhaled a sigh of relief. This was it. *Rear Window*. Its portrayal of pure cinema would be revolutionary, and perhaps even make motion picture history. By midway through production, the film's genius was obvious to everyone and a feverish excitement was building around the Paramount lot. Further indulging his reverie, Hitchcock sensed that *Rear Window* could be the film to finally win him a Best Director Oscar. So far, it wasn't hard to see why. Stage 18 had previously been home to the palatial mansion of *Sunset Boulevard* in 1950, but three years later, it was now unrecognizable. The Paramount crew had convincingly transformed the set into Manhattan's Greenwich Village.

The action would take place in a terra-cotta brick apartment building, complete with a lush grassy courtyard and changing views of the New York skyline, depending on the time of day. The set construction ran from October 12 until November 13, 1953, and involved digging thirty feet beneath the soundstage floor level, where the imaginary Manhattan street would begin. Not since Cecil B. DeMille's *Samson and Delilah* (1949) had Paramount greenlit such an elaborate design.

Not only that, this remarkable set had just saved *Rear Window* from its demise.

Some days prior, trouble began to brew when the Production Code Administration office, also known as the Breen Office (named after PCA vice president Joseph Breen), expressed serious reservations about the *Rear Window* script. Thirty-four-year-old screenwriter John Michael Hayes had worked swiftly to deliver the final version as production began on November 27, but because it didn't adhere to "the rules," it now looked as though the whole film might collapse.

Nicknamed the "Hays Code" (after Will H. Hays, president of the Motion Picture Producers and Distributors of America), its guidelines had censored American cinema since 1934. Written by Jesuit priest Father Daniel A. Lord and American publisher Martin Quigley, the Code was designed so Hollywood could police itself and avoid outside censorship. But what began as an advisory snowballed into a moral obligation all Hollywood directors were expected to follow or face the banning of their films in certain regions. With virtually no wiggle room, it spelled out in rigid form the rules regarding unacceptable conduct on violence, sexuality, colorful language, and nudity.

Script submission to the Production Code Office was stressful, even with the most squeaky-clean of screenplays. It was easy for the office to swiftly reject a picture based on what was written on the page. Since the Code executives didn't concern themselves with luxuries like artistic integrity, directors could never be too careful about how they presented things in text.

In the case of *Rear Window*, the PCA office's objections were to the "sexual suggestiveness" and "voyeuristic quality" of the screenplay. Concerning the young, sexy, scantily clad building tenant, Miss Torso, portrayed by unknown actress and dancer Georgine Darcy, they complained, "The picturization of a young girl described as wearing only black panties is unacceptable. It is apparent that she is nude above the waist, and it is only by the most judicious selection of camera angles that her nudity is concealed. This gives the entire action a flavor of a peep show, which is unacceptable." (As fans and cinephiles can attest, "peep show" was the obvious theme the director was going for.)

Hitchcock was protective of his first true opportunity to freely experiment on a large single film set. He'd worked for years to make studios wealthy and wasn't about to give in because the PCA couldn't handle the truth about human nature. And so, he dug his heels in and refused to change the script. In his mind, *Rear Window* simply described what most people would do if they saw their neighbors across the courtyard. They'd stop and watch. Without fully exploring genuine human curiosity, this picture would fall like a house of cards. *Rear Window* would become another watered-down mystery, lost in a shuffle of fifties B movies. The stakes were high, and no one was going to mess with his masterpiece.

Hitchcock had always taken the road less traveled and bucked the trends of Hollywood, and even of his home soil of London. Unlike most Hollywood directors of the fifties, he wouldn't dream of shooting one reel of film without creative storyboards in place for action sequences. His approach was slow and methodical, regardless of time pressures. This occasionally led to minor delays and flared tempers. But this time, his outside-of-the-box thinking had landed him in hot water. From the PCA office's perspective, yes, he was Alfred Hitchcock, the master of suspense, but even legends weren't above the rules.

As the fate of *Rear Window* hung in limbo, Luigi Luraschi, the Paramount liaison to the Motion Picture Association of America, had an idea. The film set, which stood forty feet high and stretched one hundred and eighty-five feet in length, had to be seen to be believed. Luigi supported Hitchcock's vision, but really, he couldn't afford to watch an investment like this go down the drain (the set cost $9,000 to design and $72,000 to build, which was unheard of in 1953). Though it was rarely done, he requested that the Production Code staff make a special trip to the set and meet with Hitchcock.

That week, the corporate suits begrudgingly made the drive to 5515 Melrose Avenue and through the grand, ornate archway of Paramount

Studios. One look at the lifelike replica of Manhattan's 125 West Ninth Street (modeled after the 125 Christopher Street complex that still stands in Greenwich Village) and they immediately began to soften. Once it was explained with a visual aid that the entire action would be filmed from the viewpoint of Jimmy Stewart, held captive in a wheelchair by a broken leg, staring out his rear window, it *finally* clicked. These "objectionable" things, like a young girl in her underwear or a gruesome murder, would be minimized by distance and camera angles. *Rear Window* wasn't a film about blatant gore or sex. Its purpose was to challenge the audience's imagination, and even their moral boundaries.

Luraschi's hunch paid off in a big way. He later noted in a studio memo, "We readily agreed that the camera location and nature of this rather extraordinary set eliminated much of the concern felt in reading the script material." The *Rear Window* set had protected the film's integrity from the wrath of the PCA, and for now, Hitchcock could rest easy. Hopefully, this film would be less painful to make than the last one.

CATASTROPHE IN 3-D

THREE MONTHS PRIOR, JUST SIX MILES NORTH OF PARAMOUNT, HITCH-cock paced back and forth on the soundstage of Warner Brothers Burbank Studios, willing himself to stay calm. *Dial M for Murder* had become the headache of all pictures. Though it was on-brand Hitchcock with a suspenseful script about a man plotting to kill his cheating wife, filming and production had been catastrophic, to say the least. It was Hitchcock's first time shooting in 3-D (a novelty fad forced on him by the studio to compete with the rising popularity of television) and quite frankly, it was destroying the picture. From the auteur's perspective, 3-D contradicted the immersive film experience instead of enhancing it. It reminded the audience that they were removed from the story and created an inaccessible wall to their emotional involvement.

The technical limitations of the process were frustrating, and the crew struggled to lug around the oversized, bulky cameras. Because they had to shoot in wide angles, the set was staged more like a theater production than a film. With the invasion of television sets, Warner Brothers previously had to close their studios for five months due to declining movie attendance and encouraged filmmakers to resort to every gimmick in the book to fill up theaters again. Hitchcock's hands were tied. Though he was miserable, his spirit wasn't broken. There was a shining beacon of hope that kept him going throughout the madness. He'd just read the thirteen-page treatment for a film called *Rear Window* sent to him by film and theater producer Joshua Logan. For the first time in years, he was simply giddy.

Grace Kelly, who worked with Hitchcock for the first time in *Dial M for Murder*, remembered, "The only reason Hitch could remain calm was because he was already preparing for *Rear Window*. He sat and talked to me about it all the time, even before we had discussed my being in it. He was very enthusiastic as he described all the details for a fabulous set while we were waiting for the camera to be pushed around." She added, "I was just an interested listener, and because I was under contract at MGM, I didn't even think about whether there was a role for me in it."

Rear Window was adapted from mystery writer Cornell Woolrich's 1942 short story initially named "It Had to Be Murder." By the mid-forties, Cornell, who also went by the pen name William Irish, was one of the originators of the paperback noir genre. His books were often nightmarish with zigzag plots and possessed a gothic bleakness often compared with Edgar Allan Poe. Though a prominent name in mystery, he would always play second fiddle to the master stylist of crime at the time, Raymond Chandler. Also, Cornell wasn't for everyone. Some readers couldn't get past the inconsistencies of his storytelling, which sometimes took bizarre tangents, but Hitchcock was entranced by "It Had to Be Murder." Making the antihero a typical Peeping Tom confined to his apartment by an injury (and who witnesses a hideous murder from his window) struck the director as pure genius.

Besides sharing a mutual love of the creepy, Hitchcock and Cornell also had social clumsiness in common. Though Hitchcock's interpersonal awkwardness and issues with actresses are well documented, Cornell was also a man who struggled to connect with others and maintain friendships. He spent most of his life as an alcoholic who rarely left home. With the amount that Hitchcock had borrowed theme-wise from Cornell's work over the years, one might assume the two shared a unique creative kinship, but that wasn't likely on Cornell's part. After *Rear Window*'s theatrical release, he bitterly complained, "Hitchcock wouldn't even send me a ticket to the premiere in New York. He knew where I lived."

Rear Window's protagonist, L. B. Jefferies (known as Hal Jefferies in the short story), was nothing short of a curmudgeon, and like Cornell, he had a vivid imagination. Hitchcock knew that bringing this complex man to life on-screen would take a chameleonlike actor who still appealed to the masses as a ticket-selling star. Consequently, in early 1953, Hitchcock and one of his favorite leading men, Jimmy Stewart, jointly acquired the rights to *Rear Window*, with Jimmy set to star as Jefferies.

Having reentered the studio system in 1945 after serving in World War II, Jimmy had spent the last few years trying to carve out a new place for himself in Hollywood. "I guess I'd only be suitable for playing grandfather to Mickey Rooney," the thirty-seven-year-old joked to a *New York Times* reporter in 1947. Coming back to the ever-changing mecca of Hollywood was a tricky transition at the best of times, but the war had changed everything. Even *It's a Wonderful Life* had flopped at the box office, despite the fact it became one of the most beloved Christmas classics of all time years later. But in 1946 after a grueling war audiences wished to put behind them, they struggled to embrace its dark themes and moments of despair.

Though Jimmy was nominated for an Oscar for *It's a Wonderful Life*, he still felt himself floating, grasping for a sense of identity in this now unfamiliar town. But help was on the way. He gradually began to play against type and dip his toe into morally ambiguous waters with Hitchcock's *Rope* (1948) and Anthony Mann's Wild West hit *Winchester '73* (1950). Now, starring as *Rear Window*'s L. B. Jefferies would not only be a shot in the arm for Jimmy's career, but it also would challenge him to dig deep to portray the complexities and contradictions of being a flawed human.

HIRED ON THE SPOT

HOLLYWOOD VETERAN HERBERT COLEMAN STOOD ON THE *DIAL M FOR Murder* soundstage in 1953 and watched Grace Kelly and Ray Milland rehearse a scene. Hitchcock leaned back in his director's chair stationed under the camera with his name emblazoned across the back and studied the actors with stern focus. He was difficult to read with his hooded eyes and curiously blank expression. Herbert would later recognize this as Hitchcock's meditative process while the wheels of brilliance turned in his head. It was usually best not to disturb him in these moments. "You have it," Hitchcock finally said, his quiet but authoritative voice barely audible.

Herbert had been on the Paramount payroll for over thirty years and had risen through the ranks as a script clerk to then become one of Hollywood's most in-demand assistant directors. Hitchcock requested a meeting with Herbert in light of the buzz that surrounded him after he'd been honored by the Directors Guild of America for his work on William Wyler's *Roman Holiday* (1953).

As Grace and Ray left the soundstage and headed toward their dressing rooms, Hitchcock, in his uniform black suit and tie, pushed his stout body out of the chair and walked over to introduce himself. He politely greeted Herbert but didn't shake his hand. When they made their way to Hitchcock's production office, they met with Mac Johnson, who'd been hired as art director to design the *Rear Window* set. He presented the plan for the bustling street, alley, and Jimmy

Stewart's second-floor apartment, which would technically be located on the soundstage's ground floor.

Hitchcock suddenly turned to Herbert. "Do you have any questions, Mr. Coleman?" In a sudden outpour of anxiety, Herbert expressed his concerns about the timing and scheduling surrounding a one-set shoot. This seemed an extremely ambitious project and making a feature film on this type of set was clearly out of his depth. As he listened, Hitchcock's face gave nothing away. Finally, he responded. "You'll decide the number of days we need to produce *Rear Window* after you've read our script, Mr. Coleman." Herbert was hired on the spot and would be Hitchcock's right-hand man for years to come.

Before filming began, Hitchcock invited Herbert to his cottage-style home, which overlooked the Bel-Air Country Club golf course. When he anxiously rang the doorbell, he was put at ease when a friendly, pint-sized woman with auburn hair answered in a pair of white shorts and cotton T-shirt. In a voice of radiant warmth, she said, "You must be Herbie Coleman. I'm Alma. Hitch is waiting in the living room." He liked her immediately.

As Hitchcock's wife led him to the living room, Hitchcock was dressed exactly the way he had been on-set, in a starched white shirt, blazer, and tie, not a button undone. Even in the comfort of his home, an awareness of self-branding never escaped him. To Herbert's surprise, it was a relaxed afternoon of chilled white wine, casual conversation, and a tour of Hitchcock's personal art collection. With an editing background herself, Alma's influence on Hitchcock's work was something Herbert was curious about. He wanted to know more, but not a word about *Rear Window* or film at all for that matter was spoken that day.

Later, Herbert drove back to his oceanfront home in Newport Beach as the sun beamed down. He had a slight buzz from the afternoon. Hitchcock was a peculiar man, but there was no question of his genius. Herbert wasn't sure what to make of the *Rear Window* concept. There was no telling how it would land with a fickle postwar audience, but intuition told him there was something special there, though it was hard to define.

Film editor George Tomasini would join the team next and end up working with Hitchcock on ten consecutive pictures until his death after cutting *Marnie* in 1964. Another key hire on the *Rear Window* crew was Clarence "Doc" Erickson as production manager. And of course, legendary designer Edith Head, a star in her own right, would design the costumes. Famous for her dark-framed glasses and impeccable taste, she dressed the biggest film actresses in the world, from Bette Davis to Elizabeth Taylor. With a growing concoction of exceptional talents, the stars were beginning to align.

Preproduction for *Rear Window* was now moving along, but amid Hitchcock's excitement, something gnawed at the back of his mind. If he was going to make a one-set revolutionary film experiment *and* attract a wide audience of moviegoers, there were still some considerable hurdles in his way. For one, he had no muse. And the last one had abandoned him.

Hitchcock had been romantically obsessed with Ingrid Bergman when they made box office hits like *Spellbound* (1945) and *Notorious* (1946) together. As many attested, Hitchcock had a habit of this. Though some thought it was a harmless fantasy, others thought he went too far. "Nothing happened, nothing came of this fantasy romance—he often had to fall in love with his leading ladies," Herbert later said. It was a pattern that had begun with Madeleine Carroll in 1935 and was repeated with Ingrid from 1944 through 1948.

Ingrid's talent and elegance had fed his creativity, or so he believed. He even secretly studied her personal life (her relationship with the famous war photographer Robert Capa would later serve as the inspiration behind L. B. Jefferies and Lisa Fremont's central love story in *Rear Window*). In 1949, Bergman caused a Hollywood scandal by leaving her husband for director Roberto Rossellini. When she moved to Italy to make films with him, Hitchcock was crushed. In the years following her departure, he'd searched far and wide for that "Hitchcockian" quality in another actress but came up empty-handed. Where would he find someone with a presence as commanding yet feminine as Ingrid's? It was like hunting for a shadow in the dark, and after a fruitless search, he had begun to resign himself to a muse-less creative life.

The second challenge, not just for *Rear Window*, but for all of Hollywood, was the extensive number of screenwriters who'd been blacklisted from the industry in the past six years because of their communist beliefs. A Hollywood professional could be blacklisted for doing as little as expressing curiosity in a communist-based organization or attending one of their meetings. Prolific talents like screenwriter Dalton Trumbo were no longer permitted to take credit for their work, or even work at all. Some even faced jail time and a life of ostracization.

Wisconsin Senator Joseph McCarthy initiated a witch hunt in 1947, resulting in an investigation of hundreds of suspected communists. It became a challenge to pick through the most talented writers, who were becoming less available by the day. In October 1947, ten motion picture producers, directors, and screenwriters including Dalton, Edward Dmytryk, and Herbert Biberman appeared before the House of Un-American Activities Committee refusing to answer questions regarding their possible communist affiliations. After spending time in prison for contempt of Congress and being blacklisted by the Hollywood studios, they were infamously referred to as the Hollywood Ten. An air of fear and surveillance infiltrated the years as the late forties gave way to the early fifties.

Amid an atmosphere of mistrust in the industry, *Rear Window* required a screenwriter who could create suspense at a primal level, while simultaneously weaving in a genuine love story that spoke from the heart. Though he'd be the last to admit it, Hitchcock was in a definite career slump. His independent company, Transatlantic Pictures, had failed, and his last film, *I Confess* (1953), though it featured Montgomery Clift's matinee-idol looks—hadn't been much of a box office draw. He realized he'd need to adapt to the changing postwar fifties, but he couldn't do it alone. He needed an injection of new blood, someone who could bring something fresh to the table. As luck would have it, lightning was about to strike twice for Hitchcock.

In what could only be described as a cosmic alignment, Hitchcock was introduced to industry newcomer John Michael Hayes in the spring of 1953. Hitchcock and John Michael shared the same agent, Lew Wasserman at MCA. Lew had a hunch that combining these two very different talents may create the synergy *Rear Window* needed to jump off the page. John Michael was young and not a Hollywood veteran by any stretch. However, he had a solid background in radio mystery, and he was hungry and hard-working. He also had a knack for believably connecting with characters' inner lives. Besides, Hitchcock could get him for cheap. Wasserman's gut feeling proved correct when the two men hit it off. "I brought him accidentally . . . or however, through my own devices a fresh viewpoint on things—on suspense," John Michael later reflected.

Meanwhile, on the *Dial M* set, Hitchcock gradually got to know another Hollywood newcomer, Grace Kelly. In the film's most iconic scene, an in-home attacker approaches her from behind, attempting to strangle her to death with a scarf while she answers a late-night phone call. Thwarting his plan, she stabs him with a pair of scissors sitting nearby. This scene marked one of Hitchcock's most violent moments up to that date. Predictably, in the end, he was forced to trim the sequence to decrease the violence and satisfy the PCA, but he still got his point across. As he observed the dailies of Grace's performance as the resourceful Margot Wendice, he noticed something rare.

Any fool could see that Grace's beauty and elegance were breathtaking, but what truly dumbfounded Hitchcock was her grasp of the power of subtlety. It was that elusive quality he loved in actors. She wouldn't just be a leading woman, but a leading *lady*. He'd make sure of it. "Until I met Grace, I just wanted to get through this thing (*Dial M*) as quickly and unceremoniously as I could," said Hitchcock. "Then I realized, here was a girl I could really do something with."

Again, those familiar feelings began to flood Hitchcock's mind and bring him back to the days of Ingrid Bergman. Not only had he found a new muse, but here was the ultimate "Hitchcock Blonde." Hitchcock typically preferred to work with blondes; in his mind, they simply photographed better against dark, somber backgrounds. With the unique blend of a cool, controlled persona and a sensual blazing heat just beneath the surface, twenty-four-year-old Grace eclipsed the rest of Hollywood. *Rear Window*'s assistant director Herbert Coleman later said, "Everyone in the production company of *Rear Window* fell for her. Not only Hitch. Everyone wanted to bring her a cup of tea or run an errand. She never asked, much less did she demand anything, but everyone wanted to show how much they admired her. I think sometimes it made her uncomfortable."

In the *Rear Window* script, Grace's character, Lisa Fremont, observes Jefferies's shapely neighbor whom he's nicknamed "Miss Torso" across the courtyard, balancing the attention of multiple male suitors. She sighs in recognition and reflects that a woman's hardest job is "juggling wolves." Perhaps John Michael Hayes's turn of phrase subconsciously referred to the wolves of Hollywood. These were the wolves that Hitchcock's team was eternally juggling, smoothing things over with, and keeping at bay.

TROUBLE ON STAGE 18

SINCE PRODUCTION BEGAN, THE *REAR WINDOW* TEAM HAD MANAGED TO ward off the PCA office with a grandiose set, and with the anti-communist blacklist still in effect, Hitchcock had miraculously found the ideal screenwriter, but every element of preproduction was one battle after another. There was the meticulous casting of the supporting actors who would play the eccentric neighbors, left to Herbert, of course. Also, the challenge of adding a love story to a film about a gruesome murder. Even when filming began, a new whirlwind of issues circled

Stage 18. The revolutionary set may have solved political problems with the PCA, but it created a slew of technical worries for the crew.

For the courtyard, laborers had to dig thirty feet below the stage level, so far that they struck water, and a small electric motor had to be installed to pump out the sump between takes, so as not to cause noise disturbance. Adding to that, entirely new camera techniques of synchronized movement would be needed to fully capture each neighbor's apartment on the set. Lighting to differentiate between day and night was an arduous task as well. Paramount Publicity reported, "More than one thousand giant arc lights were needed to light the set from overhead, while more than two thousand smaller variety lamps were necessary for supplemental lighting." The actors practically melted beneath them.

Jimmy Stewart remembered, "The heat of the lights was really intense. Suddenly in the middle of it, the lights set off the sprinkler system on all stages. Everybody stopped as we plunged into wet darkness, but it never fazed Hitchcock!" As the stages became fully drenched, the director calmly told his assistant to get the sprinklers shut off, but in the meantime, to bring him an umbrella, for Pete's sake.

Adding to that, Hitchcock's deliberately lagging pace was misunderstood by many (his ex-producer, David O. Selznick, on whom he'd based *Rear Window*'s villain, Lars Thorwald, once called him the "slowest director we have ever had" and "a fundamentally lazy man"). When filming initially began to run behind schedule, the studio head, Y. Frank Freeman, was compelled to prompt a pointed memo to Hitchcock to hurry things up. It simply read, "Daily shooting average has dropped to 4.85. An average of 6.75 is needed to complete picture on a 24-day schedule." This would mean the budget would go over. It was nothing new for Hitchcock, but this being his first Paramount film, it hadn't made the best impression. But no matter. Hitchcock had an inkling the box office return on this picture would more than make up for it.

Another more personal matter were the rumors that often swirled around Grace Kelly's love life—some true and many false—for getting involved with her leading men. Grace was mysterious and unreadable to the public, like an incarnation of an all-American Greta Garbo. Because of that, the gossip columns felt it only natural to invent stories about her life off-camera and create a persona that didn't always align with reality.

There was talk through the grapevine that during the filming of *Dial M*, she had gotten involved with her married costar, Ray Milland. However, there is no record of Hitchcock, a lover of juicy gossip, or other members of the production ever mentioning it. Even as far back as her debut in *High Noon*, a photo had been taken of Grace sitting on Gary Cooper's knee while they practiced a scene. Because they weren't in costume, the gossip columns concluded that a secret affair was the obvious explanation. Her need for privacy didn't suit the tabloid fodder, and manufactured stories haunted her, even long after her death.

The gossip rags always left Jimmy Stewart alone. With his down-home likability and war record in the air force, no hint of scandal could touch him, even if it tried. Jim Katz, former president of the Universal Classics division and a close friend, confirmed that he lived up to his on-screen persona. "He had a nice wife and lovely family," said Jim. "He was just the nicest guy." Jimmy embodied the urban legend of the film star who managed to lead a quiet life while maintaining a Hollywood career that transcended time and trends. "I had many, many instances over the years working with famous actors and directors, and more times than not, meeting them was disappointing," Jim said. "Jimmy Stewart was the opposite. He was everything you thought he would be."

Even with the brightest stars in Hollywood attached, such an experimental film with its political issues and messy technical hurdles could alienate audiences if mishandled—not to mention at the height of the conservative postwar era. The creative and financial risks would have caused most directors to throw in the towel by now. But not Hitchcock. He thrived under the pressure of creating something no one else had done. *Rear Window* would not only appeal to the entire moviegoing public, but it would make film history. This new journey would be nerve-racking, unfamiliar, and at times inconceivable, but Hitchcock had entered a new chapter and was up to the challenge of making the impossible possible.

Hitchcock was never fazed by the madness around him, no matter how hysterical the stuffed shirts got over timetables or how anxious actors became before the camera rolled. He faced each daily problem, whether creative or technical, with a detached scrutiny. Herbert later wrote about Hitchcock, "He was unlike most of the directors I'd worked with. His composed features showed absolutely no emotion, no reaction to the tense scene he was watching."

Over a decade later, while attempting to put into words the significance *Rear Window* held on a personal level, Hitchcock told French director François Truffaut, "You have an immobilized man looking out. That's one part of the film. The second part shows how he reacts. This is the purest expression of a cinematic idea."

After thirty years of contemplating his thoughts on life through a camera lens, some of it rewarding, and some of it, like *Dial M for Murder*, decidedly not, Hitchcock would soon realize his biggest dream of all—making pure cinema on his own terms.

CHAPTER TWO

An Auteur Goes Window Shopping

TIED UP

JIMMY STEWART WAS WORRIED. THE YEAR 1948 HAD GOTTEN OFF TO A bumpy start with the filming of *Rope*. It was his first time working with Alfred Hitchcock and so far, the tension on the Warner Brothers sound-stage was palpable. He wasn't used to this way of doing things. These drawn-out scenes with mountains of dialogue were migraine-inducing. And though he had top billing, Jimmy wouldn't make his entrance un-til twenty-eight minutes into the picture. *Rope* was filmed chronologi-cally, so when he was finally called to the set after committing endless lines to memory, all he could do was sit, wait, and hope for the best. But as he looked around, he realized it wasn't just him. Most actors on set seemed visibly anxious about the upcoming scene.

The role was intriguing enough. Jimmy played the philosophical Professor Rupert Cadell, a man who attends a dinner party and even-tually discovers his two students are guilty of murdering a former class-mate. In oversimplifying Cadell's teachings, which drew on Friedrich Nietzsche's questioning of conventional morality, they use it to justify strangling a young man to death with a rope.

For added effect, the victim's body is hidden in an antique wooden chest in the party room. As the guests file in, a spread of hors d'oeuvres is served on top of it so that in a morbid sense, they're essentially eating off a dead man's coffin. The single set featured a large window with panoramic New York views that filled with orange evening sky as day transformed to night. The romantic horizon of *Rope*'s backdrop was like a promise of things to come with *Rear Window*'s more elaborate set six years later.

The technical innovator that he was, Hitchcock had long desired to capture a theatrical production on film. When the chance arose to adapt the 1929 play *Rope* to the screen, he was determined to film it seamlessly, mirroring the experience of watching a stage performance. To create the illusion of a single continuous shot, *Rope* was filmed in a series of ten-minute-long takes (the maximum amount of film that a camera could hold in 1948). To everyone's frustration, if the take was interrupted or a line was missed, they would need to begin the scene again.

Furniture and props were placed on casters and the crew was forced to wheel them out of the way as the oversized camera awkwardly moved around the set. To fulfill Hitchcock's vision, the reel changes were disguised by actors walking in front of the camera. For other cuts, the camera closed in on an actor's back while the cameraman reloaded the film and zoomed out again from the same actor's back. "From the beginning, he told me he was going to do it as a play, and that interested him because it hadn't been done," said screenwriter Arthur Laurents. "It seemed to me to be a gimmick, but who was I? He was the great Hitchcock."

By this point in his life, Jimmy had won an Academy Award for *The Philadelphia Story* and served as a bomber pilot in World War II, but working on a production like *Rope* was an unequivocal first. To appease the master of suspense, each actor held their breath and prayed they'd summon the correct dialogue when it was their turn. Hearing Hitchcock bellow "Cut!" at the end of each scene was a sweet solace of relief.

After what seemed like an eternity, it was time for Jimmy's dominant entrance. With an air of calm, he waited alongside costars John

Dall and Farley Granger as the crew marked the scene, but anxiety brewed within. In this scene, guests inquire as to the professor's whereabouts, when he suddenly appears as if out of thin air, as one of the culprits, Phillip (Farley Granger), clumsily plays French composer Francis Poulenc's "Perpetual Movement No. 1" on the piano.

"Okay, everybody," announced the assistant director. "Here we go." Director of photography Joseph Valentine and cameramen Ed Fitzgerald stood by and waited on Hitchcock's cue.

Jimmy took a breath and braced himself.

All was silent. Hitchcock called action.

The soft music began to build and then fell silent as he walked toward the piano. All eyes were on Jimmy. He stopped on his mark, speaking the words he'd painstakingly labored at. "Your touch has improved, Phillip—"

"Just a minute," Hitchcock cut in ending the scene. "I'd like you to make your entrance differently."

Jimmy punched the air in frustration. "Hey, look," he complained to Hitchcock, "I've waited three weeks for this!" But, ever the professional, he gathered himself and walked back to his old mark to begin again.

At one point, the continuity pressures even got to Hitchcock. While speaking to Dick Cavett in 1972, the auteur reminisced about the opening scene, which filmed seven hundred and fifty feet without a cut. It began with the murder and followed the culprits into the dining room and kitchen. "You hold your breath, fearing something will go wrong," he said. "As the camera came back, I said, 'Thank goodness this shot's over,' and then as we pan around, there's an electrician standing there . . . right in the window!" This kind of mishap was an anomaly though, as the crew went to unimaginable lengths to ensure no interruptions. The stagehands had the most significant jobs on set, as they continually moved around candlesticks, trays of drinks, and even the walls, which were also on rollers. They juggled this with simultaneously climbing over cables to catch falling objects and remove every distraction from the camera's eyeline.

In a nuanced performance by John Dall and Farley Granger, it was unclear to audiences of the postwar era that the two murderers were lovers, as the subtext was evident to very few moviegoers. *Rope* screenwriter Arthur Laurents later said, "I don't think the censors at that time realized this was about gay people. They didn't have a clue what was and what wasn't; that's how it got by." Because it went over the heads of the PCA office, no objections were made and *Rope* remained as it was.

Although Jimmy and Hitchcock were beginning to develop a solid professional friendship, this wasn't an experience he'd soon forget. "*Rope* wasn't my favorite picture," Jimmy told his friend Henry Fonda and others whenever someone asked how filming went. At the time, the general public may have agreed—if its lackluster performance at the box office was anything to go by.

THE ANTI-METHOD ACTOR

AFTER THEIR FIRST COLLABORATION, HITCHCOCK WAS RATHER SMITTEN with Jimmy Stewart. Immediately, he mentally shifted Jimmy to his list of top leading men, alongside Cary Grant. There was no doubt he was special. Jimmy was an everyman with a rough exterior that contradicted the vulnerable inner life within. Whenever he saw the actor on-screen, Hitchcock felt he was watching his feelings about the human experience. And the respect was mutual. After *Rope* failed at the box office, Jimmy told gossip columnist Louella Parsons that it had been nothing more than "an experiment. I'm glad I did it and I'll go on the record as saying I'll make a picture for Alfred Hitchcock anytime."

In the auteur's films, the "Hitchcockian" man is generally conflicted in his predicaments, whether psychologically or romantically (usually both). He knew Jimmy could pull that off, but he had another advantage over the others—the elusive ability to transcend time. "Jimmy Stewart knew how to act in a supremely natural, understated manner that was down-to-earth and that's why his performances hold up today," said film historian and Turner Classic Movies contributor Sloan De Forest. "A lot of actors in that era could be very affected in their performances or heightened style. It wasn't necessarily bad, but, it's what we would consider artificial now." In a film like *Rear Window*, a one-note actor who spied on neighbors would potentially come off as a shifty-eyed lecher. But Jimmy's paradox of qualities could transform L. B. Jefferies into a relatable human being.

Though some actors struggled under Hitchcock's directing style, Jimmy was fully at home with it. It was a well-known fact the auteur often provided actors with little in the way of emotional motivation. Right before the camera rolled, he sometimes sat expressionless and silent, like a ghost in his director's chair. There were no pep talks and certainly no discussion of a character's subconscious beliefs or underlying intentions. This suited Jimmy just fine. He liked being given the space and trust to follow his journey in character development.

However, this style didn't always mesh with the new generation of Method actors like Montgomery Clift when he worked with Hitchcock in *I Confess* (1953) nor with Paul Newman on the set of *Torn Curtain* (1966). The two original champions of Method Acting, Lee Strasberg and Sanford Meisner, won devotees like Marlon Brando and James Dean, who religiously attended their classes throughout the fifties. These actors often wouldn't audition for a role without doing a run-through with their gurus first. Strasberg originated "emotion memory" exercises, while Meisner taught actors to visualize the character's history, thoughts, and feelings in the text.

Undeniably, a new wave of acting had migrated west from the studios of New York. These actors, drawing from their own life experiences for their performances, wanted to delve into a character's Freudian backstory, much to Hitchcock's irritation. To this, his response was, "It's a movie. You're an actor. Act." "That was also very much Dad's attitude towards acting," said Jimmy's daughter Kelly Stewart Harcourt. "It's a craft. He felt that you're not supposed to actually *become* your character. He viewed Hitchcock as a real craftsman and genuinely enjoyed the process with him."

Notably, many actors, like Anthony Perkins and Kim Novak, who fully surrendered to Hitchcock's direction once they entered the set often received the best reviews of their careers. "There seemed to be a real trust in Hitchcock from the people he directed and his ability to pull things out of you," said filmmaker and director of *Rear Window Ethics: Remembering and Restoring a Hitchcock Classic* Laurent Bouzereau. "He got some of the best performances from the actors he worked with."

Objectively speaking, every actor has a unique journey or detour to convincingly play a character. As acting styles changed in Hollywood, Method Acting wasn't necessarily viewed as superior to Jimmy Stewart's or Cary Grant's process or vice versa. And though Method stars, like Marlon Brando and Marilyn Monroe, soared in popularity throughout the fifties and sixties, Hitchcock stood his ground. His stance was that he'd never be on board with actors who deviated from the script or cost the film money by spending hours in their dressing room doing authenticity exercises.

UNDER THE RADAR

AS IS PAR FOR THE COURSE IN THE CINEMATIC WORLD, THOUGH *ROPE* wasn't a hit on its release, it was reexamined decades later as a standout classic. When it was reviewed a second time in 1984 by the *New York Times*, critic Vincent Canby wrote, "Hitchcock loved to put himself, as a filmmaker, into positions as impossible as those in which he placed his characters. One cannot understand the truly bold originality of the man without seeing it." And referring to its homosexual undertones, which went completely under the radar in 1948, Canby noted, "*Rope* is immediately explicit without actually committing any offenses the Production Code people could object to."

With the context of the sheer tension Jimmy and the rest of the cast experienced within those ten-minute takes, the silver lining was now clear. Hitchcock's one-set experiment added tremendously to the story's heightened emotional build-up because it was genuine anxiety portrayed on the screen. *Rope*'s unique appeal was birthed from the un-manufactured tension and suspense projected by a terrified cast and crew.

When asked by the *New York Times* in 1983 which of the four Hitchcock films he made between 1948 and 1958 was the most stress-inducing, Jimmy hadn't changed his position on *Rope*. "As the end of the reel came closer and closer I was conscious of everyone's getting sort of glassy-eyed. All of us thinking, 'Oh God, don't let me go up on my lines *now!*'" But he ultimately laughed off the difficulties in the end. "When I finished the picture I was talking to Hitch," Jimmy said. "I said, 'You know I think you missed the boat a little with this one-set thing. You should've built bleachers around it and soaked them five, ten bucks to watch us do this!'"

But the struggles hadn't been so lighthearted for everyone involved with *Rope*. Shortly after the release of the film, screenwriter Arthur Laurents suddenly found himself caught in the HUAC's (House of Un-American Activities Committee) crosshairs when, in 1950, *Red Channels*, a right-wing pamphlet published by three ex-FBI agents, listed him as a subversive. He even briefly lost his U.S. passport in 1952. This all came about when the *Daily Worker*, the official publication of the Communist Party USA, reviewed *Home of the Brave*, his 1945 Broadway play about anti-Semitism in the army. Laurents eventually escaped Hollywood and found steady work as a playwright on Broadway. But he'd have the last laugh in the seventies, achieving great success with the hugely popular *The Way We Were* (1973) and earning an Oscar nomination for *The Turning Point* (1977).

As postwar America marched on amidst a communist witch hunt, popular entertainment experienced a significant surge. The number of TV sets in homes eventually rose from six thousand in 1946 to twelve million by 1951. Television was now a legitimate threat to the motion picture industry. Movie theater attendance dwindled as Hollywood began to lose its audience. On Sunday evenings, families preferred to gather around the living room TV set for *The Ed Sullivan Show* instead of piling in the car and venturing out to the drive-in.

Never one to back down from a challenge, Hitchcock made *Rope* his first film in Technicolor to lure the public back to theaters. It was another experiment for a director whose black-and-white noir films had typically been the stamp of his brand. The film cost a million and a half dollars to make, and he would co-produce it with Sidney Bernstein for their company, Transatlantic Pictures. At a time when all television was broadcast in black-and-white, the ability to produce photographic color was the main advantage film had over the comforts of home entertainment.

In the late 1940s, fewer than twelve percent of Hollywood features were produced in color, but that would change by 1954 when that figure skyrocketed to over fifty percent. All thanks to the pressures of television. Hitchcock would eventually cash in on the small screen by exploiting his wry British persona on the TV series *Alfred Hitchcock Presents* throughout the 1950s. As his own best publicist, he was always ten paces ahead of the crowd.

BOTTLE BLONDE

ON THE OPPOSITE COAST, ON THE BUZZING ISLAND OF MANHATTAN, young, attractive women with stars in their eyes were taking advantage of the late-forties TV boom. There had recently been a surge in New York–based networks covering the whole country and the price of television sets continued to fall with the upswing in mass production. Wartime manufacturing freezes were lifted and it was the ticket item no one could live without. This meant a serious demand for more advertising. Madison Avenue was now swarming with agencies like BBDO, Young

& Rubicam, and Ogilvy. Since housewives were a major demographic, modeling agencies, like those founded by Eileen Ford, needed more young women to promote their products.

The Barbizon Hotel for Women became a sanctuary for fresh-out-of-college girls, who journeyed to the bustling city from various corners of America. It was a twenty-seven-story Gothic-style building that elegantly stood on Lexington and Sixty-Third Street. At twelve dollars a week, only the privileged could afford such rent. Since the roaring twenties, the Barbizon Hotel had been a refuge for the daughters of well-bred families who flooded Manhattan in search of a more glamorous life.

In later years, the Barbizon would retain a pop culture status for being home to the likes of Liza Minnelli, Sylvia Plath, and Ali MacGraw. Naturally, men weren't permitted beyond the lobby, though a young J. D. Salinger was known to stake out the building's coffee shop, and once brazenly claimed to have sneaked to the upper stories of the building to meet girls.

On a crisp, spring day in 1948, one such girl made her way out of the Barbizon's glass doors into the morning sunlight. At five foot six and a half inches, she wore glasses and a tweed pencil skirt with a cardigan that hung loosely on her lean frame. Toffee-colored waves of hair bounced around her shoulders as she walked briskly toward the American Academy of Dramatic Arts. It was located on Fifty-Seventh Street and Seventh Avenue on the upper floors of Carnegie Hall. Young Grace Kelly was a serious student of acting. Every time she entered the school, she felt a rush of excitement. After all, this place had been the training ground of her heroes, Spencer Tracy, Katharine Hepburn, and Lauren Bacall.

Grace wanted nothing more than to become an actor and follow in the footsteps of her beloved uncle George Kelly, who made a living in the theater as a playwright and director, even winning the Pulitzer Prize for Drama for *Craig's Wife*, which he also directed. Grace persuaded her family to travel to New York on February 12, 1947, for the opening night of the Broadway revival. The title role was played by Judith Evelyn, whom coincidently, Grace would reunite with when Judith portrayed the depressed Miss Lonely Hearts in *Rear Window*.

Grace's father, Jack, a pragmatic man, wasn't particularly enthusiastic about her chosen profession. A former rowing Olympian and self-made multimillionaire through his Philadelphia bricklaying and construction business, he didn't understand show business or the people it employed. It was clear Grace would need to go it alone and prove herself to her family. That would have to mean financial independence. But, like her father, Grace was no stranger to perseverance or hard work. "She told me once that she had two-hundred and fifty interviews and tryouts before she got her first paying acting job," said Grace's cousin and former secretary of the navy John Lehman. "It takes a lot of tenacity and she had a passion about it."

During her first year at the Barbizon, Grace made friends with Carolyn Scott, a fine-featured brunette, whose room was next door to hers. Carolyn had just signed with the Eileen Ford Modeling Agency. Grace, being more familiar with New York from her visits to watch her uncle's plays, showed Carolyn how to navigate the city, while Carolyn taught Grace the ropes of high fashion. "My mother was no stranger to fashion because she would literally copy all the magazines," said Carolyn's daughter Nyna Giles. "She would get the *Vogue* patterns and make everything down to the gloves and the dresses. It was amazing." Carolyn encouraged Grace to pursue the same modeling path to supplement her income. Grace immediately signed with the Walter Thornton Model Agency, the same one her mother, Margaret, had modeled for as a youth.

"My mother got Grace into modeling, partly so that she could be independent," explained Nyna. "To have her own money, and fund her acting lessons and theater career." In perhaps one of the shrewdest moves that would benefit Grace's future career, at Carolyn's suggestion, she dyed her light brown hair a golden shade of blond. Suddenly, Grace was an elegant creature, appearing in toothpaste and cigarette advertisements across the country.

As a model, Grace learned how to dress and what clothes complimented her figure. This metamorphosis, which at first glance may have seemed like a means to an end on her artistic path, actually transformed her whole appeal as an actress. Grace was now on her way to becoming the Hitchcock Blonde. It would only be a matter of time.

THE BIGGEST DEAL IN HOLLYWOOD

IN THE EARLY SPRING OF 1953, HITCHCOCK SIGNED A NEW STUDIO CONtract to get his box office clout back on track. His agents at MCA Artists began a search party for the most lucrative deal in Hollywood. MCA president Lew Wasserman generally handled Hitchcock's business, but this time, agents Arthur Park and Herman Citron were thrown into the mix to help locate the best opportunity. The joint effort paid off, and MCA struck gold with a multi-picture deal with Paramount Pictures. But there was a catch. Paramount offered the deal on the condition that Hitchcock would develop a script out of a story from Cornell Woolrich's *After-Dinner Story*, a series of short noir mysteries. Each story offered a distinct touch of creep that the studio knew Hitchcock would go for. Within a week, a copy of the *Rear Window* treatment landed on Hitchcock's desk and he went ape for the story. In a serendipitous case of the right place at the right time, contracts were drawn up to begin filming *Rear Window* at Paramount later that year.

Meanwhile, Jimmy Stewart had just wrapped shooting on *The Glenn Miller Story* when Hitchcock called, rather out of the blue. He offered him a unique role on a one-room set. Jimmy's stomach sank. *Another* one-room set? But this time it would be different. Once Joshua Logan sent him the *Rear Window* treatment, Jimmy began to warm to the idea. After one read-through, he had to admit L. B. "Jeff" Jefferies had his name written all over it.

But, according to Joshua, Jimmy was still a bit skittish after *Rope* and would need further persuasion. Luckily, Joshua and Jimmy's connection went back to their days at Princeton University. Jimmy had been studying architecture, but the two became fast friends through the plays they put on with a campus theatrical group.

"I convinced Jim it was a good idea for a film," said Joshua. He explained that the role would fully confirm his departure from what Jimmy had been known for—a bright-eyed innocent of prewar lighter fare. He'd already proven with *The Glenn Miller Story* he had the grit to play tougher, more selfish characters. Joshua suggested his friend should grab the opportunity while it was in his hands.

Jimmy was no stranger to bleakness, though. *It's a Wonderful Life* presented the challenge of suicidal ideation when George Bailey looked down from the Bedford Falls Bridge and considered ending it all. But *Rear Window*'s L. B. Jefferies's resistance to closeness combined with his ironic habit of spying on others' lives would take Jimmy's craft to a place it hadn't gone before. He meditated on the unknown path ahead. At least one thing was for sure. This time, he could relax, knowing there wouldn't be excessively long takes—he was sure to confirm that with the studio. Hitchcock had learned from the *Rope* experience and would work out technical details in preproduction so filming would go more smoothly this time.

When it came to casting his leading men and women, Hitchcock had an almost clairvoyant sixth sense. He immediately knew his other favorite star, Cary Grant, wouldn't make logical sense in *Rear Window*. He was too charming, too dapper—the type of man Hitchcock fantasized himself *becoming*. But Jimmy was different. When he was on-screen, Hitchcock recognized something in him that he saw in himself. Something that no other director had fully exploited yet. His likable common man appeal veiled repression of dark desire, something Hitchcock wrestled with himself.

When he stumbled upon that quality in Jimmy during *Rope*, he knew it had to be pushed to the surface. *Rear Window* could maximize this, as Jefferies struggles with his reluctance to form bonds, and in certain moments, the audience questions his moral compass. But

Hitchcock could keep the audience on his side by simultaneously portraying the Jimmy Stewart everyone knew and loved. In a scene where Detective Doyle has convincingly thwarted the theory that Thorwald is a murderer, Jefferies begins to question his conscience and whether it's ethical to watch a man with binoculars and a long-focus lens. Lisa provides a spot-on response. "I'm not much on rear window ethics," she replies, turning her back in frustration.

The rights to *Rear Window* were subsequently sold for $10,000 to a production company formed by Hitchcock and Jimmy Stewart called Patron Productions (coined from the combined surnames of Hitchcock's agents, Arthur Park and Herman Citron). By the time the treatment was accepted, Jimmy now had enough faith in *Rear Window*'s potential success to forgo his usual salary in exchange for part ownership of the film. "I was intrigued by the story—a man is confined to a wheelchair, and he has nothing to do but watch what happens in the apartments . . . and he sees a murder take place," he later said. "What's he gonna do? That's an intriguing idea for an actor."

Hitchcock and Jimmy were a professional match made in Hollywood heaven. "He and Hitch were like brothers," said Hitchcock's daughter, Patricia. "You could even occasionally see a little smile appear on Hitchcock's face when he and Jimmy were together." The two men bonded on their almost identical work ethic, though off the set, they had little in common in their personal lives. "Hitchcock and his wife came over occasionally, but they weren't best buds or anything," Jimmy's daughter Kelly remembered. "I didn't see them a lot growing up, so they weren't bonded to each other as friends necessarily, but they had incredible respect professionally."

Another obvious reason for Hitchcock's male lead casting choice was the fact that L. B. Jefferies was a World War II veteran, just like Jimmy. When Jefferies first suspects the murder, the natural thing to do is call on his old war buddy Detective Doyle to help him crack the case across the courtyard. Even with a disappearing wife, a large trunk, and strange comings and goings at all hours of the night, Doyle is convinced that Lars Thorwald is an innocent man and that Jeff has become delusional with cabin fever. At one point, as they spar over Thorwald's guilt, Doyle says in exasperation, "How did we ever stand each other in that plane for three years during the war?"

THE 453RD BOMBARDMENT

IN MARCH OF 1941, AT AGE THIRTY-TWO, JIMMY STEWART REPORTED FOR combat duty, just a month after he'd won the Best Actor Oscar for *The Philadelphia Story*, which he starred in with Katharine Hepburn and Cary Grant. At six foot three inches, he had second and third helpings of spaghetti at mealtimes to fill out his lanky frame so he could pass the army physical. And without thinking twice, Jimmy exchanged his lucrative MGM contract for the twenty-one dollars a month salary of a regular soldier. MGM studio head Louis B. Mayer had pleaded with him not to go, but military service ran in the Stewarts' bloodline. He'd fight for his country, just like his father did during the Spanish-American War and World War I.

"Mayer was so desperate to say something that would keep me from enlisting," Jimmy recalled. "He told me, 'You're just giving up this wonderful screen career you've made for yourself, and all you'll be doing is sitting at some clerk's desk on a military base, and then you'll regret what you're doing.'"

Initially, his celebrity status did hold him back for a period, as the War Department filled his schedule with regular appearances on radio shows to raise morale and encourage enlistment. But by sheer stubbornness, Jimmy earned his place in the air force piloting bomber planes in December 1942. He became commander of the second combat bomb wing and led a thousand heavy bombers at a time in combat over Germany.

When World War II came to an end on May 8, 1945, Lieutenant Stewart, currently based at the 453rd Bombardment Group in England, had recently been promoted to full colonel. He'd led and protected a group of soldiers, who included soon-to-be Hollywood star twenty-four-year-old Walter Matthau. Full of mixed emotion, Jimmy boarded the transatlantic liner *Queen Elizabeth* in Portsmouth along with fifteen thousand other American servicemen and women. They set sail for the long journey home, where they would dock in New York Bay.

From a distance, the war now seemed like a surreal nightmare Jimmy couldn't escape. Everything he had seen had changed him on a granular level. The lives that were lost right in front of his eyes—often men he'd bonded with, and listened to, as they talked about getting back to their families just days before. The images of the horror were permanently etched in his mind. There was also the unimaginable stress of putting his own life on the line, not sure if he'd make it home alive.

When he returned to California, like most veterans, Jimmy didn't talk about the war. In those days, it was considered taboo to ask soldiers about their experiences, and no one had even heard of the term "post-traumatic stress" in 1945. Everyone was encouraged to move on to brighter days and tuck away unexamined trauma. In the coming years though, it appeared Jimmy found a cathartic way to channel his lingering pain onto the screen as his characters developed further depth and complexity.

But in 1945, the make-believe world of Hollywood felt uncomfortable. As Jimmy tried to embrace normalcy, he began to question whether he still had the same passion for show business. Perhaps it was time to pack it in. Everything about it seemed trivial now. Besides, things had changed dramatically in the film industry since Jimmy had reentered the scene. The fickle tastes of Hollywood had moved on, and he'd outgrown his boy-next-door persona. While all his friends were settling down, Jimmy found himself single, starting over, and exhausted from the war. "You get rusty in the business, just like any other one, and boy, was I," he told the *New York Times* of his time away from Hollywood. "Memorizing parts—hell, I couldn't even remember my hat size."

But when Frank Capra offered the cinematic gift of *It's a Wonderful Life*, Jimmy felt the gentle pull of destiny. He'd always viewed his relationship with his audience as a partnership, and he couldn't let them down. Americans needed to believe in life's possibilities now more than ever and perhaps he could help. "Merry Christmas, Bedford Falls!" he called as George Bailey ran through the snow-filled streets during the uplifting final scene. The film helped Jimmy jump back into the waters of Hollywood headfirst. He was back on his path now. "You could believe in him as being the America everyone wanted to believe in and he never let his fans down," said his daughter Kelly. "He was this constant for his public."

Now, in early 1953, Jimmy sat with the *Rear Window* treatment in his hands. He was now back in the safety of his home with a loving family and a reignited Hollywood career. The *Rear Window* idea hinted at something special, but unconventional. Looking down at the page, the path forward was difficult to make out. Although Jimmy had a knack for keeping both feet firmly on the ground, shooting another film like *Rear Window* on a one-room set came with its risks. And with Hitchcock's habit of experimentation, it would either be too far outside of the box for the public to wrap its head around *or* it would be a brilliant success that hit a nerve with the whole world. Either way, there would be some sort of impact.

Jimmy still wasn't fully convinced he wouldn't end up in another *Rope* scenario. There was also the fact that Hitchcock hadn't cast the leading lady yet. She'd have to be a strong scene partner and sharp with dialogue as there wouldn't be much else happening scenery-wise in that crummy apartment. But Jimmy was sure of one thing. Whatever Hitchcock had planned, it would be genius. But would the public get it? The curiosity was killing him, but he'd have to wait until the shoot in November to find out.

Never one to be wrapped up in Hollywood hyperbole or top film surveys that changed course with every passing decade, Jimmy just wanted to do good work. Unsurprisingly, when *Rear Window* was eventually a meteoric success, it wouldn't faze him all that much. And he certainly didn't buy into the publicity of being the star of "one of the greatest films of all time."

Jimmy left his characters in the studio where they belonged and was always home in time for dinner. There were no security guards at the Stewart residence, which stood at 918 North Roxbury Drive, just north of Sunset Boulevard in Beverly Hills. Before moving there, he had considered the ritzy Pacific Palisades, but his wife, Gloria, insisted the children have a normal suburban childhood—as normal as Beverly Hills could get, anyway.

Lucille Ball and Jack Benny lived across the street. A little farther up the way were José Ferrer and Rosemary Clooney, who lived next to Ira and Leonore "Lee" Gershwin, and Agnes Moorehead (who played Jimmy's mother in *The Stratton Story*). And she was just down the road from Thomas Mitchell (who played Jimmy's Uncle Billy in *It's a Wonderful Life*). It was a star-spangled street, but this barely registered with Jimmy's children, who didn't pay much attention to their dad's celebrity status. In those days, it was common for fans to show up at the house and ring the doorbell, and if Jimmy was around, he'd sign an autograph or two.

Kelly and her twin sister, Judy, rarely visited their dad at the studio, though on one occasion in 1961, they'd visited the set of *How the West Was Won* to watch him film scenes. Even in the presence of legends like Gregory Peck and John Wayne, it didn't hold much appeal for the ten-year-old girls, whose tastes gravitated to the other side of the MGM lot. "They were filming *Bonanza* across the street, and my sister and I had this huge crush on Michael Landon—Little Joe," laughed Kelly. "We didn't really care about seeing Dad work. All we wanted to do was go across and meet Michael!"

But as she grew older, Kelly developed a strong fascination for the work her father did with Hitchcock. It was hard not to. The auteur's image was everywhere. She often wondered who the man behind the larger-than-life persona was. "Dad didn't talk very much about moviemaking," remembered Kelly. So, one day, she finally asked him her burning question. "I said, 'Well, what was Hitchcock like to work with?'" Jimmy paused and thoughtfully answered. "He was a true professional." Kelly continued, "Dad explained that Hitchcock always had in his mind what he wanted it to look like . . . and then left it up to the actors."

CHAPTER THREE

A Preview of Coming Attractions

THE SCREEN TEST

AT THE TIME, IT APPEARED TO BE MEANINGLESS. IT WAS EVEN DISCARDED by Twentieth Century Fox on first viewing and thrown to the bottom of the rejection pile. But in the end, the *Taxi* screen test meant everything for Grace Kelly's career. In 1949, after a revolving door of endless auditions, Grace finally made her Broadway debut in *The Father*, which received favorable reviews. Since then, she'd mostly made a living through television appearances. But one day, she received a casting call on the far west side of Manhattan in a barnlike studio for a peculiar-sounding film.

The role was for an Irish girl who comes to New York with her infant son. She spends much of the film riding around in a taxi trying to locate her husband with a bad-tempered cab driver in tow. "I wanted to try an Irish accent, and I found the character very sympathetic, but I didn't get the job," Grace said later. The role would go to the more experienced Irish actress Constance Smith.

In the early fifties, it was common for studios to exchange passed over screen tests, in hopes that one studio's trash would be another one's treasure. This diamond in the rough that captured Grace's elegant style and less-than-convincing Irish accent would eventually catch Hitchcock's attention. But not before director John Ford beat him to the punch. He immediately cast her in *Mogombo* costarring Clark Gable and Ava Gardner. "This dame has breeding, quality, and class," he said. "I want to make a color test with her—I'll bet she'll knock us on our asses!"

Mogambo was a mixed experience for Grace. She made a life-long friend in the free-spirited and brash Ava Gardner. She was a woman who was in many ways Grace's opposite and made her forget her self-consciousness when they were together. Though the gossip columnists had a hay day when they heard that Grace dined with Clark Gable during the African shoot, nothing was ever confirmed about a romance. Even Ava Gardner gave nothing away in interviews many years later. "Clark's eyes were on Gracie, and hers for that matter on him," she said in a cryptic turn of phrase. But being blunt of nature, had there been a consummated affair, she likely would have confirmed it.

Working with John Ford had been a demanding task. By age fifty-eight, he was edgy, short-tempered, and in poor health. If an actor had questions about dialogue, depending on his mood, he sometimes responded with outrage, or by tearing pages out of the script, automatically shortening their role. His style was beginning to get under the inexperienced Grace's skin. "If Ford said something at the outset, I would not have to figure out where I was standing and why, but he really gave me no direction, no hint," she said.

By the time the *Mogambo* shoot wrapped in March 1953, Grace was already packed and ready for home. It would be back to television work in New York, as theatrical and movie offers weren't exactly pouring in after *Mogambo*. One day, while working on the TV special *The Way of the Eagle*, her film agent, Jay Kanter, urgently rang the set and demanded she come to the phone immediately.

"Gracie, pack your bags! Alfred Hitchcock wants to meet you!"

She was to fly out to Los Angeles on June 8. Hitchcock needed a new leading lady for his feature *Dial M for Murder*. Though he hadn't yet seen *Mogambo*, he had seen that *Taxi* screen test. He'd also caught her in a scene or two from *High Noon* (1952), a classic western and McCarthy-era allegory starring Gary Cooper.

By the time the two finally met that June morning in Burbank, Grace did her best to remain composed but was shaking with nerves on the inside. What would the master of suspense expect of her? She so wanted to work with him. As they began to talk, she gradually relaxed into the conversation. It seemed the last thing he wanted to do was talk shop anyway. "He was very dear and put me at my ease," remembered Grace. "We talked about food, travel, wine, music, fashions— everything it seemed, except the character of Margot Wendice in the movie." There would still be some formalities, but after that meeting, he knew he had his Margot.

As Hitchcock began to observe Grace in the dailies for *Dial M for Murder*, he was the most impressed with her restraint. She had the refinement of an actress well beyond her years. The fact that she was maddeningly photogenic didn't hurt either. A classy woman like Grace could provide certain advantages too. He could be more colorful with love scenes played by an elegant lady. Nothing she did could ever be considered vulgar, even if it was.

According to Hitchcock, she was also the most cooperative actress he ever directed. When he was feeling playful, he'd take delight in trying to shock his new ingénue, though he wasn't often successful. "One time he turned to me when he'd been telling Ray Milland some very raw kinds of things," she recalled, "and he said, 'Are you shocked, Miss Kelly?' I said, 'No, I went to a girls' convent school, Mr. Hitchcock, I heard all those things when I was thirteen.' And of course, he loved that sort of answer."

THE ROLE(S) OF A LIFETIME

BY THE END OF FILMING *DIAL M FOR MURDER*, HITCHCOCK WAS CERTAIN he'd found a new muse to replace Ingrid Bergman. He wouldn't even entertain the idea of another leading lady for *Rear Window*. But one unforeseen obstacle now stood in his way: Elia Kazan.

Elia had become a pivotal figure in Hollywood since directing *Gentleman's Agreement* in 1947, which received eight Oscar nominations. With his emphasis on real-world social issues, his style couldn't have been more oppositional to Hitchcock's crowd-pleasing suspense. He was also gaining a reputation as a Hollywood star-maker.

Fresh off a Best Director Oscar nomination for *A Streetcar Named Desire* in 1952 (which he lost to George Stevens for *A Place in the Sun*), Elia had given Marlon Brando the career-defining role of a lifetime. Now he planned to do the same with Grace for *On the Waterfront*. Even Hitchcock would admit he had some stiff competition in the younger filmmaker. The Academy hadn't fully recognized Hitchcock as a director yet, despite the fact he had twenty years of experience over Elia. With shooting dates already confirmed, securing Grace in *Rear Window* could escalate into a bare-knuckle brawl.

The main obstacle was that both pictures would be filmed at the same time on opposite coasts: *Rear Window* in Hollywood with Jimmy Stewart and *On the Waterfront* in New York with Marlon Brando. In truth, if Grace had the choice, she'd never leave New York. She'd always preferred Manhattan to Hollywood—the four seasons, the museums and culture, and hailing a cab at two a.m. if she wanted to. She adored the authenticity of it.

Though she would spend the better part of the next three years on the West Coast, Hollywood simply didn't agree with her. As a strict renter, she never invested in Californian real estate because it didn't feel like home. "I saw so many unhappy people—miserable people, really—and so many alcoholics and nervous breakdowns," she said years later. "In addition, I didn't like the eternal sunshine of Los Angeles and being dependent on a car to go all those long distances from one part of town to another." Driving was not her favorite activity and she avoided it whenever possible.

But if she was honest with herself, it wasn't just about her preference for the Big Apple. Grace was in love. Not long after filming *Mogombo*, she met Oleg Cassini. He was an internationally renowned fashion designer, who'd recently divorced his second wife, actress Gene Tierney. When their eyes met, she fell almost instantaneously. Coming from Russian and Italian aristocracy, he was dark, handsome, and socially in demand. Just her type. Multilingual and socially well-versed, Oleg had much to discuss with her, even though she was sixteen years his junior. He was in New York and a loved-up Grace wanted to spend as much with him as possible. So, the decision was made . . . or was it?

On the Waterfront contained some grim and violent scenes that didn't quite align with Grace's sensibilities. She would also have to play a traumatized character dealing with her brother's death in the rough settings of Brooklyn and New Jersey. These things felt completely foreign to her. With *Rear Window*, on the other hand, she would portray a high fashion society girl, a real mover and shaker within the exclusive circles of Manhattan. Now, this was a life she understood.

Grace sat in her Fifth Avenue apartment one afternoon staring at both screenplays until the words of each began to blur into one. The decision was beyond impossible. Suddenly, the phone rang, shaking Grace out of her hazy state. It was her agent, Jay Kanter, and it was crunch time. A whole corporation of people was waiting on her decision. Again, he patiently asked her which part she wanted.

"I have to have your answer by four o'clock this afternoon, Grace."

Grace was tongue-tied. The indecision was maddening.

"I want to stay in New York, but I love working with Hitchcock. . . ."

Jay loved Grace like a sister, but he might need to get stern with her if she kept him hanging much longer. He told her she had exactly one hour to make her decision and hung up the phone.

As Grace sat and watched the clock, she felt the time slip through her fingers. She thought about Hitchcock and the fun they'd had on *Dial M for Murder*. She didn't know Elia Kazan and wasn't familiar with his filmmaking methods. Though he was a prolific director, the film honestly didn't *feel* like her. With Hitchcock, she'd be working with a director she already trusted, someone she knew was on her side. Not another John Ford fiasco. Then, as if someone had switched on a light, the answer revealed itself just as the long hand of the clock reached twelve. She immediately called Jay. She'd never been more certain of anything in her life.

On November 23, Paramount Pictures released a press announcement confirming Grace Kelly's upcoming role in *Rear Window*. She would be paid $20,000, prorated over seven weeks from preproduction to the film's completion. Paramount had negotiated with MGM to loan her out and she would have to be in Hollywood for wardrobe fittings in late November.

In the early fifties, Grace's entrance to Hollywood couldn't have been timed better. The public was currently starved of elegance and class. When she made a quick and forgettable debut in *Fourteen Hours* in 1951 and then played Gary Cooper's Quaker wife in *High Noon* (1952), the era of the sexy bombshell bubble was about to burst. People were growing tired of pinups and actresses who spelled out sex. Hollywood needed Grace Kelly. Metro contract player Van Johnson noted, "The public has had so much sex pitched into its face recently that it's gone for Kelly in rebellion against a broadside of broads."

Hollywood newcomer Audrey Hepburn shared a lot in common with Grace. They were the same age and made their debuts at the same time, both leaving an indelible mark on the era of elegance. Audrey's top billing in *Roman Holiday* in 1953 marked a significant moment, earning her a Best Actress Oscar. Simultaneously, 1953 had nonetheless been a good year for Marilyn Monroe. Fox released *Niagara*, *Gentlemen Prefer Blondes*, and *How to Marry a Millionaire*. In the stark contrasts of their public personas, Marilyn was deliberately positioned as a counterpoint to the sophisticated Grace. Steering her career through a seductive image, Marilyn navigated the industry from the opposite end. Yet, the few who got to know her recognized an intellectually sharp woman with a complexity that transcended the public facade she projected.

Another actress making a splash in the early fifties was Rita Gam. With dark, exotic beauty that contrasted with Grace's all-American appeal, she first emerged opposite Ray Milland in *The Thief* in 1952. She would go on to star opposite Gregory Peck in the Cold War thriller *Night People*, the same year Grace appeared in *Rear Window*.

Rita and Grace were initially introduced in New York by Rita's first husband, director Sidney Lumet, while they both worked the trenches of modeling and television. Even then, Rita immediately picked up on Grace's ability to change her demeanor between "Gracie" and the Hitchcock Blonde. "Off camera, she reminded me of a small-town high school teacher," recalled Rita of their first meeting. "Her hair was pulled back into a ponytail, her face was scrubbed clean except for a little dash of lipstick, and she wore glasses."

Two years later, when Grace landed in Los Angeles to begin preparation for *Rear Window*, she rented an apartment on Sweetzer Avenue in West Hollywood, sharing it with her secretary and friend, Prudy Wise. But once things were unpacked and settled, Prudy went back to New York. Adrift in a sprawling, unfamiliar city, Grace grappled with a suffocating sense of isolation. She'd remembered hearing that Rita Gam was temporarily living in the Beverly Hills Hotel. She'd liked her when they'd met, but other than that, she was practically a stranger. Summoning the courage for a spontaneous outreach, Grace phoned her and extended an invitation for a casual cup of coffee. "We clicked immediately," recalled Rita. "The friendship was virtually instantaneous—and Grace, who didn't like living alone, invited me to share her apartment."

Rita moved in straightaway and became a valuable friend to Grace. The two women bonded on the adversities of casting calls and went out on the town together in the evenings to blow off steam. As they navigated a constant influx of dinner party invitations from the Hollywood suits, Grace always had a plan for a quick getaway if needed. Always a believer in safety in numbers, she often put on her glasses, got behind the wheel, and insisted on doing the driving, though she detested the freeways. Grace ensured they weren't stuck in any compromising situations and could leave parties if something didn't feel aboveboard. "Grace schooled Rita on keeping the wolves of Hollywood at bay," said Rita's son, Michael Guinzburg. "Though, you never know. They may have had some boyfriends too at that time."

With her new roommate in tow, Grace began to acclimatize to California living. She would also gradually adjust to the meteoric fame that accompanied her career growth after the release of *Rear Window*. But it would still bewilder her family whenever she came back to visit her childhood home on Henry Street in Philadelphia. "Whenever we would get together over at the Kelly house when she would come to town, there were always paparazzi outside," remembered her cousin John Lehman. "She got used to it very quickly, and it didn't really bother her, but it was sure something new to us!"

In between costume fittings, as Grace got off book with her dialogue and immersed herself in the character of Lisa Carol Fremont, she began to feel a sense of ease, but a longing still tugged at her heart. On November 12, Oleg Cassini sent her a telegram for her twenty-fourth birthday.

The Earth became alive for me and created the loveliest thing in the world—you. I love you, my darling—will call you tonight.

Grace missed Oleg terribly, but now it was time to focus. And who knew, perhaps Hollywood wouldn't be so bad after all.

A POLITE WORD FOR KILLIN'

NOW THAT JIMMY AND GRACE HAD OFFICIALLY BEEN ANNOUNCED AS *REAR Window*'s leading stars, it was time for Hitchcock to turn serious attention to casting supporting players. It would be no easy feat, as these character actors would be just as imperative to the plot as the top billers. Enter Stella, Jeff's insurance company nurse and confidante—a character who would inject much-needed comic relief into a tension-laden story. A genuine New Yorker, Stella embodied toughness and quick wit, unflinching in the face of blood and gore. Hitchcock would need the best supporting actress in show business to shoulder such a responsibility and bring Stella's complexities and sharp one-liners alive.

Since her breakthrough role in *Miracle on Thirty-Fourth Street* (1947), Thelma Ritter was considered the most maternal of all character actresses in Hollywood. On-screen, she was a constant fixture as the supportive woman of a certain age. She was often a mother, maid, or helper of some type, but always with an underlying edge. Her characters were cynical, protective, and sardonic in their witty zingers, which she executed flawlessly.

As a theater-trained actor, like Grace, Thelma had attended the American Academy of Dramatic Arts. In 1950, she received rave reviews and an Oscar nomination for the role of a former vaudeville performer and the fiercely loyal assistant to the larger-than-life Margo Channing in *All About Eve*. Even at the height of Bette Davis's charisma, Thelma stole the scenes she was in, which was no easy feat. It was only natural then that Hitchcock was desperate to cast her as Stella in *Rear Window*.

When casting began, Thelma was quickly hired and received $25,694, the highest salary of all the cast members. It was her first time working with Hitchcock. She would work with him again in May of 1956 on an episode of *Alfred Hitchcock Presents* called "The Babysitter." Thelma later commented that the auteur never told you if he liked what you did in a scene but if he didn't like it, "he looked like he was going to throw up."

When Stella first enters the scene in Jefferies's apartment, it's as his conscience and sense of reason. She does her best to convince him he's making a mistake by casting Lisa aside. Flabbergasted at the thought of Jeff ending things with her because she's "too perfect," she sighs in her thick Brooklyn accent at what she views as a masochistic move. "I can hear you now. Get out of my life, you wonderful woman. You're too good for me."

Stella, initially the voice of opposition to Jeff's murder mystery "fantasy," gradually reveals herself as a voyeur with a shared curiosity as evidence begins to mount. Acting as a counterbalance to Jeff's obsession with Thorwald, her skepticism shifts to fascination as suspicious activities unfold. Even amid serious events, she manages to inadvertently turn murder into a stand-up comedy routine.

LISA: What's he doing? Cleaning house?

JEFF: He's washing and scrubbing down the bathroom walls.

STELLA: Must've splattered a lot.
[Both Jeff and Lisa look at Stella with disgust.]

STELLA: Come on, that's what we're all thinkin'. He killed her in there, now he has to clean up those stains before he leaves.

LISA: Stella . . . your choice of words!

STELLA: Nobody ever invented a polite word for killin' yet.

The next main supporter to be cast in solving the mystery was NYPD detective Thomas J. Doyle. The role went to popular supporting actor Wendell Corey. Known for playing the downtrodden husband to Joan Crawford in *Harriet Craig* (1950), he was one of Hollywood's most reliable sidekicks. His reserved acting style helped bolster the stars around him to even greater heights.

Behind the scenes, Wendell Corey's career ambitions went beyond acting. He was later president of the Academy of Motion Picture Arts and Sciences from 1961 to 1963 and even dabbled in politics when he was elected to the Santa Monica City Council in April 1965. But performance was his first love, and he worked steadily in film until his sudden death at age fifty-four in November 1968, due to cirrhosis of the liver as a result of alcoholism. Detective Doyle would always be his defining role.

THE VILLAIN

THROUGHOUT FILM HISTORY, THE ROLE OF THE VILLAIN HAS OFTEN BEEN the most challenging of all to cast. Hire someone too empathetic or one-dimensional and it can throw off the whole balance of the picture. Hire someone too sinister-looking, and the story becomes too predictable or on the nose. But Hitchcock's unexpected choice of Raymond Burr for *Rear Window*'s antagonist was surprisingly effective. Previous villains in Hitchcock films were often tall and attractive like Joseph Cotten in *Shadow of a Doubt* (1943), or had an element of class to them, like Bruno Antony in *Strangers on a Train* (1951). But Lars Thorwald circles a completely different orbit. He's a down-on-his-luck, depressed shmuck who sells jewelry for a living. Jefferies's initial spying sessions indicate that his invalid wife berates and taunts him simply for existing.

Poor Lars Thorwald has the power to lure the audience into sympathizing with him. He's a man trapped in his own life, but then again, he's also a killer. This tactic would be repeated in *Psycho* in 1960 when at first, the audience feels for Norman Bates, as he explains to Janet Leigh's Marion Crane that he doesn't have a life of his own because he's a prisoner of his mother and must obey her every whim. Norman, in actuality, is a voyeuristic murderer as he spies on Marion from the next-door cabin. It displays evidence that the world of Hitchcock is an entity where each film is echoed in one another. One seems to have a conjoined parallel to the next. The ethical view Hitchcock presents of the *Rear Window* world is perplexing. No one is completely innocent and therefore, no one ever fully escapes their fate. Villains have moments of sympathy and heroes are partial to poor decisions.

Film noir regular Raymond Burr had a special knack for threatening and intimidating some of Hollywood's biggest stars on-screen. He had recently done so to great effect in *A Place in the Sun* (1950) as district attorney Frank Marlowe. Determined to prove that George Eastman portrayed by Montgomery Clift has drowned and murdered his girlfriend (Shelley Winters) in cold blood so he could be with another woman (Elizabeth Taylor), he reduces George to a bundle of frayed nerves. By the time Marlowe finishes interrogating him on the courtroom stand and violently slams down and breaks a boat oar used as a prop to prove his guilt, a shell-shocked George is barely a functioning man.

Hitchcock knew that Raymond Burr had the goods to overpower any Hollywood star, no matter how great in stature. The casting paid off in a big way. He was offered $8,541 for the role of Lars Thorwald and immediately agreed to it. Taking the role would be one of the shrewdest moves of his career. Raymond's turn as the sad and pathetic, yet disturbingly cold-blooded Thorwald earned him rave reviews on *Rear Window*'s release. "Since enacting his role of the perpetrator of the 'perfect crime' in *Rear Window*, Raymond Burr is due to become even more of a personality on the screen than heretofore," Edwin Schallert stated in the *Los Angeles Times* on August 27, 1954, a few weeks after the film premiered.

Raymond was a burly man, and once costume designer Edith Head and makeup artist Wally Westmore gave him the *Rear Window* makeover of a haggard appearance with white hair, frumpy suits, and round spectacles, whispers began around the studio. He bore such a strikingly uncanny resemblance to producer David O. Selznick, it was eerie.

When Hitchcock moved to Los Angeles from London with Alma and his daughter, Patricia, in 1939, he and David began a turbulent director and producer partnership. The producer was known for his controlling nature, especially since his monstrous achievement of *Gone with the Wind* (1939). Though it was an unhappy time for Hitchcock, their relationship bore the successes *Rebecca* (1940), *Suspicion* (1941), *Spellbound* (1945), and the unparalleled *Notorious* (1946).

Hitchcock never publicly admitted to it, but he was sending a subtle message to his former producer whom he weathered a seven-year bitter partnership with before being set free of their contract together. In Hitchcock's mind, David Selznick had committed the ultimate sin—

interfering with his work. Even though he was long free of him, it was evident through the presence of Lars Thorwald that Hitchcock wasn't one to let go of a grudge.

THERE ARE NO SMALL PARTS

IT'S BEEN SAID BY CRITICS THAT *REAR WINDOW* IS ONE OF HITCHCOCK'S greatest love stories disguised as a thriller, where murder is the Mac-Guffin. The mystery of Anna Thorwald's disappearance is the plot device that's going to get Lisa to convince Jefferies that she is the right woman for him. But Grace and Jimmy couldn't carry this narrative on their own. They needed help in the form of the everyday people living across the courtyard who would reflect the multiple facets of their relationship back to them.

With the main players firmly committed to *Rear Window*, it was time to cast the equally important roles of the neighbors. As initially agreed upon, Patron Inc. footed the bill for the salaries of the featured and starring roles, while Paramount covered the smaller roles and extras. But these "bit player" parts weren't as minor as they seemed on paper. The complex neighbors were the objects of Jefferies's voyeurism. They had to be compelling and interesting enough for the audience to read into their stories and be pulled into the small universe Hitchcock had created in this life-sized dollhouse.

Herbert Coleman would be in charge of scouting the right talent. First, he'd need the sexy dancer across the courtyard who Jefferies has nicknamed "Miss Torso." Hitchcock didn't want her dance moves to be too professional. He instructed Herbert, "When you're satisfied you have the right girl for Miss Torso, keep her away from the dance department. Give her a record of our music and let her create her own dance."

Herbert auditioned an endless number of girls but something always felt off. Many were too polished with their erect postures and perfect turnout. He needed something a little edgier and off the beaten path. One day, he came across the headshot of a blond, glamorous dancer, curiously wearing a feather boa. Her name was Georgine Darcy. Herbert called her to come in immediately. She had no real acting experience but was a natural interpretive dancer with the chiseled figure of a Greek Muse. Though Georgine had studied with the New York City Ballet, she could also move in ways that expressed youth, innocence, and sex all at once. Naturally, the auteur hired her.

Hitchcock encouraged Georgine to improvise as much as possible when they filmed scenes. "She told me how she just went and did the scenes and she pretty much innovated everything," remembers Georgine's friend and former Universal Classics president Jim Katz. In the opening sequence, and one of *Rear Window*'s iconic fashion moments, Miss Torso, with her back to the audience, fastens her pink bra while wearing a cheeky pair of matching shorts. She then proceeds to dance with a childlike exuberance that contrasts with the suspense to come. Years later, during *Rear Window*'s restoration, Jim Katz located some of the original costumes in the Paramount costume vault. "I found the pink shorts!" he said. "Well, Georgine couldn't wait to try them on and of course, they fit. And she was almost seventy at this point!"

Next was the role of the struggling musician, who would provide a backdrop of music that dictated the changing mood throughout *Rear Window*. Hitchcock insisted on casting a genuine composer who could act—a rare combination, even in Hollywood. Luckily, it didn't take long to find Ross Bagdasarian, who often went by the stage name Dave Seville. Born in Fresno, California, to an Armenian American family, he was a singer-songwriter who'd had bit parts in movies like Billy Wilder's *Stalag 17* (1953) and had written hits for some of the biggest musical stars of the day.

The plan was that he'd repeatedly be seen at his piano playing a haunting melody throughout the film which would reveal itself as a fully composed song at the end. But with the time limit of one hour and fifty minutes, it would prove a challenge to weave this story in with the narrative. When Hitchcock did his traditional cameo, this would be of his quirkiest, as he randomly enters the composer's apartment to fix his clock while Ross continues to toil away on his piano, writing the world's most impossible song.

In his real-life compositions, Ross had already written the hit "Come On-a My House" for Rosemary Clooney, which reached number one on the Billboard charts for six weeks. In the future, he would most notably write and perform the "Chipmunks Song (Christmas Don't be Late)," the first holiday single to reach number one on the Billboard Hot 100. He'd also build a popular brand on the Alvin, Simon, and Theodore Chipmunk characters throughout the sixties.

Though according to common folklore, Hitchcock had a low estimation of actors and referred to them as "cattle," he also made exceptions for many he worked with. One of them was Ross. His son, Ross Bagdasarian Jr., who inherited the Chipmunks empire and made it a modern-day success with his family, remembers his father's collaborative relationship with Hitchcock. "Hitchcock and my dad really respected and enjoyed one another. Because my dad was a songwriter and musician I think Hitchcock looked at him differently," said Ross Jr. "He was one of the few songwriters in those days who owned his music publishing. That was very rare."

Next, Judith Evelyn was added to the cast as Miss Lonely Hearts, the depressed spinster, and Jesslyn Fax as Miss Hearing Aid, the nosy, opinionated sculptress. Grace and Evelyn would have a delightful reunion in Grace's dressing room one afternoon with a champagne toast. Of course, the two had recalled meeting back in 1947 when Evelyn starred in her uncle George's Broadway revival of *Craig's Wife*. The smaller, but vibrant roles of the bride and groom, the sleeping couple on the fire escape, and party guests at the composer's home went to performers Herbert had worked with in the past.

Each meticulously cast neighbor of *Rear Window* represents something different about human nature and the relationship between Jefferies and Lisa. Miss Torso radiates newness and vitality, while she fends off the wolves in suits, as Lisa must do in her own life. And it's the

Thorwalds who symbolize the dark side of humanity and Jeff's fears about marriage. The newlyweds embody love and optimism, as well as the emotional strains of time on a relationship. Miss Lonely Hearts on the bottom floor represents sadness and isolation. She is nearly assaulted by a man she meets at an intimate restaurant across the street, and in one of the darkest moments of *Rear Window*, almost commits suicide with an overdose of pills. But she changes her mind when she hears the music of the composer traveling through the apartment complex. The two end up together as he has literally and metaphorically saved her life. This struggling composer has coincidently written a song called "Lisa."

Every character is interconnected through the themes of relationships, marriage, and love. Though at times, the neighbors' scenes are distant and brief, there are no small roles in *Rear Window*. "Every one of these actors is important," noted Ross Bagdasarian Jr. "I think when you make sure that each one of these moments is strong, you have a movie that's more interesting to watch."

Finally, the victim of the piece, Thorwald's wife, was played by Irene Winston in a brief appearance from across the courtyard. With her attractive resemblance to Lisa, Jefferies watches her nagging her husband as she lies in their bed in a cream satin negligee (similar to the one Lisa would later wear). In a snapshot of Jefferies's worst nightmare about intimacy, she laughs at the sheer absurdity of something he has said. Later, in the blackness of the night, Jeff sits motionless in his wheelchair, Lisa's perfume still lingering in the air, when an unsettling scream pierces his thoughts. Mrs. Anna Thorwald has met her untimely death.

THE SCREENPLAY

ON A BALMY EVENING IN THE EARLY SPRING OF 1953, SCREENWRITER JOHN Michael Hayes sat in the Polo Lounge at the Beverly Hills Hotel. He was instructed by MCA to meet Alfred Hitchcock there at seven thirty that evening. He'd made the thirty-minute drive from his home in Burbank and arrived a few minutes early. He wiped the sweat from his brow as he mentally went over all the prep work he'd done after reading and rereading the *It Had to Be Murder* short story. Again, he began to recite to himself the points he'd make to impress Hitchcock.

By eight o'clock, Hitchcock still hadn't arrived. John Michael began to wonder if he'd mixed up the day or time. Though he wasn't much of a drinker, when the clock struck eight thirty, John Michael turned to martinis to calm his anxiety. He was about to give up all hope as he settled the tab for his second cocktail, and headed out of the hotel when suddenly, Hitchcock pulled up in a taxi. The young screenwriter sprinted up and introduced himself. Never one to apologize for minor details like tardiness, Hitchcock took control of the meeting. "Well, come on. Let's get going." He led John Michael back to the dining room, with a staff of waiters following in their trail. Everyone knew Hitchcock was a big spender at the Polo Lounge.

Just like Grace's experience, John Michael's first meeting with the director introduced him to a man who didn't want to discuss anything that even hinted at *Rear Window*. But it was all part of a strategy. Getting to know people on a casual level was a litmus test for him to see if they were compatible. "I like a man who drinks," Hitchcock said as he ordered a round of double martinis, then another. John Michael was beginning to feel queasy. He didn't have the stomach to keep up with Hitchcock, but he'd need to fake it to get through the evening.

"Have you seen any of my movies?" Hitchcock suddenly asked as he sliced into his Dover sole paired with white wine, his favorite drink. John Michael nervously summoned an anecdote about his former life as an army theater projectionist during the war. It was his job to screen *Shadow of a Doubt* regularly. By now, he was able to describe every aspect of the film with every frame committed to memory. Intoxicated with excitement and alcohol, John Michael then took Hitchcock through an analysis of *all* his films, from *The 39 Steps* to *Notorious*.

The liquid courage even prompted him to critique them and provide notes to Hitchcock on their weaknesses, something he knew even then, he'd regret in the morning.

After dessert and brandy were served, Hitchcock still hadn't mentioned *Rear Window*. And at the end of the meal, he made a sudden departure. He said his cordial goodbyes and was off in a taxi, as quickly as he came. It was as if the whole thing had never happened.

John Michael's heart sank as he tried to sober himself up with a coffee before attempting the drive home. Not only had *Rear Window* never come up, but thanks to a combination of nerves and booze, he'd "reviewed" each of Hitchcock's films as if he were some sort of dour film critic. He'd blown it. John Michael spent the rest of the weekend moping around the house, explaining to his wife he may need to find a new profession altogether.

On Monday morning, the phone rang. It was MCA agent Arthur Park.

"You're in. Hitchcock loved you. You start work tomorrow."

John Michael's heart nearly jumped out of his chest.

"We never talked about *Rear Window* or anything."

"You're fine."

He was elated. A feature picture with Alfred Hitchcock was a dream come true for any screenwriter. It just left one problem. He'd have to learn how to hold his liquor.

John Michael met Hitchcock on the Warner Brothers lot a few more times before beginning a new treatment on *Rear Window*. During their meetings, he gradually discovered Hitchcock's main concern with *Rear Window* was finding a way to intertwine a great love story with a heinous murder. John Michael made it his mission to help solve this narrative problem. He was officially put on the Paramount payroll on June 8, 1953, at a weekly salary of $750.

After a year of working together, when John Michael finally summoned the courage to ask Hitchcock about the night of their first meeting, Hitchcock explained, "I went to a cocktail party at Jules Stein's house. That's why I was late. You know, I was dieting and had several drinks. I remember meeting you and going to eat, but I don't remember anything after that. But you talked a lot, and on the assumption that a man who talks a lot has something to say, I hired you." John exhaled a sigh of relief. Without Hitchcock's regular dieting routine, his career may have ended that night.

CHAPTER FOUR

Lisa Fremont and the Case for Feminine Intuition

RIGHT OFF THE PARIS PLANE

EDITH HEAD WAS OUT OF BREATH. SHE'D BEEN WORKING DOUBLE TIME, running back and forth between Paramount's adjoining soundstages for two of its biggest releases of 1954: *Rear Window* and *Sabrina*. Both required the most influential costume designer in Hollywood. No one else could fill her shoes, so Edith made it her business to be in two places at once. *Rear Window* wouldn't officially begin shooting until November 27 and *Sabrina* would wrap up on December 5. The overlap was inevitable, and she'd need to simultaneously balance her attention between two of Hollywood's most powerful filmmakers.

First, she met with *Sabrina*'s director Billy Wilder for their usual consultation. A couple of months prior, she'd been informed that the film's star, Audrey Hepburn, would be bringing in fledgling designer Hubert de Givenchy for the dresses and gowns she wore after her Parisian Cinderella transformation. As a matter of fact, Audrey had already been to Paris and selected them from his workroom herself. The news stung Edith to the core. Apparently, her designs weren't up to snuff. But she gradually accepted the decision after viewing *Sabrina* (and especially after she was given credit for it with a costume design Oscar the following year). After all, Wilder had reasoned that for authenticity reasons, Audrey's French makeover would call for a *legitimate* French couture designer.

Edith was a petite woman, always in a gray or black two-piece suit with her trademark dark-framed glasses, and a sullen expression. As one of the most intimidating women on the Paramount lot, the glasses added to her mystique. No one could ever read her. She claimed that wearing them helped her see what clothes looked like on black-and-white film, though she continued wearing them well into the sixties and seventies. Edith had reason to intimidate those around her. In her career, she would collect thirty-five Academy Award nominations for her costume work, winning eight, more than any woman in Oscar history.

A former art teacher at the Hollywood School for Girls, Edith had applied for a job as a sketch artist for one of Cecil B. DeMille's films in 1923. Lacking confidence in her abilities, Edith "borrowed" some sketches from her classmates at the Chouinard Art Institute where she took night classes. Designer Howard Greer hired her soon after. Later, when faced with a blank drawing canvas, she came clean to Howard about the sketches. "You see I have the most awful confession to make. I was faced with my first interview, I was seized with panic. I was afraid that if I didn't have a lot of wonderful sketches, I'd never get the job," she told him. Howard decided to keep Edith on his staff anyway. "She might easily have saved her breath and her confession," Howard later wrote. "For her own talents soon proved she was more than worthy for the job."

Edith may not have been the most skilled sketch artist on the lot, but she was well-educated, had real-world experience, and put in the longest hours. She would become not just a designer but a fashion expert. As her reputation spread like wildfire across the industry, stars like Mae West and Bette Davis would personally request her to design their gowns and help mold their character's style.

In the coming years, Edith's star rose further with her book *The Dress Doctor* (1959) and her many appearances on the CBS television series *Art Linkletter's House Party* where she doled out fashion advice to everyday women. ("Women today are not slaves of fashion as they used to be," she told the *Los Angeles Times* in 1952. "The younger generation is not afraid to stand up and say, 'Maybe full skirts are out, but I'm going to wear mine because I like them on me.'")

Once Edith shuffled back to the *Rear Window* stage, she immediately felt at home. She'd now be meeting with Hitchcock, a perfectionist, just like herself, and the actress she most adored on the lot, Grace Kelly. "She was Miss Head's favorite to dress," said Rita Riggs, Head's former assistant, "because she was the perfect 1950s beauty. She had the perfect waist, the perfect plucked eyebrows, and she fell right into the mold."

Grace's timeless look and embodiment of "the mold" ironically stemmed from an independent mindset and a simple quest to find what suited her best. She refused to wear heavy eyeliner or painted-on eyebrows, which were popular at the time. Except for her ruby-red lips, *Rear Window*'s makeup artist Wally Westmore kept Grace's makeup relatively natural. She also refused to smoke in any of her films. For *Rear Window*, she made a compromise with Hitchcock. In the scene where Lisa lights a cigarette, she holds it for a few seconds and immediately puts it out. With a clever cutaway to Jefferies, the cigarette never actually touches her lips.

From the beginning of her career, Grace had a clear image of herself and her boundaries. Edith admired this about Grace, as well as her cultured upbringing and knowledge of art and literature. On the set of *Rear Window*, the two women established a friendship that would last a lifetime. Some days in between scenes, Grace would come to Edith's costume salon with her lunch, and the two would dine and talk for hours about museums, music, or the latest books. "It was always a pleasure to see her kick off her shoes and relax," said Edith of Grace. "Off-screen she was not the best-dressed actress in Hollywood, but she was very fastidious about the way she looked."

While instructing Edith about *Rear Window*'s Lisa Fremont,

Hitchcock told her to "make her look like a piece of Dresden china, something slightly untouchable." In contrast, Jimmy's dull blue pajamas would blend into the walls and allow Grace to shine in her glamorously chic costumes, while portraying the opposition of two different worlds. By the time Grace came to Los Angeles in late November for fittings, Hitchcock had already advised Edith about the colors and styles of the five iconic costumes for his leading lady. Just like Edith, he left no stone unturned regarding detail and how it needed to appear on camera to advance the story. No costume could appear in a film without his full approval.

Hitchcock valued Grace's input, especially after she'd complained about the off-the-rack wardrobe from *Dial M for Murder* being ill-fitting. Of course, he knew she was correct. The costumes for *Rear Window* would need to be elevated to an otherworldly level. Unlike most actresses in Hitchcock's films, Grace would be allowed input on the final wardrobe selection.

She loved to wear fabrics that were light and airy, with an ethereal quality, like weightless full skirts in chiffon. It was a theme that would begin with *Rear Window* and continue for the rest of her career. In her most iconic fashion moments, she wore watered silk and unlined linen in pastels and whites that flattered her delicate features. This look was something Hitchcock was also partial to in storytelling. He detested bold shades or loud patterns and felt they distracted from the scenes.

One of the reasons Edith Head and Alfred Hitchcock excelled as a duo was her appreciation of his precise vision. "Hitchcock is the only person who writes a script to such detail that you really could go ahead and almost make the clothes without discussing them," Edith said. "It's so completely lucid, like, 'she's in a black coat, she has a black hat, and she wears black glasses.'"

By combining Edith's know-how, Hitchcock's eye for what worked on camera, and Grace's instincts on what suited her best, the *Rear Window* wardrobe was born. It began with a showstopper of an evening dress that went down in fashion history. An off-the-shoulder black bodice and white layered tulle skirt with a cinched-in waist and black floral embellishment. It was "right off the Paris plane," as Lisa describes it after she makes her first entrance in all her aristocratic radiance. Accentuating her neck is a string of elegant pearls, and a sheer white wrap hangs loosely around her arms.

At the sixteen-minute mark of *Rear Window*, as Jefferies sleeps like a baby in his wheelchair on a muggy summer evening, a shadow crosses his face. At first, it appears like a threat. Should the audience be worried? On the contrary, all they feel is awe as the next frame features Grace Kelly's angelic face as Jefferies begins to awaken. In that special dress, with her piercing blue eyes, scarlet lips, and hair spun from gold, she accurately represents the woman Stella had earlier described as "only perfect." This is one of her most iconic fashion moments in cinema.

In that moment, she plants perhaps the most sensual kiss in cinematic history on his lips. Hitchcock liked to say he got the dreamy effect of the scene by shaking the camera. Truthfully, the kiss appears care of a double printing process. This scene would be imprinted on everyone's minds forever and Grace Kelly and Lisa Fremont would be synonymous in image and identity. Though she poses no danger to Jefferies, there is however anxious foreshadowing for what's ahead as she tells him, "I'm going to make this a week you'll never forget."

As the plot builds, to indicate that Lisa keeps up with Parisian trends, the costume she wears on her second visit to Jeff's apartment is a little black dress with sheer capped sleeves and a waist-cinching belt. The dress with its *Sabrina*-like quality was perhaps Edith Head's way of thumbing her nose at the naysayers who thought she couldn't replicate French couture.

Lisa's third costume would carry a more professionally austere and high-fashion quality. A pistachio-green blazer and pencil skirt with even more pearls and a heavy jangly bracelet that's somehow impossibly elegant on her petite wrist. The look is topped off with a pillbox hat secured tightly with a pin into Grace's upswept hair. The pistachio shade—one of Hitchcock's favorite colors—would be repeated on Tippi Hedren's suit in *The Birds* in 1962 as a way to reproduce Grace's image. In his lack of appreciation for her effort, all Jeff can say on Lisa's arrival is, "What'd you do to your hair?" He then quickly changes the subject back to his Thorwald obsession before she can respond.

Later in the scene, Lisa removes the green jacket to reveal a white halter top with a high neckline, which showcases her back and lithe frame. Edith would reuse the flattering halter look on Grace's beach attire in her next Hitchcock film, *To Catch a Thief*.

When Lisa plans to spend the night at Jefferies's, she later emerges in a sensual cream peignoir nightgown to entice his desire. The way Grace wears it, it's still classy enough to pass as an evening gown. Later, as the plot thickens with Thorwald now aware that he's being watched, Lisa reenters the apartment wearing a white dress embroidered with gold flowers. It features another waist-defining belt and a full skirt, though notably more subdued than the evening wear from her first entrance. This costume allows for more agility, enabling her to showcase her athletic side as she climbs into Thorwald's apartment to prove her courage to Jeff.

In the film's concluding scene, a significantly more casual Lisa is presented to the audience. She lounges in her reading attire of blue jeans, penny loafers, and a relaxed coral button-down shirt. Her red lips are toned down and there isn't a pearl in sight. Though it may initially appear like a reverse makeover to make a man happy, she looks just as chic and elegant in her leisurely costume.

Just like the ruby slippers in *The Wizard of Oz* and the Givenchy black dress in *Breakfast at Tiffany's*, the *Rear Window* wardrobe has remained a time capsule of cinematic costume history. In modern days, Golden Hollywood fashion remains in high demand with auction houses where private buyers and institutions bid radically high prices on original costume pieces and sketches.

Christie's former pop culture specialist Katherine Schofield noted that *Rear Window* is by far one of the biggest sellers in the international auction market. "Because the outfits were and are so identifiable because there aren't that many in the film," said Schofield, "you've got Grace Kelly in the image, it's a Hitchcock film and you also have the designs by Edith Head which are beautifully created and they are collectible in their own right."

But fashion history doesn't usually take place without a few differences in opinion along the way. When Hitchcock tasked Edith with designing Lisa's cream peignoir nightgown, the costume would need to fit in a small handbag. Initially, they had trouble getting the peignoir in and out of Lisa's miniature travel case before they created an origami-like solution where it just barely fit. The next issue with the nightgown was a little more sensitive.

During rehearsal when Grace wore the peignoir on set, something about the bosom didn't look right to Hitchcock's critical eye. Not wanting to upset Grace, he asked Edith under his breath to add some enhancement to the bust. "Edith came to my dressing room and said, 'Grace, there's a pleat here and Mr. Hitchcock wants me to put in falsies,'" remembered Grace. "I told her I wouldn't wear them, and Edith said she didn't know what to do—he was the boss." Edith studied the garment with intensity before she finally spoke. "I'll try to take it in here and pull it up there." In the newly adjusted nightgown, Grace stood up and walked with regal posture back to Stage 18 without any falsies. Hitchcock was pleased when he saw her. "That's more like it! See what a difference they make?" Grace and Edith shared a knowing glance. They never told him they had "enhanced" nothing.

Though her gift for garment design and on-set problem-solving was undeniable, Edith was a peculiar woman. Throughout her career, she didn't often share credit with assistants or colleagues, giving the impression she saw herself as the sole master of Hollywood couture. Case in point, when Edith accepted the Oscar for best costume design in 1955 for *Sabrina*, she declined to mention Givenchy's name in her acceptance speech. Indeed, there wasn't much of a speech at all. When Bob Hope announced her name with glee, she walked briskly up the aisle to the podium and accepted the statue as the *Sabrina* theme, "La Vie en Rose," played in the background. Then, with minimal eye contact, she said a quiet "Thank you" under her breath. Before Bob Hope could push her to the microphone to deliver an acceptance speech, she'd already made a beeline toward the stage left exit.

READING FROM TOP TO BOTTOM: LISA. CAROL. FREMONT

LIKE MOST ICONIC FIGURES IN CINEMA, LISA FREMONT WAS MOLDED FROM an assortment of real-life individuals. Depending on who you asked, you'd likely get a different account of who she was based on. According to Hitchcock, Lisa's persona and aspirations were heavily influenced by businesswoman and "perhaps the nation's first 'supermodel'" (according to the *New York Times*) Anita Colby. John Michael Hayes claimed Lisa's intelligence and heart were inspired by his wife, Mel Lawrence, also a blond fashion model. And, like many other Hitchcock characters, Lisa's existential worries about her romantic future with Jefferies mirrored the general anxieties of the auteur, himself. Yet, by the time she materializes on-screen, her distinctive personality is shaped and personified by Grace Kelly. In many ways, the two women couldn't have been more similar.

Grace Kelly came from a wealthy and prominent Philadelphia family. Lisa is a New York socialite, strongly suggesting that she comes from a privileged background. Lisa's wardrobe is impossibly glamorous and sophisticated, mirroring Grace's tastes and classic American style. Both women also had their dance cards filled by their vibrant circles of society friends in the metropolis of Manhattan.

As Jeff and Lisa peer out his rear window on one of her nightly visits, he points to Miss Lonely Hearts in her life of desperate solitude. He reassures Lisa, "At least that's something you'll never have to worry about." "Oh, you can see my apartment from here all the way up on Sixty-Third Street?" she responds solemnly. It's clear that Lisa resides either at the Barbizon Hotel or at least on the same street—the same building where Grace had lived six years prior.

When Jeff dismisses Lisa as a Park Avenue fashionista, he narrows down her main interests to "the latest scandal, a new dress, and a lobster dinner." He reduces her to a stereotype, based on her looks and career choices, and it's up to Lisa to prove her intellect and adventurousness to Jeff. Until she proved her abilities as an actress, Grace weathered the same path of resistance with her father. Jack Kelly looked down on theater people and viewed acting as an inelegant vocation. But no one knew the fire and knack for Hollywood wolves that shy, reserved Grace held within, least of all her family.

At age eighteen, undeterred by her father, she informed the family she was moving to New York City. Finally, her father gave in and let her go. After all, most would-be thespians came home within a year, dejected by the cutthroat acting world. "Oh Jack—it's not as if she's going to Hollywood after all," her mother said soothingly. "Let Grace go. This won't amount to anything and she'll be home in a week."

Like Lisa, Grace would have her work cut out for her in proving them wrong. Her parents would soon find they had grossly underestimated her tenacity in show business and life. "When her *Rear Window* character easily gets across the courtyard and up the fire escape to investigate the villain, *that* was Grace," noted Grace's nephew JB Kelly. "She was no shrinking violet."

Lisa is also her own woman. She has earned her career and money independently. She's not trying to land Jefferies for codependence or financial gain. She is just a woman who wants to be with the man she loves. The story is a relationship of equals and Lisa isn't merely Jeff's passive arm candy. "People have interpreted Grace Kelly's character as nagging or pushing him into marriage," said film historian and Turner Classic Films contributor Sloan De Forest. "But what's interesting when you watch the film and really pay attention, she never even says the word 'marriage.'"

As John Michael Hayes began to write dialogue for Lisa Fremont, he may not have been aware of these similarities when Hitchcock asked him to spend time with Grace on the set of *Dial M for Murder*. But the coincidences of art imitating life were remarkable. There wouldn't be a girl with a rarer combination of an adventurous spirit and icy exterior that personified Lisa Carol Fremont.

CAREER GIRL

ON HER FIRST VISIT TO JEFFERIES, AS LISA RECOUNTS HER DAY, SHE CASU-ally mentions her lunch date with Slim Hayward, a real-life American socialite who took Howard Hawks, then Leland Hayward, as a husband. She was a member of the exclusive New York Swans clique as Truman Capote had lovingly coined them (before exposing their secrets in thinly veiled fictional accounts and being exiled from their entourage forever). The circle also included Babe Paley, Lucy Douglas "C. Z." Guest, and Lee Radziwill, who were the ultimate influencers of their time. They were impossibly slender, impeccably dressed, and legendary for their long, boozy lunches at chic spots like El Morocco and 21 (the same 21 where Lisa Fremont orders Jeff a lobster dinner and knows each waiter by name). Most of the Swans were infamous for their romantic entanglements with powerful men and shoulder-brushing with the Hollywood elite. In the forties, Slim Hayward was regularly photographed hobnobbing with Jimmy Stewart and other stars at supper parties at the Waldorf Astoria Hotel.

Anita Colby was the career girl version of a Swan, and she mixed with the same hierarchy of privileged Manhattanites. She could often be seen briskly walking Fifth Avenue with somewhere important to be or kicking back at the Stork Club among the figures of café society. Everyone among the wealthy elite, from aristocrats to film stars, knew Anita Colby.

Born Anita Carole Counihan, she grew up in Brooklyn as the daughter of *New York World* cartoonist Bud Counihan. Following in his footsteps, she studied at Pratt Institute of Art to become an illustrator as well. Along the way, she took up modeling. With her delicate bone structure, perfectly arched brows, and effortless glamour, she began to dominate the growing mid-thirties modeling industry. She was soon the highest-paid model in the business at $50 an hour and often made $1000 a week. To all Manhattan bookers and photographers, she was known as "The Face." But beauty wasn't enough for ambitious Anita. She wanted to be "The Brain" and "The Boss" too.

In 1935, Anita moved to Hollywood to try her hand at a film career. After a bit part in *Mary of Scotland* (1936), she instinctively knew cattle call auditioning wasn't for her. She'd need to think bigger. Moving back east, she took on an ad salesperson job for *Harper's Bazaar* and learned the ropes of the business of beauty. In the forties, David O. Selznick hired her as "Feminine Director" to train contract actresses like Ingrid Bergman, Joan Fontaine, and his soon-to-be wife, Jennifer Jones, on beauty and publicity. Now, not only was Anita the first supermodel—she was also the first media training professional in show business. She worked on nationwide advertising campaigns for the film *Cover Girl* in 1944 and by January 1945, she'd made the cover of *Time* magazine. "Everything I have, I paid for myself," she boasted to the *New York Daily News* in 1946.

Coincidently, Anita had even been courted by Jimmy Stewart in the mid-forties. In November of 1945, he attended the Hollywood premiere of Hitchcock's *Spellbound* with Anita on his arm. Rumors would also swirl about Anita and Clark Gable soon after. When prompted about it, she played coy with *New York Daily News*. "Actors? What's wrong with actors? They always keep appointments right on time."

Hitchcock met Anita through her work with David Selznick. Struck by her ambition, he filed her persona far back in his imagination for a rainy day. According to him, that day came when he sat down with John Michael Hayes to hash out the characters of *Rear Window* in their 1953 story conferences. (At this time, Anita had just released her wildly successful *Anita Colby's Beauty Book* published by Prentice-Hall.) On occasion, Hitchcock identified Anita as his inspiration for Lisa Fremont. This was rare for the director, who often noted the evolution of his ideas for storylines, but never characters. Though there has been confusion in the past about Lisa's occupation in the film, Hitchcock had meant for Lisa's resume to read that of a businesswoman in addition to a model.

There would later be proof of Anita's influence in court papers. When Patron Productions dissolved in 1960, the rights to *Rear Window* were dispersed to its stockholders, who included Hitchcock, Jimmy Stewart, and Universal Pictures. In 1974, Sheldon Abend, the new owner of the film rights following Cornell Woolrich's death, filed his first of several copyright infringement lawsuits involving *Rear Window*. In a deposition in which he testified in court that year, Hitchcock would confirm that he had in fact based Lisa Fremont on Anita Colby.

In John Michael's mind, the inspiration for Lisa was taken closer to home from his wife, Mel, whose blond beauty resembled Grace's. He claimed there was also much drawn from his own life in the romance between Jefferies and Lisa. Before John Michael and Mel were married, they had decided to delay the wedding until he had achieved more career-wise. One day as they drove through Los Angeles, they were involved in a collision and Mel was thrown from the car onto the highway. The moment he saw her body on the road before being knocked unconscious against the windshield, John Michael had a startling realization. Similar to Jefferies as he witnesses Lisa in danger at the hands of Thorwald, the importance of the woman who meant everything to him came into full perspective.

"I said 'Oh my God. If anything happens to her, my life won't be worth anything,'" John Michael said years later. "And I decided I was not going to wait another minute if we ever lived through this thing." Thankfully, he and Mel both survived and were married immediately after.

After this life-or-death experience, John Michael instinctively knew how to provide the moment of reckoning for the on-screen romance of Jimmy Stewart and Grace Kelly. "He saw her and thought maybe it's the last he'd ever see her because this man is capable of killing and cutting her up," he said. "When I went out and picked up my wife, we weren't going to be separated again, so I drew on that."

Jefferies may be the voyeur of *Rear Window*, but Lisa possesses a sixth sense for solving crime. Her feminine intuition and bravery help crack the case, as she risks her own life to both prove her hidden depths to Jefferies and bring justice for Anna Thorwald. Without a love story and Lisa's persistence to show Jefferies their compatibility, there is no true connection to each of the neighbors.

As she looks out from Jeff's window at Miss Lonely Hearts, Lisa sees herself, or perhaps her future reflected back. Even down to the green dress Miss Lonely Hearts wears, just like the pistachio suit Lisa wears on her third visit to Jeff's apartment, she aligns with the prominent female characters across the courtyard and their experiences. Lisa's connection to Miss Torso becomes all too apparent as she and Jefferies watch her juggle a group of oversexed male suitors in her apartment, who are after her body, but not genuine intimacy.

As they witness the scene unfold, Jeff, showing what appears to be insecurity about his own economic status, is the first to comment.

> JEFF: A queen bee with her pick of the drones. Ah, she
> picked the most prosperous one.
> LISA: She's not in love with him or any one of them.
> JEFF: No, how can you tell that from here?
> LISA: You said it resembled my apartment, didn't you?

A PASSIONATE LENS

THOUGH SHE WASN'T AWARE OF IT, HITCHCOCK'S FORMER MUSE, INGRID Bergman, also played an integral role in *Rear Window*'s evolution. Since they'd worked on *Spellbound* (1945) together, Hitchcock was overwhelmed with infatuation and studied her like a rare specimen. But, it wasn't just her beauty and talent he was fascinated by. He analyzed her romantic life under a microscope too.

In 1945, as World War II came to an end, Ingrid went to Europe to entertain the U.S. troops. While staying at the Ritz Hotel in Paris, she met famous war photographer Robert Capa and the two began a tumultuous affair (she was unhappily married to neurosurgeon Petter Lindström at the time). When she returned to Hollywood soon after to film *Notorious* (1946) with Hitchcock, Robert accompanied her, snapping photos of her on the set of *Life* magazine.

Strong and masculine with a playful charm, Robert Capa was Ingrid's ideal man, but he led an unusual life. As a war photographer, he was nomadic and regularly put himself in mortal danger. Robert began his photojournalism career in Germany in 1932, and once he skied away to safety from the Nazis, he covered the Spanish Civil War throughout the late thirties. He was a cultured man who spoke five languages but his true communication was through pictures. Romantically, the man was covered in red flags, but Ingrid was hooked.

All the while, Hitchcock paid the utmost attention to Ingrid's passion for Robert, as well as his noncommittal attitude toward marriage. Sensing her desire to settle down, Robert explained to Ingrid, "You have to be wary of me. I don't seem to be lucky for people—especially for me." The affair dissolved within a year as Ingrid firmly made her desire for matrimony known. "He told me that he could not leave me all alone," Ingrid recalled. "Especially if we had a child. To go into danger, he said he *had* to be free to do it." As Hitchcock observed the relationship break down from a distance, he was utterly mystified that Robert would walk away from a woman that he could only fantasize about. The relationship made such an impression on Hitchcock that he re-created its dynamic seven years later with *Rear Window*.

The resemblance between L. B. Jefferies and Robert Capa was uncanny. They both worked at *Life* magazine and lived in Greenwich Village (Robert lived on Ninth Street). Just as Lisa suggested that Jefferies stay in New York and work at a studio, Ingrid hoped that Robert would eventually come to Hollywood and seek employment as a set photographer. "He was a dashing fellow, a romantic kind of character," film historian and producer Joseph McBride said of Robert. "Howard Hawks once told me he wanted to make a movie about Robert Capa; it would have been a great movie."

Perhaps the eeriest similarity of all between Robert and Jefferies took place two months before the release of *Rear Window*. Robert stepped on an anti-personnel mine while on assignment for *Life* magazine in a dangerous area in Thái Bình, Vietnam. The explosion tore a hole in his chest and blew off his left leg. He died at age forty. Though L. B. Jefferies was luckier with just a fracture, it was also his left leg injury that *Rear Window* revolved around.

When asked about the Bergman/Capa affair years later, John Michael claimed they hadn't officially based the love story on the couple, but with the number of coincidences, it's unlikely that this event hadn't influenced Hitchcock when he flipped through the private files of his imagination. He'd more than likely used the inspiration he took from the relationship dynamic without disclosing its source to John Michael.

Coincidentally, Ingrid Bergman's biggest hit with Hitchcock, *Notorious* romantically aligns with *Rear Window* in various ways. Set in Rio de Janeiro, Alicia Huberman (Bergman) and T. R. Devlin (Cary Grant) work together to uncover the enemy secrets of a Nazi villain and fall in love along the way. In a congruent vein, the story is about a woman trying to prove to a man that she is worthy of his love. Just like Lisa Fremont, Alicia goes to great lengths to prove to Devlin that they should be together. Similar to Lisa's daring intrusion into Thorwald's apartment to find Anna Thorwald's wedding ring, Alicia engages in a risky romantic relationship with one of the lead Nazis, Alex Sebastian (played by Claude Rains), to gather information about their activities post-World War II. If her true identity were exposed, it could mean death.

Hitchcock also sparred with the PCA office over sexually suggestive matters of *Notorious*. The Production Code, flexing their power as usual, threatened to kill a pivotal love scene between Ingrid Bergman and Cary Grant. How on earth would Hitchcock convey such passionate desire between the two when the "Sex" portion of the Code stated, "Excessive and lustful kissing, lustful embraces, suggestive postures are not to be shown?" (The unspoken rule was that kisses weren't allowed to exceed three seconds.) But Hitchcock was a step ahead of the censors. He would bypass the Code by having Ingrid and Cary repeatedly kiss for short periods while repeatedly being interrupted by a telephone conversation.

Ingrid recalled, "We just kissed each other again . . . and censors couldn't cut the scene because we never at any one point kissed for more than three seconds . . . we nibbled on each other's ears and kissed a cheek so that it looked endless." The film technically stayed within the confines of the Code while their heated desire retained itself on-screen. Hitchcock's knack for evading Hollywood censorship was getting stronger by the day.

CHAPTER FIVE

Surveillance in the Air

FLIPPING THE SCRIPT

IN 1953, AMERICA WAS STARING DOWN THE END OF THE MCCARTHY ERA. By now, a campaign of spreading fear of alleged communist and Soviet influence had pervaded the country and become commonplace. But by the mid-fifties, Senator Joseph McCarthy would lose credibility among the masses when several of his accusations were discredited and his tactics were exposed as threatening and even abusive. Consequently, over the next ten years, Hollywood would have some serious apologizing to do. Throughout that time, several ceremonies would be held at the Writers Guild of America, where the blacklisted screenwriters of countless films were honored and finally claimed credit for their work.

But for the time being, the United States was still under intense political pressure, and an atmosphere of surveillance hung in the air. America's faith in others had faltered and many were looking for telltale signs that people weren't who they appeared to be. *Rear Window* appropriately wove that theme into its plot. It posed the question: Can we really trust our neighbors? Though Cornell Woolrich's "It Had to Be Murder" short story originated this idea, it lacked a love story, which would become the film's emotional anchor.

Though the cinematic version of *Rear Window* owes much to the short story in its haunting theme and clever plot points of a murderer who comes and goes at all hours of the night, it's also the departures from Cornell Woolrich's original tale that make the film so compatible with the big screen. Hitchcock and John Michael Hayes would have their work cut out for them, but after multiple read-throughs of the short story, they decided to keep the clever aspects of its shrewd fore-shadowing. But for the visual medium, in addition to a romance, there would need to be other significant changes to draw the audience in.

Notably, the short story doesn't reveal Jefferies's broken leg until the last sentence, when his doctor visits his apartment and says, "Guess we can take that cast off your leg now. You must be tired of sitting there all day doing nothing." Yet, even when Joshua Logan wrote the initial film treatment, he instinctively knew that revealing Jefferies's broken leg should be one of the first visual details of *Rear Window*. The opening scene captures the vibrant summer ambiance of Greenwich Village in the middle of a heat wave. The camera continues to pan up through Jefferies's window, past his cast, to a coffee table that immediately reveals his life circumstances. A broken camera, a few framed action photos, and finally a fashion magazine with a glamorous blond model on the cover. This sets up everything the audience needs to know in one single shot.

Another stark contrast between the short story and the film is the fate of Lars Thorwald. In the literary version, once he determines which apartment his voyeur occupies, Thorwald waits until Jefferies is alone before attempting to murder him, but is abruptly shot and killed by police before he has the chance. Thorwald's life is spared in the film, though the suspense is much more Hitchcockian. When he enters Jefferies's apartment, he confronts him in a terrifying moment that involves flashbulbs used as a weapon of protection and a nail-biting scuffle. As the police arrive and take Thorwald to prison, he has shoved Jefferies out of his rear window, breaking his other leg in the process.

As they began work on the script, John Michael and Hitchcock went over the treatment page by page and measure by measure with a fine-tooth comb. Carefully eyeing his large sketch pad, Hitchcock laid out each camera setup for individual scenes. This was where the auteur's art direction background from silent film always came in handy. "He didn't wait until we got onto the set. He had the whole thing done when we finished working on the script in his office," remembered John Michael. "He put the sketches in a large book. The cameraman and the assistant directors looked at the sketches and Hitchcock told them what he wanted done."

Even the editors who normally weren't brought in until after filming was complete were invited to the preproduction meeting where Hitchcock unveiled the visuals of each action sequence for the entire production. This turned out to be a godsend for everyone. John Woodcock, the assistant editor, later recalled attending the meeting where camera operator Robert Burks and Leonard South, a graphic artist who assisted Hitchcock, were in attendance. "My attention was attracted to what seemed like cartoon panels covering three walls of the large room," he said. "It turned out to be a storyboard—the first I had ever seen. It was kept up to date and changed to reflect any changes in the actual shooting and was used to great effect in *Rear Window*." The auteur had mentally made the cuts before the cameras were even loaded with film.

Hitchcock was unconcerned with the way things were traditionally done in Hollywood and never looked over the shoulders of other directors to compare notes. It would make him feel like a schoolboy copying someone else's homework. No, Hitchcock always did things the Hitchcockian way. Who cared how Billy Wilder or William Wyler did it? He stuck to what worked for him. Though some scrupulous directors like Orson Welles and Fred Zinnemann were known to sketch out scenes in their films, Hitchcock was mostly alone in his storyboard practices in the early fifties. Hitchcock often observed that the real fun came from inventing the visuals in preproduction. "I wish I didn't have to shoot the picture," he once said. "When I've gone through the script and created the picture on paper, for me the creative job is done and the rest is just a bore."

Next, John Michael would need to take time alone with the script and add dialogue to breathe life and personality into Lisa, Stella, and the neighbors across the courtyard as well as those from Cornell Woolrich's original story like Jefferies, Lars Thorwald, and the Detective. John Michael's earlier screenwriting experience for B movies like *Red Ball Express* (1952) and *War Arrow* (1953) didn't allow him to fully illustrate his characterization chops, but *Rear Window* was finally his chance to shine. He was a natural at quirky and intelligent dialogue, while simultaneously adding comic relief in between the suspense. Like a statue that he obsessively chiseled each day, depth and dimension began to reveal itself in the script. Each character jumped off the page as a real person with relatable emotions and problems.

In later years, scholars and critics would dissect *Rear Window*'s hidden character depths, most notably of Jefferies's psyche and the supposed Freudian symbolism of his cast. One of the most repetitive ones suggested by critics like Roger Ebert was that Jefferies's cast, as well as his reluctance toward Lisa, was a symbolic form of impotence. "Perhaps his real reason for keeping her away is fear of impotence, symbolized by the leg cast," Ebert wrote in his review of *Rear Window* during one of its re-releases. "We are reminded of the strikingly similar relationship with Scotty, the Stewart character in *Vertigo*."

There is the suggestion of this theory during Lisa's entrance as she leans over and wakes him with that seductive kiss. It's wrapped in sensuality to the point that the audience feels as if they're the ones being kissed. At that moment, Jeff's response reveals him as a man with deep-seated problems. This concept may have been consciously or subconsciously hidden in the script, but chances are Hitchcock would have publicly scoffed at the "impotence" theory. Though given his own repressed Victorian upbringing, in private he might have acknowledged the sexual symbolism in the film.

As Hitchcock obsessively studied and revised the script with assistant director Herbert Coleman before filming began, Herbert threw in his own two cents that it may not be realistic that Jefferies could resist

Lisa's borderline aggressive advances. "I'm surprised, Mr. Coleman," replied Hitchcock. "Have you forgotten Jimmy is in a wheelchair and his leg in a cast?" His mind was made up.

THE GORE FACTOR

HAVING BEEN RAISED IN A STRICT CATHOLIC FAMILY IN EAST LONDON, Hitchcock had felt inhibited much of his life. He attended a Jesuit school and was brought up by devoutly religious parents. His authoritarian upbringing would cause him debilitating anxiety as an adult, but ultimately define his style as an auteur. "The repression forced him to think of something else to do that was equally as risqué, but in a way that was much more clever and hidden," said filmmaker Laurent Bouzereau. In addition to techniques of sexual innuendo in dialogue or portraying Miss Torso in scanty attire, *Rear Window* also reflects the psychologically dark side of humanity. Hitchcock dug deep for graphic themes that stemmed from an oppressed childhood that lacked connection, friendship, and love.

The short story's depiction of Anna Thorwald's death is slightly less gruesome than the cinematic version, though equally inventive. In desperation, Thorwald resorts to burying her body in the apartment one floor above him. The floor has just been laid and hasn't yet hardened. He carves a hollow in the floor and re-cements over her body in what Woolrich refers to as "a permanent, odorless coffin."

Hitchcock's gory portrayal of the murder of Anna Thorwald doesn't pull any punches. The concept that Lars Thorwald cut his wife into pieces, limb by limb in their apartment, and then dispersed her body parts into the East River is stomach-turning, even by twenty-first-century film standards. Unsure of what to do with her head, he initially buries it in the courtyard flower bed. When a neighbor's innocent dog gets curious about the head and tries to dig it up, Thorwald then murders the dog by breaking its neck. After that whole ordeal, he settles on a hat box as a hiding place for his wife's decapitated head. None of this is ever shown or even explicitly spelled out in plain language, but it's all implied.

When speaking at length with filmmaker François Truffaut about the making of *Rear Window*, Hitchcock explained that the Anna Thorwald murder was inspired by two news items from the British press—the case of Patrick Mahon and the case of Dr. Crippen, murders that were too strange to be invented. In the first case, Patrick Mahon murdered a woman on the seafront of southern England. Similar to *Rear Window*, he dissected her body into small pieces to easily hide the remains. But in the real-life Mahon tale, he disposed them piece by piece from a moving train window. Unsure what to do with the remaining head, that night, he hid it in a fireplace by the sea and ignited a flame to destroy the evidence. In an event stranger than fiction, a thunderstorm began and lightning illuminated the dark room. When he lit the fire, the eyes of the victim suddenly opened wide as if staring at him. "That's where I got the idea of having them look for the victim's head in *Rear Window*," explained Hitchcock.

In the case of Dr. Hawley Harvey Crippen, this time the culprit was an American homeopath practicing in London with his second wife, Cora, a music hall singer. While managing Drouet's Institution for the Deaf, Crippen had a torrid affair with his secretary, Ethel Le Neve. In 1905, the Crippens moved to Camden Road, where they took in lodgers for cash. Following a party on January 31, 1910, when Cora disappeared from their London home, Crippen's story was that she had gone to the United States. "But Crippen made a crucial blunder that turned out to be his undoing," explained Hitchcock. "He allowed the secretary to wear some of his wife's jewelry, and this started the neighbors talking. Scotland Yard was brought in, and Inspector Dew questioned Crippen, who gave a fairly plausible account of his wife's absence, insisting that she had gone to live in California. Inspector Dew had more or less given up, but when he went back for some formality, Dr. Crippen ran away with the secretary."

The story ended with the inspector conducting a search of the house. There, Scotland Yard uncovered the torso of a human body, buried under the brick floor of the basement. The head was never recovered, but Crippen and his mistress were captured when the pair fled to Canada on the SS *Montrose* and tried to pose as a father and son. Crippen was later hanged for the murder of his wife at Pentonville Prison on November 23, 1910.

The bizarre twist of the Crippen story struck Hitchcock as an imaginative plot that would provide a plausible initial argument for why Thorwald may not have killed his wife. It also created a gaping hole in Thorwald's alibi, which Lisa revealed by applying her "feminine intuition" to the case. "The scene with the wedding ring," recalled Hitchcock to Truffaut, "if the wife had really gone on a trip, she'd have taken her wedding ring with her." Lisa breaks into the apartment and puts Anna Thorwald's ring on her finger and waves her hand to Jeff from across the courtyard. In her victory, killing two birds with one stone, she's showing him the main evidence and sending a casual hint that he might get the idea and propose one of these days.

SOUNDS OF URBANITES

HITCHCOCK MAINTAINED A COMPULSIVE FOCUS ON THE ROLE THAT SOUND and music played in all of his films, but never was it a more crucial storytelling device than in *Rear Window*. He hired German composer Franz Waxman, whom he worked with on *Rebecca* (1940) and *Suspicion* (1941), to provide an auditory composite of city life unfolding around the audience. The auteur also took it a step further by layering in authentic sounds of Manhattan background noise to drive the narrative.

On November 11, 1953, an urgent night wire was sent from Hollywood requesting that a crew in New York record the bustle of side streets in Greenwich Village to avoid noises of heavy street traffic. In the finished version, the faint sounds of buses, pedestrian chatter, and children playing can be heard throughout *Rear Window*. It has an immersive quality that makes the audience feel as if they too are in Greenwich Village on a sweltering summer day.

To help push the story forward, snippets of songs and street sounds drift through the Waxman soundtrack, in and out of courtyard windows, and dictate the emotional state of various neighbors. *Rear Window* includes thirty-nine songs, ballets, and "improvisations" that are pieced together with elegant unpredictability.

Franz Waxman was an efficient man whose attention to detail rivaled Hitchcock's. Over his career, his one hundred and fifty film scores included the greatest hits of Golden Hollywood like *Sunset Boulevard* (1950), *Dr. Jekyll and Mr. Hyde* (1941), and *The Philadelphia Story* (1940). But *Rear Window* was a unique challenge for the composer. Each song would blend into the scenes seamlessly and needed to dictate an atmosphere that could change frantically from lightheartedness to suspense. He'd also need to somehow convey that the music was heard by chance by a listening voyeur outside the windows of the courtyard. Nothing could be forced on the audience.

The opening *Rear Window* theme, "Prelude and Radio," is a blend of hot jazz and Gershwin with booming clarinet and energetic strings. The song paints a picture of buzzing urban life in an asphalt jungle. The scene quickly cuts to the struggling songwriter through his apartment window, who is shaving while changing stations on the radio. Tuning away from a grating advertisement ("Men—are you over forty? When you wake up in the morning, do you feel tired and run-down?"), he switches to the jazzy upbeat tune that seems to levitate everyone's mood in the building as they wake up and face the day. Miss Torso begins her aerobic stretches while making breakfast and the man sleeping on the fire escape due to the heat is woken by his alarm clock.

The audience will become well acquainted with the song the composer continually struggles to write. "Lisa" is the haunting theme that continually intertwines itself through *Rear Window*. And it's not just the name that connects Lisa and Jefferies to the song. This infectious melody grabs the moviegoer's attention in the lightest and darkest of moments. From the composer's suite, the song continues to take shape as Jefferies resorts to his telephoto to observe Thorwald unpacking knives and saws. The song even saves Miss Lonely Hearts's life when she contemplates suicide. As she considers an overdose of pills, the rhapsodic melody stops her in her tracks with its reminder of the beauty life can unexpectedly bring. "Where do you think he gets his inspiration?" Lisa asks as the song gently makes its way up to Jefferies's apartment one evening. "From the landlady—once a month?" he deadpans.

Franz Waxman meticulously wove in melodies from films he'd scored in the past, though they're added to *Rear Window* so uniquely, it's as if they're being heard for the first time. "Mona Lisa," a song initially featured in *A Place in the Sun* (1951) with Elizabeth Taylor and Montgomery Clift, is heard drifting from the composer's apartment during a drunken sing-along when he hosts a boisterous party one evening. "Many Dreams Ago," a melancholy ballad that first appeared in another Elizabeth Taylor film *Elephant Walk* (1954), envelops a sorrowful scene where Miss Lonely Hearts reflects on her hopeless feelings about life. Suddenly, the camera veers up to Thorwald in the apartment above her, suspiciously packing a suitcase. This instantly transforms the nature of the song, making it a cynical plea of a man who very well may have killed his wife.

Of course, *Rear Window*'s score had to make room for a mischievous Hitchcockian inside joke. He does so with subtlety when the Livingston-Evans song "Lady Killer" is inserted in the scene where Detective Doyle presents Jeff with definitive evidence that Thorwald did not kill his lady.

THE SET

THOUGH FRANZ WAXMAN WAS ONE OF THE BUSIEST MEN IN HOLLYWOOD who mostly worked from home, he often brought his curious, young son along to see the action when he dropped into film studios to meet with directors and executives. In late 1953, John Waxman was just fourteen years old when his father brought him to the set of *Rear Window*. John poked his head through the Stage 18 door and looked up in astonishment at the cartoon-like metropolis. Since no filming was in effect, he was free to walk across the courtyard and get lost in his surroundings. He climbed the stairs to Jeff's apartment to get a better view of everything. John peered out of Jefferies's rear window in amazement at the neighboring apartments. He'd tagged along with his father in the past to visit movie sets, but he'd never seen anything like this. "It was so much bigger than I had imagined, particularly from L. B. Jefferies's point of view," he said, "and I didn't get that impression from watching the film later."

The set may have appeared more gargantuan in the flesh, but it was just as fascinating and lifelike on film. On camera, the *Rear Window* set held an animated quality and emerged as the film's most prominent feature. Just like a Disney version of a Manhattan street corner. It had taken six weeks to build with Hitchcock overseeing every minute detail of construction. In the beginning, challenge after painstaking challenge caused the crew to question whether this film should have been taken to an outdoor location after all. There was so much trial and error with differentiating night and day lighting, attempting to essentially dig a ditch in the set basement (which hadn't been attempted before), and even figuring out how Hitchcock would direct every actor from each apartment without running himself ragged.

The set was built from Jimmy Stewart's point of view, and in that sense, the audience's. The moviegoer takes on Jimmy's role as the Peeping Tom who watches along with him. For production, it was decided it would be most efficient to make Jeff's apartment the center of operations for principal photography. All lighting, sound, and camera work was operated from this room. It was fitting that Hitchcock sat in here with Jimmy as they both observed the simultaneous movies that played out before them.

Each of the apartment complexes had running water, electricity, and support from steel girders, so they could technically be lived in. Since they were fully functioning, Georgine Darcy claimed to have essentially lived in her small apartment, and never left the studio during most of her time working on *Rear Window*.

A remote switch controlled the lights in each apartment and a change in the overall set lighting from night to day took about forty-five minutes. Robert Burks set up stage lighting with a skeleton crew ten days before shooting and prelit all thirty-one complexes. "We had a switching setup that looked like the console of the biggest organ ever made!" remembered Robert of the contraption.

By the fateful day in November when Luigi Luraschi initiated the tour of the set for the Production Code Office that would save *Rear Window* by proving its adherence to the script, the set was finished and glowing in all its splendor. It was an urban forest of roof gardens, streets, and fire escapes that were astounding in their realness. As Luigi took the group around on the set on the first day of principal photography, it was clear to see many of the incidents like Miss Torso's sensual dance would be dwarfed by distance and camera angles. In a later memo on their end, the PCA readily concurred with Luigi's sentiment. Their memo concluded:

We readily agreed that the camera location, and the nature of this rather extraordinary set, eliminated much of the concern we felt reading the script material. It is noted that the entire view action will be photographed from a viewpoint of a man, looking out the window of his apartment.

The PCA's reversal in opinion on the *Rear Window* script was rare in those days, but it demonstrated the power of visuals and the painstaking work the crew had done to make something so artificial appear so real to life. It seemed that whoever circled Hitchcock's orbit and occupied his perspective inevitably began to see things from his point of view, even the ruffled suits of the Production Code Administration.

When the black-and-white *Rear Window* trailer was created especially for television broadcast, it began with a camera panning the courtyard, and slowly moving up to the apartment complex. It was the set that was featured to bring in moviegoers, not Jimmy Stewart or Grace Kelly. When press releases were issued to promote *Rear Window*, the set was featured only second to Alfred Hitchcock.

LOCATION, LOCATION, LOCATION

IN THE EARLY DAYS OF THE COURTYARD DESIGN, IN LATE SEPTEMBER, DOC Erickson went to New York to take photographs of the building they had scouted on 125 Christopher Street, which was replicated in the Hollywood "West Ninth Street" courtyard and complex (for legal reason, they wouldn't use the actual street name). The team also assigned four New York photographers to shoot the real Greenwich Village from every angle in all its beauty and disarray, in different weather, and in all lighting conditions, from morning to night.

Hitchcock even replicated the businesses that surrounded 125 Christopher Street. In *Rear Window*, the police are able to arrive quickly when Jefferies calls them (initially because he and Stella fear Miss Lonely Hearts may take her own life, but they arrive just in time to partially break Jefferies's fall once Thorwald pushes him out his window). In actuality, the original complex is also located across the street from the NYPD's 6th Precinct. The real-life 125 Christopher Street courtyard behind West Tenth Street would receive its well-deserved cinema starring role forty years later in 1993 with Woody Allen's *Manhattan Murder Mystery*, as an homage to *Rear Window*.

One of the most "New York" of all New York locations that would be brought to life in *Rear Window* was the 21 Club. For decades it had been the place to see and be seen by the Manhattan swans of society and celebrities alike. Located on West Fifty-Second Street, and hard to miss with its row of ornamental horse jockeys lining the entrance steps, it hosted patrons like Judy Garland, John F. Kennedy, and Bill

Clinton throughout history. Since it was a favorite of Grace's too, it was only natural that Lisa Fremont would be a regular there. In the scene when Lisa has two entrées of Lobster Thermidor with Pommes Frites à la Julienne delivered to Jeff's apartment, she tips the waiter for the cab. "Thank you for waiting, Carl." The waiter, dressed in an authentic 21 Club pea jacket, smiles, nods, and enters. "Kitchen's on the left, I'll get the wine," Lisa calls as though this is a nightly ritual for her.

The 21 Club has often been referenced in cinema to depict a character's place in New York society. In *Breakfast at Tiffany's* (1961), the perpetually late call girl Holly Golightly makes a mad dash to meet a friend (or client) there from her Upper East Side apartment. It also lent itself as a shooting location for films like *All About Eve* (1950) and *Wall Street* (1987). For *Rear Window*'s 21 Club reference, Hitchcock, as usual, kept things as authentic as possible. He insisted the 21 Club air-express a wine bucket, two dinner plates, half a dozen dinner napkins, and a pea jacket for the actor playing the waiter. Down to every detail, Hitchcock wanted to show a woman with the utmost taste and an eye for the finer things in life. Lisa Fremont wouldn't have it any other way.

Another equally famous New York location referenced in *Rear Window* is an iconic West Village haunt. "Meet me in the bar at the Albert Hotel," Jeff grunts to Thorwald over an anonymous phone call as a tactic to lure him out of his apartment. The Albert Hotel made the ideal location for Jeff to stand up Thorwald, and buy time while Lisa hotfoots it to his apartment to sniff for clues and recover Anna Thorwald's ring while he's away.

Located at 23 East Tenth Street, the hotel was just a stone's throw from the real-life Christopher Street complex. Since it opened in 1887, the Albert Hotel became famous for other pop culture moments as well. Thomas Wolfe based the Hotel Leopold on the Albert in his novel *Of Time and the River*. The Mamas & the Papas composed "California Dreamin'" while staying there, and the presence of artists like Andy Warhol and Jackson Pollock maintained the Albert Hotel as one of the

Village's most happening spots throughout the fifties and sixties. With its quiet dining room, it was the perfect meeting place for the tense conversation that would never happen concerning Anna Thorwald. It seemed Hitchcock had thought of everything.

STAGE 18, FRIDAY, NOVEMBER 27, 1953, NINE A.M.

TENSION MOUNTED ON STAGE 18 AS THE FIRST DAY OF SHOOTING AP-proached. Thankfully, the set had surpassed both Hitchcock's and Mac Johnson's expectations. It was a relief considering it had cost twenty-five percent of the entire budget. In additional hires, Hal Pereira was brought on to assist Mac with art direction and Robert Burks was officially secured as director of photography. When he arrived at the studio, Hitchcock stood and admired the oversized dollhouse that loomed above him. It had been clear from the beginning that the film required a studio set, and he was pleased that he'd gone with his instincts and blocked out inane suggestions to take it to the streets of Manhattan.

Greenwich Village of the fifties was a vibrant place, but it was noisy, filled with lights, blaring horns, and general craziness. Re-creating this whirlwind in a controlled environment was the right call. With the restrictions of a real-life apartment complex, he wouldn't have been able to get any of the lighting or interior shots he needed to capture the voyeuristic element. Stage 18 was the safe and efficient Hollywood version of a bustling metropolis. Taking over a real apartment building for several months and trying to capture its interior and exterior elements would have been sheer madness. And he'd pulled off interesting single-set films in the past, like *Rope* and *Lifeboat*. Sure, they weren't every critic's cup of tea, but with a set this size, he could take the complexity a step further by weaving multiple stories together.

With most big pictures, scenes were filmed out of sequence according to timing and efficiency with locations, but because *Rear Window* was limited to one set, and all the actors signed on for the length of the full production, it could be filmed chronologically. Contrary to David O. Selznick's opinion, Hitchcock ran a tight ship and his methods were so predetermined and hyper-organized that there was rarely wasted film. This time around would present new hurdles though, he thought as he walked back to his office. Such as, how would he be able to speak to and direct each actor who occupied individual rooms while synchronizing the shooting of each of their scenes? Luckily, his crew had figured it out for him.

At an earlier production meeting, he'd explained his dilemma to Herbert Coleman. He'd have big stars and many cast members with whom he'd need to have intimate conversations, discussions where he'd rather have privacy. "You wouldn't expect me to speak with them using a loudspeaker, would you, Mr. Coleman?" he said, with a stern voice, hiding a half smile. It would be somewhat amusing to see how the team dealt with such a unique problem.

Herbert had immediately taken action and conferred with the head of the Paramount sound department, George Dutton. Luckily, George had a genius idea. The sound crew had little receivers they normally used for dance sequences when they hid them in actors' ears so they could hear the tempo of the music while performing. Hitchcock would use these same devices to instruct his actors, and the most fun part—when he gave directions, they wouldn't be able to say anything back.

Before filming began, while standing in Jefferies's room, facing the courtyard, Herbert showed Hitchcock the new contraption. He pointed to a microphone hanging on a corner of the set. Beneath it were buttons, each one labeled with the actors' names. All Hitchcock would need to do is pick up the mike and push the button of the actor he wished to speak to. They'd receive a signal on their end, pick up their receiver, and listen to his instruction in their earpiece.

Herbert was beside himself with pride over the revolutionary idea. But as he explained it to his director, Hitchcock's reaction was difficult to read. He later wrote, "Hitchcock didn't seem to be as happy with the idea as I thought he would be. But he was all smiles when he tried it out after we started shooting." Herbert would soon learn throughout his years working with Hitchcock that he had been very pleased with the microphone. "Thank you" and "Great job" just weren't phrases that often passed his lips.

Production officially began at nine a.m. on November 27. Grace was in the makeup chair the earliest of anyone at seven a.m., while Jimmy's makeup call was at eight. From Hitchcock's energetic focus, as he rushed around making last-minute set approvals, everyone gradually became aware of the magnitude of *Rear Window*. This picture was going to be something special. The soundstage buzzed with excitement as the cast and crew eagerly waited for the first scene to begin rolling.

When it was time, Hitchcock sat off to the side in his stationed area in Jefferies's apartment and called action. In the first complex opening shot, the camera moves strategically through a synchronized combination of scenes. The sequence in the finished film would need to be cut to three shots, the longest shot beginning with a couple waking up on the fire escape. The camera then pans to Miss Torso's apartment, and over to the alley where children are playing. Next, it moves to a woman uncovering a birdcage at a window. As the camera fluidly moved around the set, Hitchcock put his microphone powers to use, providing each actor with their own unique direction.

After establishing a colorful scene of characters, the camera pans up to Jimmy's apartment window, to the beads of sweat on his forehead, a close-up of a thermometer at ninety degrees Fahrenheit, and finally to the cast on his leg. Jimmy didn't need to work hard at portraying the discomfort of a heat wave under the scorching studio lights, which had been cranked on high for the daytime setting. Ten takes were filmed of the opening sequence before Robert Burks was satisfied that they'd captured what they needed.

As one scene of filming led to another, *Rear Window* was a productive set, the complete opposite experience of *Dial M for Murder*.

Though the auteur was known to move at a pace that seemed leisurely to some studio executives, his crew moved quickly and efficiently, completing thirty-four camera setups on the first day of filming, and twenty-one on the second. Going into December, the main delay that arose and began to slow down production was the need to reshoot multiple scenes from Jeff's perspective with a ten-inch telephoto lens. At the last minute, Hitchcock decided on a six-inch telephoto lens. This paid off in the long run. It increased definition and sharpness up to ninety feet from Jeff's apartment.

The decision to keep all the action limited entirely to the apartment complex set without any cutaways to another location wasn't officially made until much later in production. Initially, after the opening shot of the courtyard and Jefferies's cast, *Rear Window* was meant to begin in the office of his magazine editor, Ivar Gunnison. In the original script, Gunnison sits at his desk with a cablegram in his hand while his assistant, Jack Bryce, stands across the room with a cigarette in his mouth. He lights it after reaching over and lighting Gunnison's first. A big story has come up. "Indo-China—Jeff predicted it would go sky high," says Gunnison. The two men discuss the merits of Jefferies's photography and decide he's the only man for the job. From the beginning, it's been established that Jefferies is married to his career, which takes him to places like Southeast Asia and the African jungles at the drop of a hat.

Actors had already been hired with the scene in place and ready to shoot.

BRYCE: I'll pull somebody out of Japan.
GUNNISON: Bryce, the only man for this job is sitting right
    here in town. [Picks up the phone.]
BRYCE: Jefferies?
GUNNISON: Name me a better photographer.
BRYCE: But his leg!

GUNNISON: Don't worry—it comes off today.

[Bryce gives Gunnison a startled look.]

GUNNISON: I mean the cast.

But Hitchcock had serious misgivings. He hemmed and hawed over the scene for weeks. Would beginning *Rear Window* in this sterile office scene with characters who'd never reappear advance the plot *or* was the scene completely redundant and distracting? The same information would be relayed to Jeff over a phone call in the next scene. And what about the set they'd worked so hard on? Perhaps an abrupt cutaway like this would pull the moviegoer out of the small universe he'd created on Stage 18. It would be risky and a very tall order to bring the audience's imaginations back to viewing the set as an authentic neighborhood again.

Examining the reason he may have put the scene in the film in the first place, it was likely Hitchcock was having thoughts about the potential concerns the studio had about another "one set" film that may not bring in money. But the whole team was uneasy about shooting it. It's also curious to note that actor Frank Cady was cast to play Gunnison—the same actor playing half of the couple who sleep on the fire escape for much of *Rear Window*.

On the day the scene was to be filmed, Herbert Coleman had reserved an additional soundstage. He and Hitchcock walked together in silence toward the stage. Hitchcock was in deep thought as if in another world. He suddenly turned to Herbert. "Do you still think it's a mistake to cut away from the Greenwich Village set to Gunnison's?" Herbert was thrown by the question. It had been a few months since they'd last discussed it. Though they were down to the wire, honesty still seemed to be the best policy. Herbert looked him square in the eye. "Yes, Hitch," he answered.

The Gunnison office set was ready to go and the six actors in the scene were waiting, so Hitchcock went ahead and filmed the scene, knowing it wouldn't be used. "All it will cost us is a little film," Herbert reassured him. "You'll have it if you change your mind again." But Hitchcock had seen the light. Everything that happened in *Rear Window* needed to happen in that apartment complex.

Hitchcock had made the right choice. Surviving photo stills of the scene in Gunnison's office appear jarring and out of place in comparison to the *Rear Window* apartment set. In hindsight, he'd known all along it would never work. The whole genius of *Rear Window* was the sole focus on this small world of people by keeping all the action in one place. Once he scrapped the scene, Hitchcock hired the golden-voiced Gig Young, famous for his Oscar-nominated role in *Come Fill the Cup* (1951), to play Gunnison's voice on the phone call with Jeff.

For a set as intimate as *Rear Window*, Hitchcock knew it was vitally important to hire not just a competent cast and crew but people he genuinely liked. On a set like this where he wasn't filming with different people in several locations, everyone would need to get along or at least be civil. In a more confined space, he couldn't have Method actors like Montgomery Clift pushing back at direction, or a Marilyn type showing up hours after call time. Luckily, he adored Jimmy and Grace and would end up hitting it off with Ross Bagdasarian and Georgine Darcy.

Due to his excitement about *Rear Window*, Hitchcock created an on-set atmosphere of lightness and buoyancy. He treated the set like an amusement park fun house and routinely played practical jokes on the actors. In good fun, Ross Bagdasarian and Hitchcock posed for goofy promo shots, where Hitchcock is seen pouring a watering can on his head, drenching his suit. "He knew my dad was a good actor and fun person to have on set," said Ross Bagdasarian Jr. "You want to be around as many people that you are like-minded or enjoy the process because they were stuck together for a long time on one set making that movie."

Hitchcock had now entered his creative prime and having the most fun he'd had in a long time. As he became more comfortable instructing actors with a microphone and earpieces, he decided a good practical joke was in order to keep things lively. One day as production loomed on set, Hitchcock called Georgine Darcy on her headset and requested she come to his side in Jefferies's room as she waited for her next scene.

When she arrived, he was in the middle of directing the scene of the couple sleeping on the mattress on the fire escape when it begins to rain. He told the wife, played by Sara Berner, to take her earpiece out and gave the direction to the husband, portrayed by Frank Cady. Then, he asked Frank to take her earpiece out and gave his direction to Sara. He then turned around to Georgine and winked. "Watch this." He'd given them both different directions. Frank was pulling the mattress to one window and Sara was pulling it to the other and they began to fight over the direction it would go. "Finally he pulled the mattress and somebody fell into the window," said Georgine. "It was quite funny and real. Those are the kind of things he would do." The scene made it to the final cut.

CHAPTER SIX

I Think We Have a Movie

THE PLASTER COCOON

JIMMY STEWART SAT BACK IN HIS WHEELCHAIR WHILE THE SECOND HALF of the "cast" was secured on his left leg and a makeup artist, sponge in hand, sprang at him for another touch-up. Conveniently, the artificial cast had a hinge on the bottom so he could stroll around the set between shots. He grinned to himself as he looked down at the signature that read, *Here lie the broken bones of L. B. Jefferies.* He surveyed the shabby apartment and began to immerse himself in the world of Jefferies while the crew finalized the setup for the next scene. One of the first things Jefferies utters in *Rear Window* is "Next Wednesday, I emerge from this plaster cocoon." He's desperate to get out of his cement prison cell and hit the road again. Though it only covers his left leg, it's as if his whole life exists inside the cast throughout the film.

Jefferies was a man of many inconsistencies and an incredibly contradictory character to pin down. Despite Jimmy's recent foray into darker themes, this was still foreign territory. Sort of like driving without headlights. Self-admittedly, his confidence had been slightly rocked by his time away from Hollywood during the war, but his last few pictures had helped him turn a corner. He was finally feeling like Jimmy Stewart the film actor again.

It was hard to forget how narrow-minded Hollywood could be

when an actor stepped out of his "nice guy" mold, but Jimmy knew that Jefferies wasn't a bad person at heart, though his behavior sometimes contradicted that. He was just a troubled man, maybe tortured by past ghosts. While mastering Jefferies's resistance to closeness and displaying the red flags of commitment phobia, Jimmy labored at balancing this with the paradox of obsessively spying on others' lives. It took a lot of script analysis and preparation, but he pulled it off in every scene. Hitchcock was delighted with his performance (though he wouldn't show it, obviously). Jimmy viewed acting as more of a craft or a trade than an art form. Part of the skill was to transform dialogue so the acting didn't show and only believability came through. His analysis of Jeff was based on logic, but on-screen, Jimmy made it seem like pure magic.

As he mentally prepared and the crew had almost finished setup, Grace Kelly entered the room, looking very Parisian in costume number two—the black silky organza dress with sheer cap sleeves and three simple strands of pearls around her neck. Lisa and Jeff were about to have their most intimate scene where they embraced and tenderly kissed on his couch while she does everything in her power to win his heart or at least his undivided attention. It also happened to be Jimmy's favorite scene of *Rear Window*.

"Okay, everyone! Quiet please," called Herbert Coleman.

This scene would call for a more sensitive touch. In many ways, this moment was the heart of *Rear Window* and would require dead silence on set. Though the picture was on a tight schedule, Jimmy knew it couldn't be rushed.

". . . Action!" Hitch's voice piped in.

The scene opens across the courtyard as the composer, while simultaneously mopping his floor, struggles with the chord progressions of "Lisa" on the piano. It's the song that won't leave him be. The camera slowly pans to the childless couple on the fire escape whistling for their tiny dog, who appears and jumps in a basket, which they lift by turning a crank device. Then, a slight shift down to the sculptress,

Miss Hearing Aid, working on her latest eccentric piece. Finally, the camera pans back across the courtyard to Jeff's apartment where he and Lisa are in their most vulnerable embrace.

Between kisses, they speak tenderly. "How far does a girl have to go before you'll notice her?" Lisa asks. This seems like a futile question, considering the night before, he requested they keep things as "status quo." "Well, if she's pretty enough, she doesn't have to go anywhere. She just has to be," Jeff answers, evading the meaning of her question. "Well, ain't I? Pay attention to me." "Well, I'm not exactly on the other side of the room," Jeff retorts. "Well, your mind is, and when I want a man, I want all of him," Lisa whispers almost inaudibly.

Predictably, it doesn't take long before Jeff breaks up the beautiful moment. His full focus is on Thorwald, questioning why a man would leave his apartment three times on a rainy night. Mere moments later, Lisa is back on the other side of the room again. Her efforts have been made in vain.

While Jimmy watched *Rear Window* later, this scene struck the strongest chord with him. Lisa tries to seduce him with kisses and caresses while he uses his binoculars and voyeurism as a defense mechanism against intimacy. His fight to resist love is becoming more and more evident. There is shared affection on their faces, so close together, yet Jeff grasps for his equilibrium and reminds himself that he and Lisa come from different worlds.

"I would watch Dad's films with my parents and he would occasionally say 'That was my favorite scene' or he would say 'I could've done that better,'" remembers Jimmy's daughter Kelly Stewart Harcourt. "He would make little comments every so often, but he did often comment on that scene in *Rear Window* . . . or maybe he just liked being that close to Grace Kelly!"

Rear Window was Jimmy and Grace's first time working together and the two got on like a house on fire. Jimmy was thoroughly impressed by the way Grace carried herself on set as a professional who always showed up on time and knew her lines. Though the crew constantly catered to her and she flirted back when she was in the mood, she was wise beyond her twenty-four years and could see through the superficiality of it. Though some saw her as standoffish and cold, the truth was that she felt lonely and isolated in Hollywood. She longed for a deep connection instead of small talk about the weather. It also later came to light that in the rare moments she didn't greet cast or crew members with a smile, it was actually because she couldn't see two feet in front of her without her glasses.

As a Hollywood veteran, Jimmy could see Grace had incredible potential as an actress. She actively listened during their scenes and didn't merely recite her lines back like some other actresses. It was difficult to believe this was only Grace's fifth picture. Like all her characters, she was deeply committed to Lisa Carol Fremont. In 1986 he told biographer James Spada, "She was really in a class by herself as far as cooperation and friendliness are concerned. A lot of things impressed me about her. She seemed to have a complete understanding of the way motion picture acting is carried out."

Lingering rumors loaded with double standards about Grace's love life reared their ugly heads whenever she starred opposite a leading man. But contrary to any reports, Jimmy and Grace's special friendship was a platonic one. Their mutual respect shone through in *Rear Window* and in the way they spoke about each other in years to come.

Even after she left Hollywood, Grace was sure to send the Stewarts a Christmas card every holiday season, or reach out if she'd seen Jimmy in a performance she'd enjoyed. In 1977, Jimmy's wife, Gloria, told film critic Clive Hirschhorn, "In all the years we've been married, Jimmy never once gave me cause for anxiety or jealousy. The more glamorous the leading lady, the more attentive he'd be to me!"

Though Grace was his predominant scene partner in *Rear Window*, Jimmy spent much of the film alone, simply reacting to what he saw outside his window. He realized he'd need to convey an entire relationship to each neighbor with just a simple look. When Miss Lonely Hearts toasts her drink to no one in particular on her pantomime date,

Jeff toasts his wine glass back at her, though she doesn't know he's watching. When the audience witnesses Miss Torso seductively exercising in her apartment, Jeff's eyes are now filled with lust, yet when he sees Thorwald leaving his house with a trunk in the small hours of the morning, his face is that of a brave man on the search for justice.

Placing Jimmy as *Rear Window*'s voyeur gave Hitchcock the perfect opportunity to utilize the Kuleshov effect, a montage editing technique he'd been itching to fully experiment with. The idea was first put to film by Russian film theorist and director Lev Kuleshov in the 1910s and 20s. As an experiment, Kuleshov filmed an actor with a blank, deadpan expression, and instructed him to smile. He used the same shot of the actor reacting to different situations, like a bowl of soup, a child, and a beautiful woman in a swimsuit.

Kuleshov demonstrated his theory by cutting away from this actor to a child. The man smiled showing that he was a benevolent man who liked children. He then cut to a bowl of soup and showed the same smiling face; he now appeared hungry. And finally cutting to a beautiful woman, he suddenly appeared to be leering. However, in all three cases, the actor's face remained the same. Hitchcock referred to this idea as "pure cinematics and how it can be changed to create a different idea."

As each scene was prepared, Hitchcock showed Jimmy what he was about to see through his binoculars. Then, he'd show him in playback how his face had appeared so he could reflect on what he saw. "I spent an astonishing amount of time looking into the camera and being amused, afraid, worried, embarrassed, bored, the works," Jimmy later told Roger Ebert.

Hitchcock acknowledged that silently reacting to a camera with an array of emotions is more of a challenge than meets the eye. Not normally one to compliment actors, he told François Truffaut of Jimmy, "In my opinion, the chief requisite for an actor is the ability to do nothing well, which is by no means as easy as it sounds. He should be willing to be utilized and wholly integrated in the picture by the director and the camera."

CRASH LANDING

THOUGH EACH SCENE WAS AS METHODICALLY PLANNED AS HUMANLY POS-
sible, *Rear Window* wasn't an entirely accident-free set. Besides minor
cuts and scrapes, there were no serious injuries until January 7 close to
the end of the filming day. Many of the non-action scenes with straight
dialogue were now in the vault. It was time for one of the more technically and physically demanding scenes where Thorwald would push
Jefferies from his window after confronting him. The helpless Jeff in
his wheelchair could only buy so much time by setting off the blinding
flashbulbs of his camera to fend off Thorwald. "What do you want
from me?" Thorwald's voice repeatedly booms before he maniacally
comes toward Jeff with outstretched hands and hatred in his eyes.

As the scene was set up, the air was tense. This would be innova-
tive as Jimmy's longtime stand-in and friend, Ted Mapes, a well-known
stuntman, would do the physical work. But Hitchcock would still need
to make it appear as if it was Jimmy falling from the window, something
that would need to be worked out in postproduction.

"Okay, everybody," announced Herbert Coleman. "Here we go!"

A wardrobe supervisor brushed a piece of dust from Raymond
Burr's frumpy gray suit. It was time for his close-up and finally his turn
to be on Jeff's side of the courtyard for the confrontation.

"Thank you, everybody," Herbert's voice boomed throughout the
set again.

"Ready? Roll camera!"

The cameraman flipped a switch. "Camera rolling . . ."

A slate was dropped in front of the lens.

Hitchcock took a last look around Jeff's apartment to ensure everyone was on their mark.

". . . Action!"

Raymond mustered all the intensity he had and walked toward
Jimmy's stunt double, Ted, in the wheelchair. He picked him up and
began shoving him out the window. This was looking good. Just the

darkness and fire the scene called for. This might be the scene that made the cut.

"Aaggh!!" Suddenly, a yelp filled the set.

"Cut!"

Raymond keeled over in pain. He'd pulled his back and was in desperate need of medical attention. He had badly strained it trying to lift Ted. Ever the hard worker, Raymond stayed on set the rest of the day but would require medical attention again on January 11. Finally, he took a day off to recuperate and the scene schedule order was reorganized to ensure principal photography would still wrap up by January 15.

The frames of this famous scene that show Jimmy to be falling from the window were done by creating an effect that combined live action with a pre-photographed "black velvet" background. Paramount special effects expert John P. Fulton used the "traveling matte" technique to believably create it. He photographed the patio, shooting straight down from Jeff's window, with the detective and policeman at the bottom, ready to break his fall. The velvet material covered the area where Jimmy would have fallen, creating a "black hole" in the scene. As the camera rolled, Hitchcock instructed them to act as if they had just caught him.

A few days later, on Paramount's Stage 3, the crew shot Jimmy as he hung from a windowsill above mattresses covered in black velvet. Later, the editing team would superimpose this image onto the first and give the illusion that Jefferies was falling out his rear window. For a sense of realness, Ted and occasionally even a dummy stood in for Jimmy during the scene.

The memorable final scene of *Rear Window* where Jefferies is shown asleep in two casts was actually a last-minute addition. "That wasn't in the script," Jimmy told the *New York Times* in 1983. At the eleventh hour, the usually premeditative Hitchcock had a change of heart. "On the day we were going to shoot, he came up to me and said, 'What would you think about breaking another leg?'"

When Grace was faced with on-set stunts, she was insistent on performing her own. Even though Herbert Coleman had hired a stunt double for
the physically athletic scene when she sneaks into Thorwald's home by
climbing up to his fire escape—no easy feat—she was adamant. Climbing the ladder over the balcony and through the window into Thorwald's apartment was challenging enough, but Grace did so in a floral
dress and a pair of high heels, adding to the dangerous element. Sharing
the same sentiment as the audience, Jefferies whispers across to her from
his window, "Lisa!! What are you doing?!" But it's too late. She's about
to put herself in mortal danger for the man she loves.

"This was close to the end of the picture," Jimmy remembered
years later. "Grace said, 'Well, I've been thinking about it, and how's
this?' She climbed up the fire escape, opened the window very carefully, and climbed in on her hands and knees. Hitchcock said, 'I
should've shot it,' but she said, 'Fine, I'll do it better the next time.'" As
she performed the stunt with the effortlessness of an acrobat, the scene
only took a few takes before it was in the can.

Through the grapevine of the village-like set, it got back to Grace
that Herbert Coleman wasn't happy that Hitchcock had allowed her to
go through with the stunt. It was dangerous and Grace was a beautiful and fragile creature whom every man on set fell over themselves to
watch out for. But Grace didn't see it that way.

When lunch was called that afternoon, the lights went out on set.
Everyone headed to Paramount's Café Continental to tuck into a Swiss
cheese sandwich or tenderloin steak. The set was empty except for a
group of crewmen at their usual lunchtime poker game in Miss Lonely
Hearts's apartment. Herbert settled into Jimmy's wheelchair across
the courtyard for a quick nap. He had fallen asleep when he suddenly
felt someone sitting on his lap. Then, he felt a soft kiss planted on his
cheek. He opened his eyes and it was Grace. "Don't be mad at Hitch,
Herbie," she said. "I talked him into letting me climb the ladder." A

still photographer was on hand to snap a picture of the moment. All was forgiven.

The next day, when Herbert arrived in her dressing room, Grace presented him with a copy of the photo. Even in this early point of her career, Grace had a knack for diffusing situations and influencing the narrative around her. Taking after her father, she applied the "Kelly charisma" to everything she did. It was in her blood. "Even though she didn't pick up the athletics from my grandfather, she did pick up his attitude and sense of carrying yourself in the public eye," said Grace's nephew JB Kelly. "She carried herself that way as a movie star and princess and it made her very successful."

As the holiday season approached, Grace began to grow more confident in her abilities and it showed in the dailies. For most of the *Dial M for Murder* shoot, she wasn't sure if she was pleasing Hitchcock. He often asked her and Ray Milland for multiple takes of scenes without offering an explanation. Most of the time, she walked away convinced that it was her fault, and not due to a technical interruption. But now, she was beginning to understand her director on a deeper level. Hitchcock's inability to compliment an actor on a good job—even when he liked what he saw—had worried her in the past. But as *Rear Window* moved along, she came to realize it often had nothing to do with her performance. It was just a Hitch thing.

THE GOOD LIFE

THOUGH GRACE HAD TRIED, SHE STRUGGLED TO ENJOY CELEBRITY LIFE. It was the American dream to become a Hollywood star, but something about it felt hollow to her. She was uncomfortable in a town full of freeways and showbiz types she failed to connect with. All the nervous breakdowns she'd already witnessed . . . Some of the people she knew here were in pain and could only sedate themselves with barbiturates and martinis.

Thank goodness for Rita Gam. At times, it was hard to make genuine friends in show business, but having Rita as a confidante and housemate gave her solace. Grace also longed to untangle her love life and settle down with a man she loved. During the filming of *Rear Window*, things had stalled with Oleg Cassini. Living on separate coasts created difficulty in receiving a full commitment or even a hint of anything that resembled marriage. The relationship was on and off for months. Not helping matters was his tendency toward mad jealousy anytime she dined with another actor, even in a group.

Grace missed New York terribly and would get sudden urges to leave town. It's not that *Rear Window* wasn't an incredible opportunity, but she wanted to be somewhere she could feel free to explore and navigate without getting stuck in traffic. On set, Grace often chatted with Ross Bagdasarian about the beauty of his hometown, Fresno, California. "For some reason, she was very interested in where my dad grew up," said Ross Bagdasarian Jr. "She had this affinity for Fresno and was always wanting him to show her what the wine vineyards were like. I think she liked the country more than her look would have you believe."

During its downtime, the *Rear Window* set was always star-studded, whether Danny Kaye stopped by while filming *White Christmas*, or William Holden took a break from wrapping up *Sabrina* on the adjoining soundstage. William was a troubled man with a love of hard liquor, but he never struggled to attract beautiful women. He'd always been friendly with Jimmy, but it was Grace he developed an immediate eye for on his first visit to Stage 18.

Grace was charmed by his witty sense of humor and his ability to have everyone in stitches whenever he entered the room. He also had impeccable manners, which appealed to her upper-class background. He had a knack for making the object of his affection feel like a goddess. Now his sights were set on Grace.

The day after *Rear Window* wrapped, as luck would have it, Grace moved across the Paramount lot to begin work on *The Bridges at*

Toki-Ri. Her costar was William, who played her husband, a navy hero during the Korean War. When the *Sabrina* shoot was completed in December, he had just ended an intense romance with Audrey Hepburn due to his having a vasectomy (this was a deal breaker for Audrey, who wanted children more than anything). Without missing a beat, William turned his affections to Grace. The two began a relationship as they worked together. He was a married man, but he and his wife were open about his affairs and lived mostly separate lives, much to her dismay.

Though untrue rumors have always circulated about some of her show business "trysts," Grace's children confirmed her relationship with William Holden in the 2007 tribute book *Grace Kelly: A Life in Pictures*. ("She succumbed to the actor who was twelve years her senior. The friendship rapidly turned into a fiery passion.")

Grace and William's romance lasted three weeks. It was his heavy drinking that ended things rather abruptly. Grace instinctively realized once and for all that she couldn't heal others with her sympathy and she'd need someone who was up to the challenge of meeting her halfway. Though she longed for a genuine bond in the isolated Hollywood hills, little did she know, she wouldn't have to wait long for her fairy-tale ending.

THE GRAND FINALE

ON JANUARY 5, THE LAST SCENE WAS READY FOR FILMING. *REAR WINDOW* ends the way it begins with a single pan of the courtyard that concludes in Jefferies's apartment. In a single shot of synchronized activity, the last scene reveals how the neighbors' lives have changed over time. After hearing his beautiful song in her darkest hour, Miss Lonely Hearts is now with the composer in his apartment and listening to a recording of "Lisa" on vinyl. The couple, whose dog was mercilessly killed by Thorwald, now have a new precious dog to shower with love. Miss

Torso is welcoming home her true love, a compact army private, who seems more interested in what's in the refrigerator than making love to her. The Thorwalds' apartment is being painted over, in hopes of cleansing away any lingering demons from this tragic event.

Finally, the camera ends on Jefferies sleeping in his wheelchair, now with both legs in casts. Lisa is beside him, casual in her indigo jeans and a simple red button-up, reading William O. Douglas's *Beyond the High Himalayas*. Sharing an inside secret with the audience to show she hasn't changed her tastes for Jeff, she quickly switches her reading material to *Harper's Bazaar* magazine.

The final scene took principal photography a week to film. The official final day of shooting would be January 13, 1954, which mostly focused on reshoots of Hitchcock's cameo in the composer's apartment and shots of Jimmy for the promotional trailer. Though they began much further behind in their timeline, the *Rear Window* team worked efficiently between November 27 and January 13. When principal photography closed, they were just fifteen days behind schedule and only slightly over budget. Hitchcock would need to go back later and reshoot an additional take with Miss Lonely Hearts alone in her apartment and another close-up of Stella on February 26, but for now, production was mostly complete.

As *Rear Window* wrapped, Hitchcock was still in high spirits. He'd been in the business long enough to know when he had a hit on his hands. In a tongue-in-cheek gesture, he presented Herbert Coleman with a photo of himself, which he signed, *To Herbie. From your assistant, Hitch.*

At the end of the last day, Grace, Hitchcock, and Herbert walked through the exit doors of the soundstage together and into the January mist. A light rain had begun to fall. It was the end of this bright, artificial world, one that would live forever in the corners of their imaginations. Everyone had grown so accustomed to living on the *Rear Window* set that it felt peculiar to leave it behind. Grace looked back at the set one last time through the open door. "You know, Hitch. It's like leaving a home you've grown up in," she said. They stood outside and watched every light go out on the set before they turned and went home.

During the editing process, Hitchcock sat with George Tomasini and directed over his shoulder. "Okay, cut three frames there. Add seven there." It was clear to George he already had the entire film precut in his mind. With so many interwoven stories and suspenseful moments in one film, *Rear Window* was a tricky beast to edit. There wasn't room for even a millisecond of error. Hitchcock knew that going in. After an eternity of meticulous starting and stopping, the film got to a point where it could be viewed all the way through. As the last frame faded out, Hitchcock sat with his typical blank expression. Did he approve of it? George couldn't tell. Finally, Hitchcock looked directly at him. "I think we have a movie."

SPARRING WITH THE PCA

IN EARLY 1954, BESIDES SUBMITTING FINISHED SCRIPTS TO THE PCA BEfore production, it was industry standard for filmmakers to submit a finished cut of their films too. If the picture passed their "test," it would receive a seal of approval. If not, it would receive editorial recommendations that filmmakers could implement before they resubmitted. This step wasn't exactly optional for mainstream filmmakers, as many movie theaters of the early fifties required that films have this PCA seal of approval. This made it virtually impossible for directors to ignore their edits if they wanted their work to be seen by a mass American audience.

Hitchcock, being a perpetual envelope-pusher and always up for a bit of fencing with the PCA, was putting the finishing touches on *Rear Window* before submission for approval. In mid-February, the first cut of the film was submitted to the office and was immediately rejected. Again, they aimed at Miss Torso and her costume appearing too much like underwear, as well as scenes where she appeared to be topless, though she was lying on her stomach.

Though the PCA suits had gotten a better understanding of *Rear Window* by seeing the lavish set up close, they were still firm in their opposition to sexuality on-screen. Hitchcock was instructed to remove part of the offending Miss Torso scene. No bother. He already knew that would be cut. It had worked perfectly in distracting the censors from the precious voyeuristic core of the story. All the filmgoer had to do was look deeper to find the darkness in the narrative. His films were like a maze of mind games, always more provocative than met the eye. *Rear Window*'s dialogue, full of double entendres, was luckily something the PCA was oblivious to.

In addition, the PCA reported that Grace Kelly's peignoir nightgown was far too "provocative and unconventional." They also found the honeymoon couple to be "unacceptably sex suggestive." Hitchcock wasn't rattled by any of this. This was part of the plan. You throw the censors a scantily clad woman or a sexy ensemble and it protects your baby. The crew had already filmed "protection" footage of Miss Torso fully clothed to replace the two scenes where he'd filmed her topless. But this tactic was nothing unique in the Hays Code days. It was common practice among the top directors. "You gave the censors bait, which they focused on," said John Michael Hayes. "Therefore the things you wanted to keep didn't appear harmful. This was done all the time, not just by Hitchcock."

Luigi Luraschi jumped in as Paramount's yes-man once again as he did during preproduction when guiding the PCA tour of the set. He assured PCA representative Eugene Dougherty over the telephone that the objectionable scenes where Miss Torso appeared topless would be replaced with more wholesome images. He also confirmed the scenes with the honeymooners' sexual innuendo and Grace Kelly's negligee would be shaved down to appear more "acceptable." *Rear Window* finally received its certificate of approval from the PCA on March 30, 1954.

CHAPTER SEVEN

Opening Night of L. B. Jefferies's Last Week in a Cast

THE WHITE PICKET FENCE ERA

BY 1954, REPUBLICAN PRESIDENT DWIGHT DAVID EISENHOWER HAD BEEN in office for a full year. As the thirty-fourth president of the United States, he'd already made an indelible mark with his version of conservative postwar America. The rates of marriage and home purchases began to soar exponentially. After a traumatizing war and a political hunt where everyone doubted their neighbors, people searched for a sense of belonging through domestic bliss. So, it was settled. The all-American family unit would be a two-parent household, each with their defined roles. A man worked nine to five, while a woman's place was in the kitchen. He brought home the bacon, while she was sure to have a vodka martini with two olives waiting for him after a draining day at the office.

It couldn't have been a more interesting time to release *Rear Window*. In one of the most conservative periods of postwar American history, Hitchcock flipped fifties gender politics on their ear. Lisa Fremont proves herself to be not only a self-sufficient career girl but a woman of conviction to the anti-marriage-minded Jefferies, who isn't in the market for a wife or a conventional life of any kind. He wants autonomy. Yet it's also arguably one of Hitchcock's greatest love stories. In classic trademark humor, *Rear Window* was promoted as a "Peeping Tom" picture about a murder across the courtyard, but beneath its tense surface are the longings of alienation and the universal human condition.

Rear Window was initially previewed at the Academy Theater in Pasadena on April 1, 1954, to a test audience. By the end of the screening, the audience comment cards were varied and unpredictable. The most common theme was a strong reaction, whether the viewer was elated or perturbed. Predictably, some found it offensive with the morally flexible Jefferies and the subtle but risqué dialogue. "Too many suggestive comments," one card read. This likely referred to Stella's vivid description of blood splatter during the murder of Thorwald's wife or the sexual innuendo between Jeff and Lisa when she plans to spend the night, which wasn't in line with mid-fifties Code-enforced cinema. "Trim the kissing scenes," another echoed.

Rear Window went over the heads of some. ("Why did he kill his wife? What was in the hatbox?") These viewers would need to see the film a second time before processing these subtleties. But overall, the majority of test audience members were open-minded and immediately understood Hitchcock's experimental intentions. An eloquent card read, "This was the most unusual and refreshingly new type of movie I have seen in a long time. After a while, I began to feel a little guilty myself looking through the rear window. However, don't change a thing." Bingo. Hitchcock had gotten through to his audience.

THE STOUT SILHOUETTE

WHEN IT CAME TO THE *REAR WINDOW* AD CAMPAIGN, THE KEY QUESTION that lingered for Paramount's marketing department was: How exactly do you promote bloody murder, voyeurism, and a peep show without ruffling executive or public feathers? Though *Rear Window* had finally passed the Hays Code test with flying colors—mainly because it implied as opposed to showed life's realities—Paramount's publicity department still knew it would be a delicate dance with this one.

They'd need to infuse a sense of fun into the promotional campaign, play up Hitchcock's cheeky humor, and again, rely on that phenomenal set. Hitchcock always had a strong arm in handling the marketing of his films while strengthening his brand (unlike many directors of the time who often stepped aside and let the marketing department do their thing as they moved on to their next film). Whether through film cameos, being the main attraction of press conferences, hosting his own television series, or appearing in trailers, the never-camera-shy auteur constantly made his presence known.

In 1960, the *Psycho* trailer starred Hitchcock, as he gave his audience a tour of the set, even taking them inside the creepy depths of Norman Bates's home. It would create more suspense and curiosity than hundreds of thriller trailers in years to come. His appearances for *Rear Window* marketing and ad material weren't as overt, but he was just as involved in overseeing its details.

The *Rear Window* trailer created especially for black-and-white television mainly focused on the virtues of the set, but the theatrical trailer opened with Hitchcock sitting between two cameras with his back to the audience as he stared up at the artificial Greenwich Village, contemplating the next scene. Each neighbor is introduced in sequence by the announcer's overly dramatic delivery ("Miss Lonely Hearts, so lonely that even *death* seems like a friend" and "the songwriter who plays the same melody over and over again . . . a genius or *insane?*"). The camera then cuts to the affable, wheelchair-bound Jimmy Stewart. He breaks the fourth wall and turns to the audience. "These are just a few of my neighbors," he says matter-of-factly in character as L. B. Jefferies. "First I watched them just to kill time, but then I couldn't take my eyes off them . . . just as you won't be able to."

The primary poster designed by the art department for Paramount's 1954 campaign features a view of the courtyard from Jefferies's apartment, as he peers intensely through his telephoto lens. "The most UNUSUAL and INTIMATE journey into human emotions ever filmed . . . revealing the privacy of a dozen lives!" These lives are pictured in the apartment windows in a series of capitalized blurbs introducing each character. Another more sensationalized poster ad that resembles a noir book cover features Lars Thorwald throwing Jefferies out of his apartment window as Lisa, naturally dressed in her sexy negligee, helplessly looks on.

In a stroke of genius, Hitchcock also made a humorous promotional poster aimed at any remaining cinemas who chose not to screen *Rear Window*. It featured Hitchcock with a deadpan expression and a shaving razor in his hand. "To those unfortunate exhibitors who have not already booked *REAR WINDOW*, I would like to demonstrate the correct method of cutting your throat. . . ." The ad boasted of the staggering box office results already received in cities like Chicago, Detroit, Cleveland, Kansas City, and Buffalo.

Almost a decade later, when Paramount decided to re-release *Rear Window* in 1962, following the enormous box office success of *Psycho*, they kept the same voyeuristic approach. Hitchcock's whimsical on-camera introductions on the weekly television program *Alfred Hitchcock Presents* had significantly caught on with the public. By 1955 when the program was introduced, Hitchcock had been levitated from famous auteur to household name. People now felt like they knew him, not just as a director, but as a personality. The appearances helped pave the way for another successful *Rear Window* publicity campaign.

Hitchcock was still a famous face in 1954 and he had always made himself visible to moviegoers with his cameo appearances. His recognizable stout silhouette always made him easy to spot. But the television series later catapulted him to a movie star level of celebrity. He'd now attained the elusive "icon" status (at a time when that term wasn't exhaustively used in celebrity culture). This time, Hitchcock promoted *Rear Window* through many television and radio spots. The publicity department was jumping for joy.

Now they could emphasize Hitchcock's dry British wit, which, going by his television series, the American public was eating up. The "special material" in the 1962 *Rear Window* publicity packet included "The Alfred Hitchcock Coloring Book Contest" ("This is Alfred Hitchcock. He is the producer of *Rear Window*. He frightens people to death. He is a nice man. Be kind to him. Color him thin."); radio ads with the master's voice ("If you scream yourself hoarse watching *Rear Window* and cannot tell your friends how much you enjoyed it, please drop them a line."); and the *Rear Window* photo contest ("A tie-in with your local newspaper," reads the manual, "whereby readers are invited to submit photographs taken by themselves from the vantage point of their own rear windows.").

The main slogan for the 1962 campaign was "See it—if your nerves can stand it after *Psycho*!" But this time, the famous courtyard set is nowhere to be seen in the publicity campaign. To bring filmgoers to the theater this time, the marketing facelift for *Rear Window* relied more on Hitchcock's increasingly popular star quality.

THE PREMIERE

IN THE SUMMER OF 1954, PARAMOUNT SCHEDULED *REAR WINDOW* FOR AN August 4 release at New York's Rivoli Theatre. Though two thousand spectators crowded outside the theatre at 8:30 p.m. just before the film began, the premiere was focused less on A-list stars and more on philanthropy. Its proceeds would go to benefit the American-Korean Foundation, which provided emotional and material relief amid the aftermath of the Korean War.

The Hollywood premiere, held a week later on August 12 at the Paramount Theatre, would be a different story. After all the back-breaking work, this was the event where *Rear Window* would be screened in the attendance of Hitchcock's industry peers. The house was packed with Hollywood royalty, like Cary Grant with his third wife, actress Betsy Drake; Joan Crawford; José Ferrer; Rosemary Clooney; Rita Moreno;

Joseph Cotten; Marla English; and Henry Luce III. Hitchcock was on cloud nine, arm in arm with Grace Kelly and Jimmy Stewart, and posing for the flashbulbs, while they shared laughs and inside jokes among themselves.

The *Hollywood Reporter* had reviewed the film a few weeks prior and had raved that Hitchcock had outdone himself this time. This could only mean one thing: the recognition of an Oscar after all these years of toiling and being overlooked. That night Hitchcock was like a little boy in a candy shop as he buzzed around the crowd, grinning from ear to ear. He charmed glamorous female guests with a kiss on the hand when introduced and hammed it up for the cameras any chance he got.

This was why he'd gotten into filmmaking in the first place. To show the world his ideas were like no one else's. And people were finally getting it. During the screening, in the scene when Grace Kelly sneaks into Thorwald's apartment, while the audience witnesses him arriving home, Joseph Cotten's wife, Lenore, who was seated beside Hitchcock, suddenly turned to her husband in a panic. "Do something, do something!" she cried. Filmgoers were putting themselves in Jefferies's place. The experiment had worked.

That night, Grace Kelly wore a radiant smile too as she posed on the red carpet in a Christian Dior Caracas black dress with a crisp white collar. Fresh from the spring/summer 1954 collection, it was couture worthy of Lisa Fremont. In her post-Hollywood years when she no longer relied on Edith Head to dress her, Christian Dior would become one of her go-to designers. The look was topped off with oversized pearl earrings and Grace's signature white gloves.

The main reason she was beaming with delight may have had more to do with the familiar-looking man by her side than the film. After the short-lived relationship with William Holden had fizzled midway through filming *The Bridges at Toki-Ri*, Oleg Cassini was now back in her life. This could only mean that marriage was around the corner. With a firm, almost possessive grip, he held her arm tightly that night. He had realized his mistake in taking such a cavalier approach to the relationship. Accompanying her to both the Los Angeles and New York *Rear Window* premieres, Oleg pursued her more enthusiastically than ever. The two were madly in love and over the next year, they were constantly spotted dining out in Los Angeles and New York. But Oleg's jealousy and the Kelly family's disapproval of a divorced man as marriage material would always be a thorn in their side.

The day after the *Rear Window* premiere marked Hitchcock's fifty-fifth birthday. Never one to rest on his successes, he was already back at work shooting interior scenes at Paramount on his new picture, *To Catch a Thief* with Grace and Cary Grant. During a break from filming, his secretary brought out a large birthday cake to mark the occasion. Oleg Cassini recalled her announcement when she came onto the set. "Could I have your attention for a moment? Would you all come into the other room, please, and have a piece of Hitchcake's cock?" Realizing her mistake, she turned scarlet red and set it down in front of Hitchcock.

He chuckled at her blunder, took Grace's hand, and blew out the candles. This was one of the most fulfilling times of his career. His artistic juices were flowing and the ideas kept coming. And critics weren't complaining either. He had the most bankable Hollywood film stars he'd ever worked with, but most of all, he had a certified hit with *Rear Window*.

BIG IN TOKYO

ON JANUARY 31, 1955, WHEN JIMMY AND GLORIA STEWART TRAVELED ACROSS the world to attend Tokyo's *Rear Window* premiere, they didn't know what they were in for. The crowd at the Hibiya Theatre was so enthusiastic and overwhelming, that security had solidly blocked the entrance doors until a police riot squad had to clear it. Everyone was desperate to get a look at Jimmy Stewart, the man of the decade. Paramount International immediately sent a night wire to New York, but Jimmy and his wife, Gloria, remained composed and laughed off the madness.

Onstage, just before the film screened to a fully packed house, according to the original night wire, "Mr. and Mrs. Stewart performed magnificently before a loudly appreciative audience." Once the screening ended, the audience members who filled the standing room area hooted and hollered in an emotional tribute. *Rear Window* fever had broken outside of the American market and the rest of the world was now responding.

The wire concluded, "Please communicate to the studio our great appreciation for Stewart's visit and their cooperation." Jimmy had a reputation for going above and beyond for his fans, even in the most uncomfortable circumstances. He wasn't as hardened by the industry as other veterans. Even later on in his career in 1970, when he performed *Harvey* nightly on the Broadway stage with Helen Hayes (a character revived from the 1950 film he'd starred in), he retained the same gratitude for his fans. When an exhausted Jimmy exited the back door of the American National Theatre and Academy (ANTA) late at night, there were mounds of devotees standing in the rain, waiting to meet him. He made a point of thanking every fan and signing every autograph.

"He was always proud when people asked him for his autograph," said his daughter Kelly, "and I never ever saw him refuse to give an autograph, even later on." Perhaps it was perspective gained from the war or maybe he was just born that way. But in August of 1954, even in the back of Jimmy's mind, an anxiety-inducing question still lingered. How *would* the sometimes close-minded critics of the fifties react to a film experiment like *Rear Window*?

THE CRITICS

EVERYONE WAITED WITH HUSHED ANTICIPATION AS THE REVIEWS BEGAN to flood in for *Rear Window* after the Hollywood premiere. To Hitchcock's relief, the reviews were generally positive, though *Rear Window* received its fair share of contrary write-ups, like the *New Yorker* calling its single set "foolishness."

C. A. Lejeune, a traditionalist critic who usually raved about Hitchcock's work, cited the "Peeping Tom" aspect of *Rear Window* as morally offensive in her analysis. Published in the *Observer*, the review was somewhat of a backhanded compliment of the director. "*Rear Window* strikes me as a rather horrid film, but extraordinarily well done. Hitchcock is a director who has always reveled in contrasts; nothing delights him more than to smother his ice cream with lashings of hot chocolate sauce. Whether one shares this taste or not, one must admit it *is* a taste and *Rear Window* has superlatively got it."

Variety printed an appreciative piece for a job well done in the auteur's film experiment. William Brogdon wrote, "Hitchcock confines all of the action to this single setting and draws the nerves to the snapping point in developing the thriller phases of the plot. Interest never wavers during the 112 minutes of footage."

With Hitchcock's already abundant body of work, critics often played the comparison game with his earlier films, where, depending on their mood, *Rear Window* sometimes played second fiddle. *Time* magazine began their review with "*Rear Window* is just possibly the second most entertaining picture (after *The 39 Steps*) ever made by Alfred Hitchcock." It did have a few qualms. "To the bad are the occasional studied lapses of taste and, more importantly, the eerie sense a Hitchcock audience has of reacting in a manner so carefully foreseen as to seem practically foreordained."

As is standard practice, whenever an artist dares to venture off the beaten path, naysayers crawl out of the woodwork. In retrospect, film critic Vincent Canby later wrote, "At the time *Rear Window* was first released, there was a certain amount of self-righteous outrage directed at the film's seemingly casual attitude toward voyeurism called Peeping Tomism." Hitchcock expected this wouldn't be to everyone's tastes in such conservative times, but he knew people would be talking about it. That was the important part.

The *New York Times* analyzed the film as "insignificant, superficial and glib and the purpose of it is sensation." But they congratulated Jimmy on his performance, saying he "does a first-class job, playing the whole thing from a wheelchair and making points with his expressions and eyes. His handling of a lens-hound's paraphernalia in scanning the action across the way is very important to the color and fascination of the film." They also called Grace "fascinating." (Not surprisingly, the *Times* would retrospectively change their tune about *Rear Window*'s lack of significance later, calling it "the most bittersweet of Hitchcockian suspense-romances" in its 1983 review of its re-release.)

But no *Times* review could hold back *Rear Window*'s mass appeal in 1954. The overwhelming public response translated into solid box office revenue of $5.3 million. It came in fifth that year behind *White Christmas*, *The Caine Mutiny*, *The Glenn Miller Story* (another Jimmy Stewart film), and *The Egyptian*.

Rear Window solidified Grace Kelly as a Golden Age star when the *Hollywood Reporter* stated, "To keep it from being cold and technical, Hitchcock adds to it the warmest love story he's ever placed on the screen. Here he capitalizes on the charm, beauty, and acting powers of Grace Kelly."

In 1954, both the National Board of Review and the New York Film Critics Circle honored Grace as the best actress of 1954 for her performances in *Dial M for Murder*, *Rear Window*, and *The Country Girl*. Partially thanks to Hitchcock, Grace was now living an actor's whirlwind fairy tale before she left Hollywood for good just a little over a year later.

TO CATCH A THIEF

BY THE TIME *REAR WINDOW* WAS PLAYING IN THEATERS ALL OVER THE world, Hitchcock and his unit were now properly set up in their suite of offices at Paramount Studios. Billy Wilder had just departed the studio for 20th Century Fox to make *The Seven Year Itch* (1955), so Hitchcock was welcomed as Paramount's hottest new commodity. When he informed Grace she'd be working with him again soon, he didn't inquire about her plans first. With his new leading lady, he imagined he'd never have to search out another actress for future films. This turned out to be one of the most naive presumptions he ever entertained.

To Catch a Thief starred Cary Grant as John Robie, a retired cat burglar who now works in the French vineyards and must clear his name once several robberies are committed in his style. Though considerably lighter fare than *Rear Window*, the PCA was still sure to remind Hitchcock of its looming presence when it voiced objections to the sensual love scene between Cary and Grace.

Geoffrey Shurlock, who now replaced Joseph Breen as director of the PCA after his retirement, would only allow a certificate of approval "with the understanding that in all prints . . . the love scene between Cary Grant and Grace Kelly in Miss Kelly's hotel room will be terminated by a dissolve before the couple lean back toward the corner of the sofa." Instead, Hitchcock toned down the sensual saxophone score, emphasizing comedy over sex. This seemed to do the trick. By 1955, with the burgeoning popularity of foreign films, it also wasn't lost on Hitchcock that the PCA's power in Hollywood was slowly beginning to crumble.

When Grace starred as Cary's love interest, it would serve as an extension of her cool Hitchcock Blonde image and help raise her star even further. The romantic plot of *To Catch a Thief* aligns with *Rear Window* in that the woman is the pursuer of a man who resists intimacy. John Michael Hayes had spent hours getting to know Grace Kelly and even more time perfecting the Lisa Fremont character on paper, and he continued on the same character trajectory with Frances Stevens. She is an heiress who grew up in luxury and wealth as the daughter of an oil millionaire. Like Lisa, she has that same autonomous streak. As an act of rebellion, she makes a bold move on John to break out of her box and prove she isn't merely the prim socialite everyone believes her to be.

Edith Head continued to build on the *Rear Window* wardrobe as well. The main visual difference with Frances is she has a tan and a convertible car for tearing around the cliffs of the South of France. By day, she basks on the beach in a canary-yellow one-piece swimsuit with horn-rimmed sunglasses and a classic swimming cap. By night she seduces Cary Grant with an ice-blue evening gown with a Grecian drape over her left shoulder. The leading man may have changed, but Lisa Fremont's audacity is just as present in *To Catch a Thief* as it is in *Rear Window*.

Hitchcock's schoolboy crush on Grace seemed to be increasing with time. She remained a good sport to his sometimes crass humor and always remained focused on his good points, like his unending patience with her on set. "I didn't discover Grace," Hitchcock once said, "but I saved her from a fate worse than death. I prevented her from being eternally cast as a cold woman."

As 1954 came to a close, Grace had gradually become a global sensation. Metro contract player Van Johnson understood the reason for her climbing popularity. "There hasn't been a newcomer of her thoroughbred type for many years, as contrasted with the cuties who've flung themselves up the old way."

Women began to reject the idea of emulating the impossible-to-attain bombshell looks of Marilyn Monroe or Gina Lollobrigida. Instead, they gravitated toward Grace's simple all-American style. Suddenly, the windows of Bloomingdale's were bursting with mannequins in A-line dresses with headscarves and classic white gloves. According to Grace's cousin John Lehman, she always had a sixth sense for what worked best on her figure. Her interest in fashion was deeply influenced by other show business members of the Kelly clan. "She was born with a flair for style and appreciation of it," he remembered. "Her uncle George and uncle Walter, whenever they were back from either New York or Hollywood, where they worked on stage and screen, would always slip her a hundred-dollar bill and say, 'Now you go to the best style shop in Philadelphia and get yourself an outfit.'"

In retrospect, Grace also had the right look at the right time. Simultaneously, her European counterpart, Audrey Hepburn, was casting the same influence from a Parisian standpoint with capri pants, ballet flats, and the little black dress. Jacqueline Kennedy would soon follow suit with pillbox hats, three-quarter sleeve jackets, and oversized sunglasses (with Oleg Cassini's help as her official wardrobe designer) when she became first lady in 1961. It was unanimous. The bombshell look had its time in the sun, but now femininity and class were the name of the game.

"I don't think Grace changed from the minute I met her to the day she died," Rita Gam said. "She had an extraordinary PR sense and she had a strong sense of who she was. She allowed herself to be used by the talented fashion people of the time. And she enjoyed it. But I certainly don't think of clothes when I think of her. I think of friendship, and of a loyal good friend."

Grace, never one to be valued for the superficial, felt anxious about all the hoopla surrounding her appearance. She'd worked hard on her craft and still wanted to conquer the stage, not become a glamour model. "Frankly," she admitted, "I've always hated being known for my looks. I'd much rather be known for my ability." This wasn't lip service of a woman who secretly liked being gorgeous. Fame never went to her head. She wanted to be taken seriously and still had much to prove to the world.

VERTIGO

JIMMY STEWART'S DOWN-HOME IMAGE REMAINED CONSUMMATE THROUGH the years, just like the stable life he'd built for himself in Beverly Hills. Though he was raised in Indiana, he'd been making pictures in Hollywood since the Depression era. He met his wife, Gloria, an elegant socialite, in 1948 at a dinner party in Gary Cooper's home. Back on the market, she had recently divorced Edward McLean Jr., whose mother,

Evelyn Walsh McLean, owned the Hope diamond. The two were married within a year.

Jimmy and Gloria built a happy life together with four children—two boys, Michael and Ronald, from Gloria's former marriage whom Jimmy had adopted, and two twin girls, Kelly and Judy. Life was peaceful in Beverly Hills with its manicured hedges and lush greenery. Everyone left their doors unlocked and the worst crime committed was when Rosemary Clooney and José Ferrer broke the Beverly Hills curfew by walking home from a party at Jack Benny's without ID.

Jimmy finally felt settled in his life. The Stewarts were so invested in their large Tudor-style house that when their next-door neighbor put his home up for sale, Jimmy and Gloria jumped at the chance to buy the lot of land. Gloria was an avid gardener. Wouldn't it be ideal to have a beautiful garden full of flowers to look out at, she asked her husband. So they went ahead with the sale.

The first time they went to view the house, there was one issue, however. The neighbor had let the home go to ruins. "It was covered in dead bees," remembered Kelly. "It was like a horror house from a Hitchcock film with a crumbling stairway." Jimmy and Gloria tore down the whole property and eventually transformed it into Gloria's marvelous dream garden. Jimmy even got into growing sweet corn and tomatoes as a hobby.

As Jimmy further embraced domestic life, little did he realize the release of *Rear Window* was about to ignite a whole new chapter of his career as the "complex" and "tortured" Hitchcockian man everyone would come to know. The beauty of Jimmy's everyman appeal was that it made him like an old friend to moviegoers who wanted to see what he'd do next. Throughout *Rear Window*, he became an unflappably "cool hero" who could literally lie around in his pajamas and still save the day.

He was also a hero who fought in the air force, making him a staple of American pride in the public consciousness. This added significantly to his aura on-screen. For the purposes of *Rear Window*, it provided him leeway to do things that were morally questionable and still be forgiven by the audience by the time the credits rolled. "There's this obsession with watching what's going on with people's lives and, that's maybe very unhealthy and not all that likable, but you know . . . it's Jimmy Stewart," said filmmaker Laurent Bouzereau.

Hitchcock built on this contradictory idea with *The Man Who Knew Too Much*, a 1956 remake of Hitchcock's original 1934 classic (this time set in Morocco instead of Switzerland). As Dr. Ben McKenna, Jimmy faces every parent's nightmare—the abduction of his child and all the fear and desperation that goes along with it. It's not until the family is in crisis that his role as a man is threatened. Ben is a husband, father, and doctor with a seemingly ideal life, but it becomes apparent that he takes his wife, played by Doris Day, for granted. It's the couple's interconnection he needs to come to terms with and which ultimately aids with the return of their son.

Vertigo finally completed the image of Jimmy as the conflicted Hitchcockian man. In one of his most famous roles, as John "Scottie" Ferguson, he faces the challenge of juggling his intense personal demons and extreme fear of heights with a romantic obsession that borders on necrophilia. Mourning the death of his lover, Madeleine Elster, portrayed by Kim Novak, again, Jimmy walks a morally fine line in how far he'll go to feel her love again. For the two films, Hitchcock wanted to expand the *Rear Window* character and create what would be a trilogy starring the same actor in different scenarios, which captured the nightmares of dark romance and anxiety that taunted Hitchcock's psyche.

It was important to Hitchcock to keep the same actor for all three parts while rotating the leading woman. When Doris Day was cast as Jimmy's wife in *The Man Who Knew Too Much*, it was a shock to many. At first glance, she was more of the anti-Hitchcock blonde. "Hitchcock and I met accidentally at a party," she said later. "Neither of us had the reputation for being partygoers and I think were both surprised to meet in that setting."

Hitchcock had seen her little-known film *Storm Warning* (1951), a noir about Ku Klux Klan terror in a Southern town, and had enjoyed it. To her amusement, he was a fan of her singing as well. And he knew her voice would make a vitally important plot device in *The Man Who Knew Too Much*. During filming, Doris, like many actors before, found Hitchcock's lack of feedback off-putting. She began to worry that he disliked her performance. After all, she was America's Sweetheart, not an ethereal, icy femme fatale.

By the end of filming, when he still hadn't provided any encouragement whenever a scene cut, she'd convinced herself that Hitchcock had only cast her for her singing skills, and nothing more. Surely, he would have preferred Grace Kelly for the part. On the last day, she gathered the courage to broach the subject with him. In typical form, he replied, "I said nothing because you gave a good performance. If it had been otherwise, I would most certainly have said something."

For *Vertigo*'s female lead, Hitchcock had his eye on Vera Miles, but when she announced her pregnancy, this put a delay on production. Hitchcock had originally planned to work around the pregnancy until he saw Kim Novak in *The Eddy Duchin Story* at an October 1956 screening. With her cool, platinum hair and hypnotic gaze, she embodied the Hitchcock Blonde at every level. He cast her immediately.

Though *Vertigo* is now viewed by scholars and film historians as one of the greatest movies of all time alongside *Rear Window*, in 1958, while Jimmy and Kim received excellent notices, the film did not. It was subsequently met with both critical and box-office indifference. John McCarten of the *New Yorker* wrote that Hitchcock "has never before indulged in such farfetched nonsense." Overall, *Rear Window* and *The Man Who Knew Too Much* had been far more commercially successful. Although it wasn't nearly as well received as Hitchcock believed it would be, *Vertigo* wasn't a total financial failure. By the end of 1958, it ranked as the twenty-first highest-grossing Hollywood film, having earned $3.2 million on its initial release—$2 million less than *Rear Window.*

Despite his awareness of the collective effort behind filmmaking, Hitchcock oddly shifted the blame for his *Vertigo* disappointment onto someone else. According to François Truffaut in a 1984 edition of his book *Hitchcock/Truffaut,* Hitchcock privately put the onus for the commercial failure on fifty-year-old Jimmy, who he thought was now too advanced in his years to play the romantic lead in one of his films. Yet he'd never expressed this theory only two years prior when *The Man Who Knew Too Much* was a box office success.

In 1958, the objective truth was that *Vertigo,* with its intricate storytelling and psychological depth, was simply too complex for audiences to fully grasp. But by 1982, the film would be reevaluated and enter the British Film Academy's prestigious *Sight and Sound* magazine's top films of all-time list, in seventh place. Of course, this accolade may have been lost on Jimmy, who likely didn't take out a subscription to *Sight and Sound.*

CHAPTER EIGHT

The Cinematic Aftermath

AN ANIMATED DETOUR

ONCE THE PREMIERE EXCITEMENT AND CRITICAL RECEPTION OF *REAR Window* had quieted down, Ross Bagdasarian was beginning to feel restless. He had conquered the acting side of show business as planned. After his performance in *Stalag 17* (1953), Billy Wilder praised him as one of the most natural actors he had ever come across, the ultimate compliment from a Hollywood legend. Playing the role of the frustrated composer in *Rear Window* had been his most prominent role so far, and working with Hitchcock had been an actor's dream. Ross knew he could stay on this trajectory if he wished, but did he want to weather the ups and downs of the actor's life? He wasn't so sure anymore.

Being a man of many talents, he sometimes grew tired of the more passive role of taking direction. But music was the calling that had constantly beckoned to him. Post-*Rear Window*, Ross dipped in and out of acting gigs, like the western *Three Violent People* (1956) with Charlton Heston and Anne Baxter. He made random television appearances playing dad types on *The Pepsi-Cola Playhouse* and *The Ray Milland Show*. But beginning in 1958, whenever he appeared on television, it would be to promote the biggest songs of his music career and one of the most commercially successful Christmas songs of all time.

Ross recorded a song in 1958 called "Witch Doctor" by singing a catchy tune into a tape recorder at half speed. This created the novelty sound of a voice on helium as he sang the unforgettable earworm "Oo Ee Oo Ah Ah, Ting, Tang, Walla Walla Bing Bang." The record sold 1.5 million copies and peaked at Number 1 on the Billboard Top 100. It also prevented his label, Liberty Records, from near bankruptcy. As "Witch Doctor" became the catchy theme of sock hops and summer camps across America, people young and old went crazy for his novelty act, and Ross knew he was onto something.

Seven months later, he followed that up, using his musical stage name David Seville, and invented three fictional chipmunks named Alvin, Simon, and Theodore. This time, he overdubbed his voice three times with the same "helium" recording technique, and "The Chipmunks Song (Christmas Don't Be Late)" was born. The song won three Grammy Awards for Best Comedy Performance, Best Children's Recording, and Best Engineered Record (non-classical). It was also nominated for Record of the Year.

When Ross appeared on *The Ed Sullivan Show* in December of 1958, his acting chops came in handy when he performed as the conductor with his three chipmunk puppets. "Alvin!!" he shouted in frustration when the cheeky puppet held a miniature hammer over Ed Sullivan's head, about to strike. This would eventually become the main catchphrase of a multimillion-dollar brand, which included music, an animated series, movies, toys, and a lot of swag.

After Ross conquered another facet of the entertainment world, that familiar restlessness began to creep in again. This time, he turned his sights to fine wines. In 1963, he bought a grape ranch in California and by the mid-sixties owned Sierra Wine Corporation, a winery that supplied products to the famous Ernest & Julio Gallo Winery, among others. The Chipmunks torch would later be passed on to his son Ross Jr. to carry on after Ross Sr.'s sudden death of a heart attack eleven days before his fifty-third birthday.

Pondering where his father might have eventually ended up had he not passed away in 1972, Ross Jr. thought it likely that he'd end up full circle—back where he began in the film business. "He loved the idea of directing and when I'd watch a movie with him, he'd have great thoughts about how this shot could have been more dramatic or that scene was great," remembers Ross Jr. "When he was doing the *Alvin Show* on CBS prime time in 1961, he was very specific about how the writing should be done, how the performances should be, and how the edits and cuts and timing should be done."

TINY DANCER

THOUGH SHE WOULD APPEAR IN A RECURRING ROLE IN THE TV SERIES *Harrigan and Son* and show off her dance skills in *Don't Knock the Twist*, acting had never held much appeal for Georgine Darcy. Waiting around just to stand on a mark and then not being able to move freely just felt unnatural for her. Next to the occasional modeling job, dancing was what made her come alive. But the thought of having to sit and memorize dialogue and hoping not to flub her lines made her stomach turn.

Recalling her arrival at the Hollywood *Rear Window* premiere, she said, "There were people lined up for Paramount Pictures and someone said, 'Who are you? What's your name?' I said 'Georgine Darcy.' And they said, 'Who the hell is that??'" Understandably shaken by the less-than-warm red carpet reception, Georgine quickly ducked into the theater and took a seat to view herself on film for the first time.

By the time the end credits rolled for *Rear Window*, she was a nervous wreck. "I was never an exhibitionist. I'd never seen myself so big as I was on that screen, and I was terrified." Ironically, Miss Torso was the biggest attention-seeker of all the neighbors of *Rear Window*, as she flounced her goddess-like frame around her apartment. The shutters are wide open as though she wants others to see her sensual performance (to Jeff's delight and Lisa's annoyance). But in reality, each time one of these scenes lit up the screen, Georgine self-consciously slid farther down in her seat. Among the theater crowd, she felt the weight of many curious stares, all intrigued by this newcomer. At the end of the film, a slew of paparazzi and journalists waited out front to photograph the stars as they left, but Georgine wasn't in the mood. "When the movie finished, I went out the side door," she said.

A native of Brooklyn, Georgine began as a ballerina at the New York City Ballet, though with her sexy figure, her mother urged her to become a strip tease dancer. Before *Rear Window*, she hadn't followed films much as a teenager. At age twenty, she was working in Las Vegas in a dance revue when she received the call from Paramount about *Rear Window*. When Georgine showed up at the studio a few days later and auditioned for Hitchcock, she had no idea who the auteur was.

When Herbert had shown her headshot to Hitchcock, he was amused by her black leotard and green feather boa and agreed she might be a unique choice. There was something spunky about her and when she danced, it was hard to tear your eyes away. At their meeting, Hitchcock suggested she get an agent, but since she wasn't sure she wanted to be an actress, she decided not to. Consequently, she was paid only $350 for the role that would make her a pinup sensation.

On the *Rear Window* set, the last day of filming Miss Torso's scenes was January 14. It also marked Georgine's twenty-first birthday. With her hair in curlers and cold cream on her face, she was packing up to go home when there was a knock on her dressing room door. It was Herbert Coleman. "Mr. Hitchcock would like you to come on the set," he said with a straight face, careful not to give anything away. She quickly threw a robe on and walked out to the set. To her surprise, Hitchcock presented her with a huge "Miss Torso" cake perfectly carved in the shape of her voluptuous body. "It had the breasts and everything!" she remembered. "Everyone was there and they could've gone home. Grace Kelly, Jimmy Stewart, Thelma Ritter, Raymond Burr. Everyone was there to sing 'Happy Birthday' to me."

After the film was completed, Hitchcock made the ultimate proposition. "You know, Georgine, if you study with Chekov, and go to

Europe for a couple of years, I would make a big star out of you." But she didn't follow that advice either. "Well, what a crazy suggestion! I assumed he was just teasing," she said years later. After that, she had bit parts in four more films; *Love Me Madly* (1954), *Don't Knock the Twist* (1962), *Women and Bloody Terror* (1970), and *The Delta Factor* (1970), none of them hits.

Acting was a pastime and a bit of a lark, but Georgine knew it was time for a new path. Though she had no shortage of acting offers after *Rear Window*, she decided to get married and embrace domestic life. Her husband didn't want her to work so she spent much of her time in retirement mode. She wouldn't work in show business again until her marriage ended five years later. "She had a really good habit of marrying very rich guys," said her friend Jim Katz. She married twice—once at twenty-one, and for the last thirty years of her life, to actor Byron Palmer.

"She always dressed well and, even in her sixties, she still looked great," Jim recalled. "She was a lot of fun. While we worked on the *Rear Window* restoration in the late nineties, she lived very close to us, and we went out to dinner with her several times. She gave me this great signed picture of her, which I still have. I didn't ask for it. I just got it one day under my plate at the restaurant!"

Although multiple claims have been made that Hitchcock was manipulative and controlling toward some actresses he worked with in later years, Georgine's experience with him on *Rear Window* was to the contrary. She remembered, "He was incredibly gentle and quiet. People may think him ferocious, but to me, he was a big old penguin." The two kept in touch over the years, even having phone conversations sporadically. When Georgine heard of new books or properties that had Hitchcock written all over them, she'd telephone him right away and let him know. The two had a genuine friendship. She even attended the premiere of *The Birds* and *To Catch a Thief* to support him.

The year she passed away, Georgine was the subject of the 2004 documentary short film *Remembering Miss Torso* by director Malcolm Venville, which was introduced during *Rear Window*'s fiftieth anniversary at the Edinburgh International Film Festival. The youth and vitality she represented in *Rear Window* would forever live on the screen, even though she'd resisted her sexpot image till the very end.

AWARDS SEASON

BY THE TIME *REAR WINDOW* SCREENED AT THE VENICE FILM FESTIVAL IN late August of 1954, the buzz surrounding the out-of-the-box film everyone had to see had picked up worldwide. Though it didn't take home the Golden Lion for which it was nominated, *Look* magazine and the *Film Daily* named it one of the top ten pictures of the year in their annual 1954 polls. *Rear Window* was also nominated for a Directors Guild of America Award, and a BAFTA (British Academy Film Award), though it surprisingly wouldn't win either.

John Michael Hayes was awarded Best Motion Picture Screenplay at the Edgar Allan Poe Awards in April of 1955, but like any blue-blooded director, Hitchcock had his eye on the biggest award of all, the Oscar. The news had just broken that *Rear Window* was up for four statues, but would the Academy finally acknowledge his contributions this year?

THE ACADEMY AWARDS, MARCH 30, 1955

THE YEAR 1954 HAD BEEN AS BUSY FOR THELMA RITTER AS IT WAS FOR HER *Rear Window* costars—if not more. After playing Stella to pitch perfection, her dance card was full of personal appearances. From luncheons with the mayor to cocktail parties at the Plaza Hotel, delivering a speech for the Cerebral Palsy Drive, and multiple appearances on the *Today* show, everyone wanted a piece of Thelma. Not to mention endless radio and magazine interviews, which never seemed to let up as the months went by.

Early 1955 was shaping up to be even more hectic. She'd been asked to take on the role of mistress of ceremonies for the East Coast segment of the twenty-seventh annual Academy Awards on March 30. Thelma was no stranger to the Academy. In her career, she would be nominated for a total of six Supporting Actress Oscars without a single win. After having been nominated for the fourth time, she joked, "Now I know what it feels like to be the bridesmaid and never the bride."

Bob Hope, who hosted the Oscars a total of nineteen times between 1940 and 1978, opened the night with a few off-the-cuff jokes about the now booming movie business after the "TV scare" ("Still, television isn't worried and they'll only start to worry when the motion picture industry has enough money to sponsor this program."). He then went into a colorful commentary on the films up for awards.

"Just look at 'em. True theatrical literature. *On the Waterfront*, the story of brutality and murder, *Rear Window*, a story of murder and brutality (pause for audience laughter), *Country Girl*, a story of alcoholism, *The Caine Mutiny*, a story of insanity. Whatever happened to *Seventh Heaven*?" (Coincidently, the sentimental romance, *Seventh Heaven* (1937) starred Jimmy Stewart in his prewar boy-next-door days.)

Bob's joke landed well with the Hollywood crowd. It was now becoming clearer from this year's selection that moviegoers were gradually becoming open to the perils of the real world. These films weren't upbeat musicals or candy-coated portrayals of life that people leaned on for postwar escapism. Perhaps *Rear Window* would have a real shot at winning this year.

Bob then passed it over to the NBC Century Theater in New York, where Thelma took to the stage, and the two bantered back and forth throughout the telecast. She was in full Stella form with biting observations that only she could get away with. When Bob asked if Marilyn Monroe was there, Thelma deadpanned, "Yes, she just came in with the Brothers Karamazov." (Marilyn had recently announced she wanted to star in the film adaptation of the book, which the press had cruelly mocked her for.)

Back in Hollywood, Bob introduced the first presenter of the night, a stunningly regal and visibly nervous Grace Kelly. Decked out in an ice-blue satin gown with double spaghetti straps and a ruffled waistline—an Edith Head creation—she appeared to be walking on air. As she floated across the stage to the podium, matching pastel blue slippers peeked out from her gown and a pair of white opera-length gloves accentuated her slender arms. A few days later, Grace would wear the same gown in a photo session for the cover of *Life* magazine's April 11th issue.

In a cool tone that masked her nerves, she spoke only a few words when she presented the award for Best Documentary. The truth was Grace had good reason to be anxious tonight. She had been nominated for Best Actress, not for the equally powerful performance she gave in *Rear Window*, but for her role as Georgie Elgin, the long-suffering wife of alcoholic Broadway star Frank Elgin (played by Bing Crosby) in *The Country Girl*. With her back-to-back schedule, she'd managed to film it soon after *Rear Window* in February of 1954. As she went back to her seat, all she could do was sit and wait. What would happen next?

SLIPPING THROUGH HIS HANDS

ALFRED HITCHCOCK DIDN'T OFTEN SPEAK ABOUT THE OSCARS. IT WAS A complicated relationship. *Rebecca* had won Best Production in 1941, but the statue technically went to its producer, David O. Selznick. As a director, Hitchcock received the nominations, but never the wins. Sitting and waiting on the big night, he looked at *Rear Window*'s four nominations—Best Director, Best Screenplay, Best Cinematography, and Best Sound. No Best Picture though. It was no surprise, considering the Academy's track record with his work. They liked certain types of films and his didn't fall neatly into that category. He'd already lost in previous years for *Lifeboat* (Leo McCarey won) and *Spellbound* (Billy Wilder won). They seemed to favor witty directors like Billy, the Oscar darling of the Golden Age who'd earned six statues overall.

As the telecast moved swiftly from one category to the next, each presenter called out the winners in exhilaration. "Best Screenplay goes to George Seaton for *The Country Girl!*" "Best Cinematography goes to *Three Coins in the Fountain!*" Piece by piece the chance of an Oscar for one of Hitchcock's greatest masterpieces slipped through his hands.

Later in the night, Marlon Brando took to the stage to present Best Director. He announced his own director's name, "In New York, for *On the Waterfront*, Elia Kazan!" Kazan, the man who made thinking pictures about social issues, moved with confident grace toward Thelma Ritter as she congratulated him. His film had dominated the whole night.

On the Waterfront wasn't a film that terrified moviegoers, but it made them think. With its fixation on the struggling common man, it was the latest thing Hollywood had to offer. It was a fresh, raw style of filmmaking that shook up the scene with an edginess only the young can pull off. Hitchcock was a purist of the old school and stuck with what worked for him. In the popularity contest that was the Academy Awards of 1955, his chances of victory were slim.

Marlon Brando was also called back to the stage close to the end of the night when he took home Best Actor. Eva Marie Saint won Best Supporting Actress for the role that Grace had almost chosen over *Rear Window*. *On the Waterfront* won eight Oscars that evening (its total wins tied the record with 1939's *Gone with the Wind*). There was no reason to be on pins and needles by the time the Best Picture award was presented. It was fairly obvious to everyone that the man of the hour would be called back to the stage again.

If Hitchcock felt hurt or disappointed over the snubs, he never showed it. But when François Truffaut asked him his general thoughts on the Academy Awards in 1972 he noted the unfair advantage of year-end releases. "The disadvantage of the present formula is that the awards invariably go to pictures that were released between September and December thirty-first."

William Hays, guardian of Hollywood morality in the Hays Code era, which began in 1934. *(Photo credit: Everett Collection)*

Jimmy Stewart as L. B. Jefferies in a publicity photo taken for *Rear Window*.
(Photo credit: Everett Collection)

Thelma Ritter as insurance nurse Stella and Grace Kelly as Lisa Fremont, both of whom added feminine intuition to the sleuthing in *Rear Window*. *(Photo credit: Everett Collection)*

Anita "The Face" Colby, Hitchcock's inspiration for *Rear Window*'s Lisa Fremont. *(Photo credit: Everett Collection)*

Alfred Hitchcock, Grace Kelly, and
Jimmy Stewart on the *Rear Window* set.
(Photo credit: Everett Collection)

Jimmy Stewart and Grace Kelly clowning
around with a camera on the Paramount lot.
(Photo credit: Everett Collection)

The *Rear Window* set, a vibrant replica of 1950s Greenwich Village.
(Photo credit: Everett Collection)

Suspicious activity:
Lars Thorwald
(portrayed by
Raymond Burr)
up to no good.
*(Photo credit:
Everett Collection)*

Georgine Darcy
striking a pose as
Miss Torso, the role
that made her
a sex symbol.
*(Photo credit:
Everett Collection)*

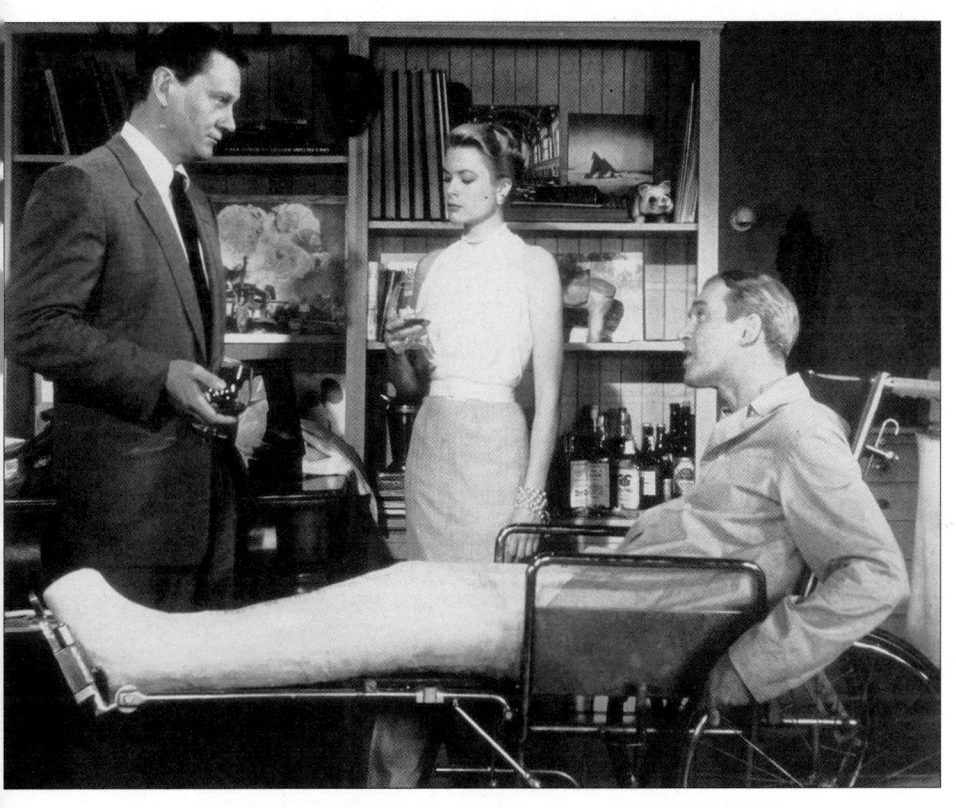

Wendell Corey is the picture of skepticism as Detective Doyle
in a scene with Grace Kelly and Jimmy Stewart.
(Photo credit: Everett Collection)

Screenwriter John Michael Hayes on the *Rear Window* set going through last-minute script changes with Alfred Hitchcock.
(Photo credit: Everett Collection)

Alfred Hitchcock working on a script as his wife, Alma Reville, looks on and provides tea in 1958.
(Photo credit: Everett Collection)

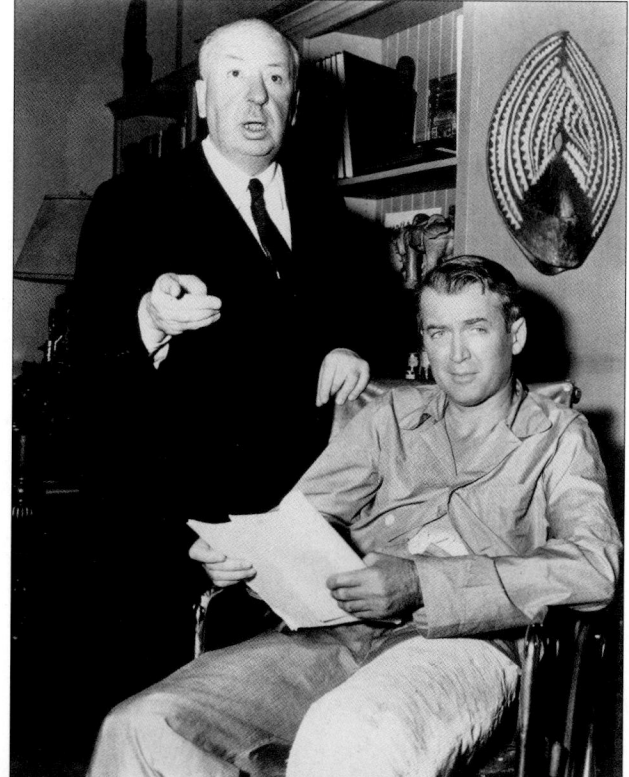

Jimmy Stewart and
Alfred Hitchcock
preparing for the next scene
of *Rear Window*.
*(Photo credit:
Everett Collection)*

sorrowful day:
rince Rainier III with his
hildren Caroline and Albert
uring the funeral procession
f Her Serene Highness
e Princess of Monaco,
race Kelly Grimaldi,
n September 18, 1982.
*Photo credit:
verett Collection)*

Grace Kelly at her wedding to Prince Rainier III in a gown designed by Helen Rose of MGM.
(Photo credit: Everett Collection)

Grace Kelly as Lisa Fremont attempting to entice Jimmy Stewart's L. B. Jefferies.
(Photo credit: Everett Collection)

Grace Kelly in the negligee that raised eyebrows with censors
during a tense scene with Jimmy Stewart in *Rear Window*.
(Photo credit: Everett Collection)

Grace Kelly looking every inch the ultimate society girl in a *Rear Window* publicity photo.
(Photo credit: Everett Collection)

Alfred Hitchcock winds the clock
in his *Rear Window* cameo
as Ross Bagdasarian,
the composer, plays on.
(Photo credit: Everett Collection)

Alfred Hitchcock with French filmmaker
François Truffaut at the Film Society
of Lincoln Center Annual Gala Tribute
to Hitchcock on April 29, 1974,
in New York.
(Photo credit: Everett Collection)

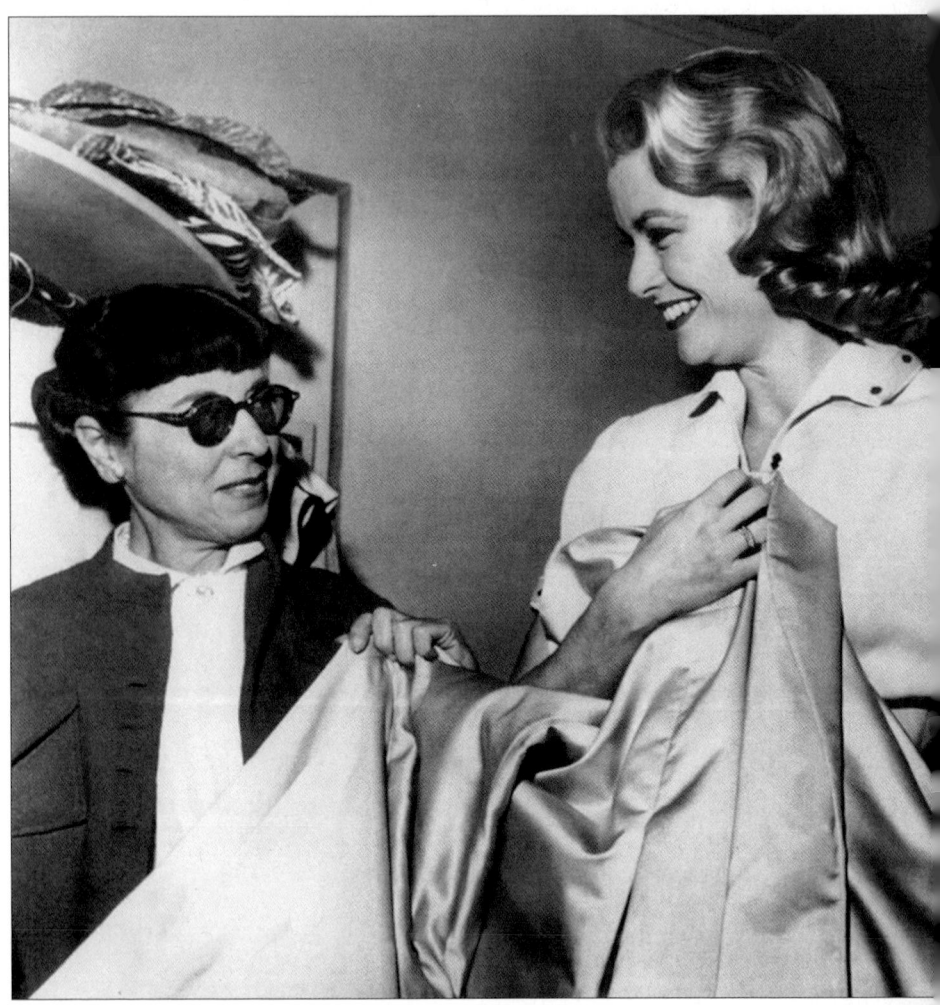

Grace Kelly with her friend, Hollywood designer Edith Head, as they hold the ice blue dress she'll wear the following night at the 1955 Academy Awards.
(Photo credit: Everett Collection)

The showstopper dress: the Edith Head creation that Lisa Fremont wears
for her memorable first entrance in *Rear Window*.
(Photo credit: Everett Collection)

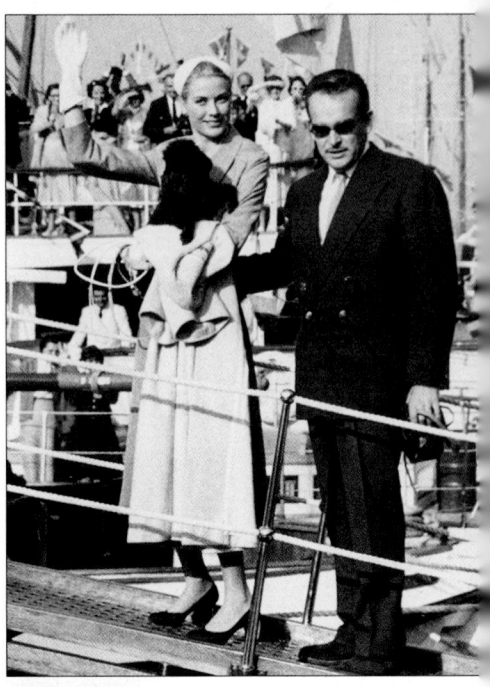

Prince Rainier and Grace board the boat for their honeymoon, along with Grace's poodle, Oliver. Grace wears the grey suit Edith Head designed for her departure. *(Photo credit: Everett Collection)*

Grace Kelly with Danny Kaye, who took a break from filming *White Christmas* to pay the *Rear Window* set a visit. *(Photo credit: Everett Collection)*

In the twenty-first century, it's become a spectator sport to debate or criticize supposed mistakes and tone-deaf "oversights" of the Academy. But the ultimate Oscar invalidation was made by Raymond Chandler in the March 1948 issue of the *Atlantic*:

"Technically, they are voted, but actually, they are not decided by the use of whatever artistic and critical wisdom Hollywood may happen to possess. They are ballyhooed, pushed, yelled, screamed, and in every way propagandized into the consciousness of the voters so incessantly, in the weeks before the final balloting, that everything except the golden aura of the box office is forgotten."

Even Marlon Brando, who became increasingly socially conscious in the coming years, would have a change of heart about the Academy Awards and follow suit in 1973 when he won the Best Actor Oscar for *The Godfather*. When Native American actress and activist Sacheen Littlefeather attended the ceremony in Brando's place to decline his award, everyone in the audience and at home was left stunned. When his name was announced, she took to the stage and explained that the actor "very regretfully" could not accept the award, as he was protesting Hollywood's portrayal of Native Americans in film.

The Oscar voting process and the Academy's decision-making have remained mysterious to many over the years. Hitchcock had the advantage of getting to make the films he wanted to make in Hollywood and usually got the stars he wanted. He'd built an extraordinary brand as a director where filmgoers couldn't wait to spot him in his next film. "In the face of so many great films and performances at the time—and frankly during all of Hitchcock's career, his success and the fact that he consistently worked, may have been perceived as enough of a reward from his peers," said filmmaker Laurent Bouzereau.

Another factor to consider with Hitchcock's losses was the period of 1955. The Academy was a more constrained group of people. It comprised mostly men with similar ages and economic backgrounds. "The Oscars have added a lot of members in recent years and they've diversified in different ways," said *National Post* chief film critic Chris

Knight. "The membership back in 1955 was probably only a few hundred people."

Adding to this perfect storm was the fact that genre films did not have a strong track record of appealing to the Academy in earlier years. It was a considerable amount of time before horror, science fiction, or even thriller films were accepted by the Academy as serious contenders. Though films like *The Picture of Dorian Gray* (1945), *The Bad Seed* (1956), and later *Carrie* (1976) had been recognized by the Academy, it wasn't until 1992 when *The Silence of the Lambs* was one of the first horror thrillers to steal the show when it took home five Oscars.

Top directors have often found themselves on a perpetually rotating axis, taking turns being honored by the Academy. When it was finally "their time" (though it didn't necessarily mean it was the best film of their careers), they took their position onstage. "I think it's often that when the industry rewards people, it's not strictly on a case-by-case basis," said former New York Film Festival president and Columbia University film professor Richard Peña. "There they are looking back over a career and saying, 'Oh, let's give it to them.' But is *The Departed actually* Martin Scorsese's best film? It's the only one he won Best Director for."

Hitchcock always labored under the burden of being "too good an entertainer" or having films that were "too successful." In what appears as an oxymoron, some in the industry felt if one was a successful artist, they shouldn't have commercially viable films. "I can remember when I first started going into film studies, some people were truly reluctant to want to take Hitchcock seriously," said Richard Peña. "There's a famous interview with Ingmar Bergman when they asked him about Hitchcock. He said, 'Yes, his films are amusing, but he's basically a child.' Well, I'm not so sure that *Strangers on a Train* is that much more childish than *Persona*."

There are additional cases as with *Citizen Kane* at the fourteenth annual Oscars in 1942 losing to *How Green Was My Valley* for best film. These losses generally don't make sense to the public or critics, but the underdog or sometimes less popular films that take home the trophy often fit into a mainstream idea of what an American film should be. Hitchcock movies of the fifties, though they were wildly popular, would have been considered too off-kilter or unsettling for the Academy, who sometimes went for a happy ending or triumph over adversity in their selections.

"He was interested in dark subject matter," noted *Star Tribune* film critic Chris Hewitt. "That wasn't something that the Academy had cared for; they looked at what represents 'the best of,' not only of our filmmaking but the best of America. That was not something that Hitchcock particularly cared to explore in his films." Hitchcock was an escapist storyteller and wasn't focused on depicting what was best about the American character. Even though the Academy loved British film, this should have worked in his favor. But when all was said and done, Hitchcock was far more interested in purely entertaining his audiences than he was in uplifting the morale of the world.

Hitchcock did his best to shrug off the *Rear Window* losses. In fact, this provided further ammunition to keep making films for the public, *not* the awards. By the time *Psycho* predictably lost for Best Director in 1961, the master of suspense had now been nominated for a grand total of five Oscars throughout his forty-year career with no golden statue to place on the living room mantel.

Finally, in 1968, the Academy, perhaps seeing the error of their ways, honored him for his "unique mastery of the art of film-making and distinguished contributions to the motion picture industry." But even then, it was a bit of a technicality. Instead of winning one of the Academy's traditional categories, he was presented with the Irving G. Thalberg Memorial Award, something of a lifetime achievement award for filmmakers. Not quite satisfied with this consolation, Hitchcock delivered a speech that rivaled Edith Head's brief *Sabrina* acceptance, one of the shortest in Oscar history: a simple and rather curt "thank you."

THE COUNTRY GIRL

JUDY GARLAND WAS HEAVILY TIPPED TO WIN THE BEST ACTRESS OSCAR for *A Star Is Born* in 1955. She couldn't attend the ceremony as she had just given birth to her third child, Joey. Instead, cameras and lights were set up in her hospital room so she could express her thanks in the likely event of her win. But in another classic case of the Oscars underdog, it wasn't to be.

When presenter William Holden's eyes lit up as he announced his costar and former girlfriend's name, Grace could hardly believe her ears. "Grace Kelly—for *The Country Girl!*" The whole world was stunned. Groucho Marx even sent Judy Garland a telegram of condolence, saying it was the biggest robbery since the Brink's Job. It didn't sound quite right to Grace either. Everyone had said Judy was a shoo-in, so she hadn't gotten her hopes up. Perhaps the envelopes had been mixed up and Bill had called her name by mistake? Before getting out of her seat to accept the award, Grace turned to Paramount executive Don Hartman. "Are you sure? Are you sure?" She had to be certain.

As Grace stood next to Marlon Brando backstage posing for the overexcited cameras with their Best Actor and Actress statues, she felt like she had the world in the palm of her hand. But in the depths of her consciousness, she knew something was missing. In answering the repetitive questions like "How did it feel to win an Oscar?" or "What is it like to be a world-famous star?" she always thought of something polite to say and told reporters what they wanted to hear. But in years to come, the concept of fame being the answer to happiness gave her room for deeper reflection. "I was unhappy," she later said. "I had fame, but you find that fame is awfully empty if you don't have someone to share it with."

By Oscar night, Grace and Oleg had separated for good. The loneliness was profound. Grace loved acting but she also wanted a husband and a family. Her sister Lizanne had recently gotten married, and while she was happy to help plan festivities, she felt a pang deep inside. She had a longing for the same type of life and for Prince Charming to come along and sweep her off her feet. If only life were that simple.

When Grace made her way to the Cannes Film Festival on May 4, 1955, to promote *The Country Girl*, *Paris-Match* magazine movie editor Pierre Galante and his wife, *Gone with the Wind* actress Olivia de Havilland, happened to be traveling on the same train. When Pierre learned that Grace was a fellow passenger, he was hit by a brain wave. Wouldn't it be a brilliant idea for the actress to meet Rainier III, Prince of Monaco, in a photo op for the magazine? What if it were possible to arrange a meeting between the two in a *Hollywood Princess Meets Real-Life Prince* type headline? Olivia loved the idea. But it would be a long shot.

When the train arrived in Cannes, Olivia ran as quickly as she could to catch up with Grace and suggest a meeting with Rainier. Grace was flattered but explained that while she was in Cannes, her schedule would barely allow her to catch her breath between interviews and appointments. She'd also have to check with MGM first. But, more out of curiosity than anything else, she tentatively agreed to the meeting.

A few minutes before their three o'clock meeting on May 6, Grace arrived at the Prince's Palace of Monaco. She looked appropriately aristocratic in a long-sleeved boatneck dress with a floral pattern, and her hair swept up and arranged with small flowers (the electricity had gone out in her hotel that morning, so without a hair dryer, she resorted to a last-minute bun).

Prince Rainier had been delayed on business in Beaulieu, but the palace staff assured her that he'd return shortly. The palace's maître d'hôtel, Michel Demaurizi, kept her occupied with a tour. He walked her through the rooms of grand apartments filled with Empire-period masterpieces collected by Rainier's grandfather, Prince Louis II. By 3:30, refreshments were offered, but still no Rainier. At quarter to four, Grace stared at the clock as she waited anxiously in the palace courtyard. She couldn't be late for the Cannes cocktail reception for *The Country Girl* at 5:30 p.m. She'd have to makes her excuses and leave.

Then, just as the clock was about to strike four, a red-faced Rainier hurried in to greet his guest with profuse apologies. "Would you like to visit the palace?" he asked. "We just have," Grace replied politely. Rainier took her on a walk through the palace gardens, as cameras zoomed in from a safe distance, allowing them to talk privately. Thirty minutes later, Grace was saying her thank-yous and goodbyes before she was whisked back to Cannes to make the reception. What a charming man, she noted. So cultured and yet, an open manner you wouldn't expect from a royal prince.

A few weeks later, Grace wrote a formal letter to Rainier, thanking him for the welcome he extended to her. Simultaneously, the prince wrote Grace a note of appreciation for allowing him to interrupt her busy schedule. So began a frequent pen-pal exchange that would blossom from a distance across the Atlantic Ocean. According to Rainier, he and Grace "revealed more and more with each letter." She found him warm and surprisingly easy to talk to. He had the kind of European charm she found refreshing after years of being courted in a more brazen style. Rainier found Grace authentic and unaffected by her life as a star. They also shared the same occasional risqué humor. Grace realized she may have finally met her match in the Prince of Monaco. Her usually disapproving father would be on board with this one.

By December 27, Rainier was spotted entering and leaving Grace's Fifth Avenue apartment in Manhattan. And on the 28th, he popped the question that had brought him to New York. "Will you marry me?" She didn't need to think about it. "Yes, of course I'll marry you." Rainier presented Grace with a 10.47-carat, emerald-cut diamond engagement ring, mounted in platinum from Cartier on Fifth Avenue. She would wear it when she starred opposite Bing Crosby and Frank Sinatra as Tracy Lord in *High Society* in 1956. On-screen, this ring symbolized her departure from acting and the new life she was about to begin in Monaco.

"I think they were very surprised," said Grace's nephew JB Kelly of her family's reaction to the engagement. "Just to hear something like marrying a prince sounds out of this world!" Once married, Grace would now become the wife of a head of state, and would assume responsibilities to the government and to the citizens of Monaco. She would officially be known as Her Serene Highness Princess Grace of Monaco—legally Grace Kelly Grimaldi.

Little did she know, *High Society* was the last film she would ever make, but when asked about her career at the time, she responded, "Of course I'm going to continue with my work—I'm never going to stop acting!" Marrying Rainier was the happily ever after she'd been searching for, though she wasn't fully aware of the sacrifice her new royal duties would cost her artistic life.

WHAT A CIRCUS

THE CEREMONY BETWEEN GRACE AND RAINIER HELD ON APRIL 18, 1956, was universally defined as "the wedding of the century" (a phrase repeated for Prince Charles and Diana Spencer's wedding twenty-five years later). Grace was the picture of serenity as she walked down the aisle of Monaco's St. Nicholas Cathedral toward her prince. She wore a refined gown of smooth taffeta and antique Brussels lace topped off with a sheer veil that covered her face. The dress was designed by Helen Rose of MGM. Edith Head had assumed she would be the one to design it until she found out the job was going to a rival studio. "The only time that I saw Edith Head upset was when Grace Kelly did not let her do her wedding gown," said Paramount Studio designer Moss Mabry.

Edith tentatively broached the subject with Grace. "Edith, MGM is *paying* for the dress . . . Would Paramount pay for it?" Grace asked her disgruntled friend. Edith paused at the question. No, they probably wouldn't, she realized. That ended the discussion then and there.

As a consolation, Grace asked Edith to design her honeymoon go-
ing-away outfit—a smart gray blazer and full pencil skirt, which she
wore when she and Rainier sailed off into the Mediterranean sunset
aboard the royal yacht. Even Edith knew that second prize was better
than nothing.

On the surface, it was a storybook wedding. The tale of the American movie star marrying the prince of a wealthy city-state captured
the world's imagination. But in reality, the frantic pace of the wedding
was taking a toll on everyone. Sixteen hundred reporters and photographers had flooded Monaco, and six hundred guests, who included
Cary Grant, Ava Gardner, and Gloria Swanson, jammed into a cathedral meant to hold four hundred. Later, fifteen hundred guests were
invited to the palace reception. Everything was in disarray.

The weather was unusually chilly for Monaco in the springtime
and the palace wasn't ready to be lived in yet. And there were hundreds of gate-crashers and jewel thieves invading Monte Carlo hotels.
"I remember looking at those first weeks as if I were just a visitor," remembered Grace. "A guest at my own wedding—but unlike guests, I
couldn't go home when all the fuss and furor became too much."

Grace's core group of friends remained important to her throughout her life, and selecting the women closest to her as bridesmaids
would hold utmost importance. Of course, she'd need her older sister, Peggy, in the wedding party to keep her centered, as well as Rita
Gam. She would also include old friends Bettina Thompson and Ma-
ree Frisby from her pre-Hollywood days. And Judy Balaban Kanter,
the wife of her agent, Jay Kanter, and of course, Carolyn Scott from her
Barbizon Hotel days in New York.

In exchange for releasing Grace from her contract, MGM was allowed to film the ceremonies for television and cinema. It would be
the event of the decade with roughly thirty million viewers, and the
publicity was overwhelming for the entire wedding party. The minute
the names of the bridesmaids were released to the media, it wasn't just

Grace who was stalked by the paparazzi. Suddenly, her friends who normally enjoyed their anonymity had lost all sense of privacy.

"Cary Grant had given a black poodle named Oliver to Grace after *To Catch a Thief*," remembered Carolyn Scott's daughter Nyna Giles. "So, my sisters with the nanny would walk the dog in the park because none of them could go out and be seen. Grace couldn't even walk her dog. It was really something for all of them. Years later, I talked to Rita Gam and, you could tell at a certain point they all got sick of being chased—they each had their own lives. Rita had quite a career as an actress."

Adjustments would be necessary for everyone involved in the royal wedding, particularly Grace's father, Jack. Despite being the father of the bride, there wasn't enough time to get acquainted with Rainier's family due to the attention they were obligated to give their European aristocratic guests. This was a culture shock for Jack, who was head of the Democratic Party in Philadelphia at the time. "He had run for mayor, not successfully, but he was the guy about town in Philly," said his grandson JB Kelly. "He didn't feel he was treated with the same respect because he came in behind on the protocol in Monaco, where they treat the royals ahead of commerce."

Jack wasn't used to playing second string to anyone and he felt uncomfortable in his new surroundings. But, as he got to know the rules of the royal palace, he gradually began to relax throughout his stay in Monaco. "He got over it. They have a protocol they need to follow, and that's their culture," explained JB. "He later realized it wasn't right for him to come in and expect anything different."

Grace also had a learning curve on the horizon. Though she would learn to love her position as Princess of Monaco and even Hitchcock would later refer to it as "the best role of her life," it was a demanding transition. As she tried to get a handle on her new life, she sometimes felt like an outsider with the palace staff and struggled with delegating tasks. However, drawing on the Kelly tenacity, Grace worked at fitting in, and by 1963, she was a fluent French speaker with no trouble assigning responsibilities to royal attendants. In addition to being a mother of three by 1965, she revived and personally directed the principality's Red Cross and the renovation of a crumbling local medical facility.

Over the coming years, Grace thrived in her new role as a humanitarian and mother. The only problem was the nagging feeling that her acting career had passed her by. But Hitchcock, who longed to be reunited with his original Hitchcock Blonde, would keep searching for a way to lure her back to the big screen, even if he had to fly to Monaco himself to make it happen.

CHAPTER NINE

Inching the Window Open in Censored America

A TURNING POINT

AS TIME MARCHES ON, THE NATURAL ORDER OF LIFE IS ALWAYS IN MOTION. The Hollywood film industry is no exception, and as the fifties closed on a period ruled by virtuousness, the pendulum began to swing in the opposite direction. This was partly due to changing tastes among American filmgoers. The postwar years saw a gradual liberalization of American culture as the silent generation gave way to baby boomers. The general public began to grow restless with the moralistic approach of Hollywood and craved a real-life take on the big screen.

A boycott by the Catholic National Legion of Decency no longer guaranteed a film's commercial failure (Elia Kazan's controversial *Baby Doll* (1956) was one of the first films to make a virtue of being condemned in its promotional material). Several aspects of the Hays Code, especially the sexual ones, began to lose their taboo as a new generation of viewers rebelled against what their parents had found entertaining. In 1956, select portions of the Code were rewritten to accept subjects like miscegenation, adultery, and prostitution. Inch by inch, the PCA was losing its grip on America's changing culture.

In parallel, foreign films that depicted people in nonmarital sexual relationships began to gain popularity in America. "These films didn't have to go before any kind of censorship board," said Columbia film professor Richard Peña. "There were a lot more independent cinemas because the studios were now forced to sell off their exhibition chains. So, because of that, these independent cinemas showed foreign films or even films that were American that just didn't go before the board."

Two Swedish films, Arne Mattsson's *One Summer of Happiness* (1951) and Ingmar Bergman's *Summer with Monika* (1953), both of which contained nudity, were released to the U.S. in 1955 and enjoyed box office success. This helped open the door to a new wave of sexually provocative European films in American theaters. Each time a new film tested the waters to see how audiences would respond, it led to a new chain reaction of releases. Next came the popularity of British films, like *Victim* (1961) and *A Taste of Honey* (1961), that challenged traditional gender roles and confronted the prejudices against homosexuality. Just a few years earlier, this would all have been in blatant violation of the Production Code.

Even in the mid-fifties when studios could sense change on the horizon, they had proactively found ways of complying with the Code while simultaneously getting around it. In 1956, Columbia acquired an art-house distributor Kingsley Productions, which specialized in importing foreign art films, to distribute and capitalize on the notoriety of the sexually liberal Brigitte Bardot vehicle *And God Created Woman* (1956).

Hollywood films gradually began to reflect changing American life as they became more explicit in their meaning. In the summer of 1955, in a shrewd move, director Otto Preminger released *The Man with the Golden Arm* before submitting it for a PCA seal of approval, but in early December that year, the PCA denied the film a Code seal, and the decision was upheld upon appeal to the MPAA. Large movie theater circuits including Loews held their ground and refused to ban the film, despite the lack of Code approval. It was their business to show the public what was new and popular after all. As a result of the controversy, feeling outnumbered, the MPAA was forced to reexamine and revise production codes, allowing future movies more freedom to explore taboo themes—all the things that made the PCA blush, like drug abuse, kidnapping, and abortion.

In 1959, Billy Wilder, who engaged in the same practices as Hitchcock in planting naughty red flags in rough-cut submissions to distract from what he wanted to protect, followed Otto Preminger's lead on the release of *Some Like It Hot*. The all-star film featuring Marilyn Monroe, Tony Curtis, and Jack Lemmon had not been granted the certificate of approval on release due to "the subject matter of 'transvestitism' and a clear inference of homosexuality and lesbianism." But the public begged to differ and the comical idea of Tony and Jack dressing like women to hide from the mob and blend in with an all-girl traveling band was a huge smash at the box office.

As the sixties approached, *Cat on a Hot Tin Roof* (1958), *Suddenly, Last Summer* (1959), and *The Dark at the Top of the Stairs* (1960) were some of the most prominent films of the age that dealt with adult and sexual subject matters not seen in Hollywood since before the Hays Code was enforced in 1934. To keep up with the changing palette of moviegoers, the Motion Picture Association knew they had no choice but to grant the Code seal of approval for these films. But now, due to an increasing number of those who'd no longer go by the book, the seal of approval had finally lost most of its authority. Public opinion was overriding the whole system and directors now had the upper hand.

Hitchcock was delighted by this news. It was an opportunity to experiment on a more visual and gory level. He could now make the film that had been taunting his nightmares. A truly unpredictable horror that followed its own rules and would delight and terrorize audiences at their core.

Psycho (1960) would begin in a completely oppositional setting to *Rear Window*. Instead of a muggy humid Manhattan block, it opens in the desert dryness of Phoenix, Arizona. When Marion Crane, portrayed by Janet Leigh, gets in her car to drive, she's escaping her life, and twenty-five minutes into the film, it begins to rain. She has suddenly entered a parallel universe. Hitchcock's uncanny gift for establishing his locations was ever-present. This drenched, heavy atmosphere signals that she's left the world she knows and is entering a new one that symbolizes her death.

When she pulls up to the Bates Motel, Marion's fate is to die under running water and be buried in a swamp. With more flexibility from the fraying Hays Code, Hitchcock was able to show the explicit elements of body parts and blood in the shower scene, as well as an opening postcoital scene in which Marion appears in a bra with her lover, Sam. The film has transgressive subject matter, where murderer Norman Bates cross-dresses, though, this isn't revealed until he attacks Marion's sister, Lila, played by Vera Miles.

Though the Hays Code was becoming largely ignored by directors, the PCA still liked to taunt Hitchcock when it had the chance. The director had a full-on rumble with the censors over the raciness of the shower scene. Another cause of concern was that Marion was shown flushing a toilet, with its contents (a torn-up notepaper) fully visible. A flushing toilet had never appeared in mainstream film or television in the United States at that time. After some negotiation, the censors finally passed the film when Hitchcock resorted to his usual trick à la Miss Torso in *Rear Window* when he removed one shot that showed the buttocks of Janet's stand-in.

Psycho received the usual mixed reviews of a Hitchcock film on its initial release, but it was a massive overnight success with theater audiences. It broke box-office records in Japan and the rest of Asia, France, Britain, South America, the United States, and Canada, and was even a moderate success in Australia. It was the highest-grossing film of 1960 behind *Spartacus*, making a box office gross of $32 million.

This gave Paramount an idea. They would re-release *Rear Window* on the coattails of *Psycho* in a new promotional campaign. In the new 1962 poster for *Rear Window*, which reused a graphic of Jimmy Stewart with binoculars from the 1954 campaign, the strongly worded copy described it as "The most unusual and intimate journey into human emotions ever filmed!" This time, the updated campaign strongly emphasized Raymond Burr's new-found celebrity from the television show *Perry Mason* and Grace's royal position as Her Serene Highness of Monaco. And, of course, Hitchcock's massive celebrity status from his weekly television program.

The 1962 *Rear Window* publicity campaign would rely on name recognition more than the set or the story itself. After this second successful theater run, Hitchcock put *Rear Window* back in its vault with no further plans for it. Throughout the sixties and seventies, other than the odd television broadcast, it became impossible to find copies of *Rear Window*, *The Man Who Knew Too Much*, *Rope*, *Vertigo*, or *The Trouble with Harry*. He had complete control of them, just the way he liked it.

THE BREAKUP

AFTER GRACE SETTLED IN MONACO AND IT BECAME CLEAR SHE'D LEFT Hollywood for good, Hitchcock felt as if he'd had the rug pulled out from under his feet. Why did talented actresses like Kelly and Bergman have to abandon him and run off to foreign countries for love? In truth, he felt no real grudge toward Grace as he had Ingrid. After all, Rainier wasn't a filmmaker the way Roberto Rossellini was. And there was a certain awe that came along with the title of Her Serene Highness of Monaco, one that might even rub off on him. He would try his best to get Grace back on set again, but would spend the rest of his career unsuccessfully attempting to replace the magic they'd created together in *Rear Window*.

Soon after Grace's departure, Hitchcock suffered another significant loss in his professional life. After the success of their *Rear Window* collaboration, he hired John Michael Hayes to write the screenplays for *To Catch a Thief* (1955), *The Trouble with Harry* (1955), and *The Man Who Knew Too Much* (1956). This was more than any writer he'd worked with since Charles Bennett back in the thirties. Hitchcock recognized John Michael's talent for dialogue and character development, which beautifully complemented his own gift for suspense and storytelling. But his inability to give credit or to congratulate someone on a job well done continually plagued him. In the end, it cost Hitchcock a relationship that would have borne more fruits had it been tended to with a few simple words of appreciation.

John Michael first saw the warning signs of incompatibility with Hitchcock on April 20, 1955. It had been a day of milestones at Paramount. The auteur had officially become an American citizen that morning, while the Mystery Writers of America had presented John Michael with the Edgar Allan Poe Award for the *Rear Window* screenplay. A brief celebration with cake and champagne was held at the Paramount office for Hitchcock's citizenship. He would later attend the ceremony where John Michael accepted his award.

On the surface, everything was good-natured. To the outside world, the two men seemed like the ideal Hollywood partnership. John Michael gave a clever and humble acceptance speech and when asked about working with Hitchcock, he described him with the quirkiness that everyone expected. He provided terms like "wine connoisseur," and "perfectionist," and described the director as "an amazing authority on such unexpected matters as the origin of waterfalls."

But things weren't as they appeared. John Michael later told biographer Donald Spoto that the following day, when he showed his trophy to Hitchcock, the auteur was dismissive. "You know, they make toilet bowls from the same material" was his assessment of the statue. Shortly after, the *New York Times* asked John Michael to write a piece on what it was like to work with Hitchcock. According to John Michael, when he showed his first draft to the director, he tore it up, saying, "Young man, you are hired to write for me and Paramount, not for the *New York Times*." Nevertheless, the two continued to collaborate on what would be some of the most commercially successful works of Hitchcock's filmography.

For *The Man Who Knew Too Much*, Hitchcock asked John Michael to update his earlier 1934 version of the film to the starkly contrasting world of 1956. He would Americanize the main characters to suit the personas of Jimmy Stewart and Doris Day while playing on Doris's singing of "Que Sera, Sera" as a clever plot point in locating their missing son. But when it came to the screenplay credit, Hitchcock insisted that his old friend Angus MacPhail, who had worked on *Spellbound* (1945), and whom he brought in as a technical consultant for the spy portions of the story, be given a co-writer credit. John Michael was appalled. He was the one who had written the script, not Angus MacPhail.

John Michael managed to get MacPhail's name removed after a Writers Guild arbitration. According to John Michael, Hitchcock threatened to never speak to him again if he went ahead with his meeting with the Guild. This tipped John Michael even further over the edge. Hitchcock and Hayes then parted ways forever, never to utter another word to each other again. Hayes later recalled: "I enjoyed working with Hitchcock professionally . . . But he was egotistical to the point of madness."

On February 21, 1959, after John Michael's abrupt departure, a curious letter addressed to Hitchcock was sent to his Paramount office. But, like salt to a wound, it only served as a reminder of John Michael's dynamic talents as a screenwriter—a screenwriter who had walked out on him. Aspiring playwright Raphael Semmes Lowry of Flushing, Queens, was inquiring about the stage rights to *Rear Window*. A letter was swiftly sent back from an assistant at Hitchcock's office to Lowry on March 11.

> *Dear Mr. Lowry:*
> *The story* Rear Window *was written by Cornell Woolrich whose pseudonym is William Irish. Prior to the production of the motion picture photoplay entitled* Rear Window, *rights were acquired from Cornell Woolrich.*

These rights included motion picture rights and certain related rights but did not include the stage rights. Unless, therefore, he has since disposed of them, Cornell Woolrich is the owner of the stage rights and he would be the proper person to contact.

Sincerely,
Sidney Justin
bc. Mr. Herb Coleman

It's unknown whether Raphael Lowry ever contacted Cornell Woolrich about the rights, but his version of *Rear Window* never made it to the stage. It's likely he was discouraged by the fact that if *Rear Window* were to be adapted as a play, it would be Woolrich's version of the story that would be told, not Hitchcock and John Michael Hayes's with its dynamic neighbors and romantic storyline.

Rear Window wouldn't be adapted to stage until over fifty years later in 2012, when playwright Keith Reddin took the original 1942 short story to Connecticut's Hartford Stage in a production starring Kevin Bacon. In the meantime, there would be no further attempts to take *Rear Window* to the legitimate theater.

The decade that followed the severed relationship between Hitchcock and John Michael Hayes was a turbulent one for Hollywood. The studio system, which had slowly eroded away since the late forties, had become virtually nonexistent along with the Hays Code. Bearing the weight of the competitive television industry and the dispossession of movie theaters by studios, the system had finally buckled under the pressures and a new filmmaking culture waited in the wings to take its place.

Independent directors with long-term contracts were now taking control of things in a Wild West scenario, but writers would need to hustle to find work under the new regime of a freelancer's world. In the wake of the sexual revolution, films like *Bonnie and Clyde* and *Who's Afraid of Virginia Woolf?* would take over by 1967, and every Golden Hollywood veteran would need to reinvent their personal formulas.

Hitchcock didn't need coaxing to change with the times. He'd already begun with *Psycho* and *The Birds*. Though *Rear Window*'s themes were perverse in a way that escaped censors, his early sixties films would mark a turning point of deviant behavior on-screen. He went back to noncommittal writer relationships and hired screenwriter Joseph Stefano for *Psycho* and author Evan Hunter for *The Birds*.

Simultaneously, John Michael Hayes was showing the world he could keep up with the Hollywood transition as he branched out from comedic dialogue to more dramatic themes. Though to many, it was a shame Hitchcock and the younger writer couldn't work out their differences, John Michael proved he could still land on his feet after the unpleasant breakup. He wouldn't need Hitchcock to stay employed or keep his momentum in Hollywood.

He was nominated for a second Oscar for *Peyton Place* (1957), a soapy and controversial adaptation of Grace Metalious's bestselling book. Next, he worked on a similarly dramatic film, *BUtterfield 8* (1960) based on the John O'Hara novel, which won Elizabeth Taylor an Oscar for her portrayal of an upscale prostitute. Another notable Hayes screenplay was for William Wyler's *The Children's Hour* (1961), in which he walked a fine line in merely suggesting the lesbian longings of Shirley MacLaine for Audrey Hepburn, rather than the overtness of Lillian Hellman's original 1934 play.

Decades later, the Hitchcock/Hayes credit controversy arose yet again. This time, it was over *Rear Window*, when biographer Donald Spoto released the acclaimed 1983 book *The Dark Side of Genius*, which dug into Hitchcock's creative and personal life. In his depiction of the *Rear Window* production, he reported that Hayes had written the screenplay entirely on his own after a few "preliminary meetings" with Hitchcock. When Herbert Coleman, whom Spoto had also interviewed and even had stay with him in Colorado during the interview process, read the book, he felt the need to set the record straight from his perspective.

In *The Man Who Knew Hitchcock*, which Herbert released in 2003, he claimed that Spoto's account of the *Rear Window* script was inaccurate. In his account, Hitchcock dictated many of the scenes to Hayes in his presence. In his words, Hitchcock described everything from the camera movements across the courtyard to a half-dressed ballet dancer and Jimmy's leg in a cast. From Herbert's recollection, Hitchcock had instructed Hayes, "I've decided to have Jimmy asleep when Grace makes her first appearance in our film." He also claimed that Hitchcock often paced the room and described scene after scene, adding all the colorful characters. Like a frustrated composer, a honeymooning couple, and a traveling jewelry salesman with an invalid wife.

Herbert Coleman described his and John Michael's next few days as a "graduate school course in screenplay development" as they absorbed Hitchcock's lessons. He alleged the final scene dictation in which Hitchcock told John Michael to then add dialogue to the script. From the mixed versions of events offered by Herbert, John Michael, and Donald Spoto, it would be difficult to know the full story without having been a fly on the Paramount office walls. Ownership is often a typical web to untangle in joint creative ventures. But the fact remains that real magic had happened between Hitchcock and Hayes, even if credit was the thing that killed their partnership in the end.

In September of 1965, Hitchcock stared down in dismay at the screenplay for *Torn Curtain*. It was an undeniable mess. He'd spent four months working on it with novelist Brian Moore and screenwriting team Keith Waterhouse and Willis Hall, but something just wasn't clicking. When his contract ended with Paramount shortly after completing *Psycho*, he signed a new contract with Universal and released the last six films of his career with them. Initially, Universal had been like a second home to Hitchcock, but it was now clear to his longtime personal assistant, Peggy Robertson, that he was struggling to compete during changing times.

Peggy short-listed a small group of proven writers she thought would liven up the script's dullness. When she handed the list to him, his eyes quickly skimmed it until they stopped on one name: John Michael Hayes. Seeing his name in print was like a slap in the face. He still felt all sorts of things that he couldn't describe about the credit debacle. Hitchcock, the master of suspense, had *made* John Michael's career, and he had repaid him by going behind his back and disobeying his orders. Though Peggy thought John Michael would be the perfect solution for fixing the script, Hitchcock outright refused to even consider calling him. "No, Peggy. That won't be necessary," he said as he crossed out John Michael's name with precision. Time had not healed this wound and it likely never would.

MARNIE

HITCHCOCK DIDN'T CONCERN HIMSELF WITH MUCH CATHOLIC GUILT OVER his fallout with John Michael Hayes. He had one relationship from the *Rear Window* days that had remained as strong as ever. In December of 1961, Hitchcock's plane landed in Nice for an important occasion. He was on his way to the Prince's Palace of Monaco where he had an appointment with his friend Princess Grace of Monaco.

It had already been six years since she had departed Hollywood. But her absence had grown heavy on Hitchcock, creating a gaping hole he was desperate to fill. He needed his stars to make films and he had a surefire plan to get her back to Hollywood. One that neither she nor her husband could turn down. It took the form of offering Grace the title role in *Marnie*, an edgy film about kleptomania and obsessive love. It would be the perfect reintroduction of Grace to a progressively evolving Hollywood. Finally, they could re-create the magic of *Rear Window* and return to the good old days of the fifties when life seemed less complicated.

Grace was thrilled to see Hitchcock. She craved her old career more than she'd anticipated, and as soon as she greeted him on his arrival, it was as if no time had passed between them. She never wanted to give up acting, yet here she was, missing it more with each passing year. Hitchcock's long journey from Hollywood to the Prince's Palace had paid off. Grace immediately accepted his offer. She couldn't wait to get back on set and disappear into a new character. And *Marnie* was like nothing she'd ever done. Grace's daughter Caroline was just about to turn five, but perhaps the family could travel to America with her to film. Of course, Grace loved her husband but nothing would compare to that feeling of autonomy, a chance to build something that was hers alone.

On the afternoon of March 19, 1962, a palace spokesman announced that Her Serene Highness would travel with her husband and children to the United States from August to November that year for the filming of Alfred Hitchcock's film *Marnie*. The *New York Times* broke the story in America the next day, along with a photo of the Princess of Monaco and a comment from Hitchcock that he very much looked forward to "making a movie again with Miss Kelly, who is a wonderful actress."

Prince Rainier talked about the role in 1997. "We talked to Hitchcock about it. She was very anxious to get back into the swing of things, and by that point, I didn't see anything wrong with it."

But after the announcement some logistical problems arose for Hitchcock and Grace regarding the timing of *Marnie*'s production that autumn. In addition, Grace found out she was pregnant in April after she'd accepted the offer, though she would sadly have a miscarriage in mid-June. She sent a deeply apologetic letter to Hitchcock on June 18, 1962. "I hate disappointing you. I also hate the fact that there are probably many other 'cattle' who could play the part equally as well—despite that, I hope to remain one of your 'sacred cows.'" Hitchcock was understanding in his response. "Without a doubt, I think you made, not only the best decision, but the only one. After all, it was 'only a movie.'"

Grace was devastated but eventually took the disappointment in stride. She had to remember her new responsibilities. There were rumblings and dramatizations in Hollywood that her husband had forbidden her to take the role, but the truth was much more complex. Grace had the freedom to follow her passions, but how would she realistically balance the demands of various foundations and helping children in need *and* being a Hollywood star? She couldn't be in two places at once. "It's not that Rainier said no, but he talked her out of it, basically saying that she already had a full-time job," remembered her cousin John Lehman. "Whether she would have come back to Hollywood, I'm not so sure. I think that she felt it would be very hard to reconcile that with the family, official, and philanthropic things she was doing."

When the news broke in Hollywood that the lead role for *Marnie* was now a free agent, actresses all over town, especially those under contract to Hitchcock, like Vera Miles, were vying for the role. But Hitchcock had his eye on someone new. One who he was sure could fill Grace's shoes.

Soon after, Lew Wasserman made a special trip to the set of *The Birds* where Grace Kelly look-alike Tippi Hedren and Rod Taylor had just filmed a scene on the bluff. As she began to walk off set toward her trailer, Wasserman took her aside. "Congratulations, Tippi," he said smiling. "You're going to be our Marnie."

DARKNESS AND DISARRAY

HITCHCOCK MADE HIS LAST EVER PROFESSIONAL APPEARANCE AT THE American Film Institute's tribute to Jimmy Stewart in early 1980 before he died that April. Having just been knighted by the queen in late 1979, his new title was still a novelty to him. During rehearsals, he delivered his introduction to the camera for the televised event, while reading from the cue cards in front of him.

"Hello, my name is *Sir* Alfred Hitchcock."

He raised his eyebrows when he read "Sir," enunciating it with pride. This was his first time addressing the public this way and he had to admit it had a ring to it. He continued to read the cards.

"I've been quoted as saying that actors are cattle and that's not what I said. What I *really* said was actors should be *treated* like cattle."

Even with an ongoing rumor of his less-than-gracious attitude toward actors, Hitchcock was willing to poke fun at himself in public (as long as it was him doing the poking, not someone else). He quickly followed up this line with, "But an exception should be made for the actor being honored tonight. His name is Jimmy Stewart."

Combined with Hitchcock's dry delivery, the joke went down well with most, except a sensitive few. Producer and film historian Joseph McBride worked on the AFI tribute and had written those words that Hitchcock spoke in his last ever appearance. "The *Variety* review of the show attacked the opening for Hitchcock saying actors should be treated like cattle," he said. "They had no sense of humor. That was a joke that he made, and he didn't really mean it."

Hitchcock's relationships with actors over the years had mixed outcomes. Some like Grace and Jimmy adored working with him in the fifties when he was energetic and in his creative prime. Even close to the end of his life, actors like Bruce Dern, who worked with him on his last film *Family Plot* (1976), had found the experience educational and even life-changing. "I can see where it's tough for actors," Dern said of Hitchcock's reputation for providing little direction. "But that's where ego gets in the way. You have to come to him; he isn't going to come to you." Bruce also praised Hitchcock's flexible approach to empowering actors to showcase their talent in their own distinctive way. "Maybe twice a week he comes up with a shot which becomes the most fascinating shot in your career."

But depending on personality dynamics or Hitchcock's mental state during filming, this certainly wasn't every actor's experience. Some claimed he was controlling, cruel, and even abusive. Tippi Hedren was among the first to speak up. Blond, petite, and Nordic-looking (just Hitchcock's type), Minnesota-born Tippi got her start in the fifties as a model with Eileen Ford.

She often worked with Grace's close friend and bridesmaid Carolyn Scott on editorial shoots for magazines like *Glamour* and *Life*. Similar to Grace, when Tippi came to Manhattan, she and Carolyn became fast friends. Carolyn's daughter Nyna Giles remembers their supportive friendship in a cutthroat industry. "Tippi was very driven and she worked all the time, but she and my mother were so happy as women to be working and making great money," she said. "They had a friendship where she would come out to our house and stay; Tippi and Grace were probably my mother's closest friends in that era."

In the late fifties, on his mission to find the "New Grace," Hitchcock discovered Tippi in a black-and-white television ad for the diet drink Sego, and asked to have her come into the studio so they could meet. Though she had no acting background, he arranged a $25,000 screen test for Tippi and cast her in *The Birds*, the feverishly anticipated follow-up to *Psycho*. The commercial that led to Tippi's discovery showed her walking down a street and hearing a catcall-style whistle. She turns to see the culprit, a small, unassuming eight-year-old boy. Hitchcock loved this ad so much, that he re-created it in the opening scene of *The Birds* at San Francisco's Union Square where a boy walks past her and gives a whistle. She reacts with amusement before going about her business and entering the pet shop.

What Tippi lacked in experience, she made up for with a strong focus and a knack for taking direction. She was a sponge to Hitchcock and everything he taught her about acting and the craft of filmmaking. But trouble was beginning to brew in the background.

According to Tippi, the first red flag presented itself over dinner in a Santa Rosa hotel during the filming of *The Birds*. Once Alma excused herself from the table to say hello to some people she knew and Tippi and Hitchcock were alone, he casually brought up a scene between Cary Grant and Grace Kelly in *To Catch a Thief*. "It was such a seamless transition from the stories he'd been telling that night that I didn't even see this coming—during a scene in which they were kissing, he said he suddenly found himself getting aroused," wrote Tippi in her 2016 memoir.

Things began to decline from there. Hitchcock, perhaps feeling the need to lock down Tippi after Grace's departure, asserted control over every aspect of her life, from her wardrobe and hair to her weight—similar to the way Jimmy's Scottie treats Kim Novak's Judy while trying to re-create her in the image of his lost love Madeleine in *Vertigo*.

Tippi claimed the auteur occasionally had her followed and even had her handwriting analyzed. Things allegedly turned sinister when he asked her to "touch him" one day as they stood in a private corner of the soundstage during shooting and even attempted to kiss her at a later point. "Sexual harassment and stalking were terms that didn't exist back then," wrote Tippi of her feelings of helplessness. "He was Alfred Hitchcock, one of Universal's superstars, and I was just a lucky little blond model he'd rescued from relative obscurity. Which one of us was more valuable to the studio, him or me?"

When biographer Donald Spoto interviewed actress Diane Baker, who worked with Hitchcock on *Marnie* in 1962, she reported that the auteur was flirtatious and came on to her during this time, though she was able to fend him off. But others like Kim Novak, who had worked with him in 1958's *Vertigo*, only saw the behavior of a professional. In 2013, she told Britain's *Daily Mail*, "I never had a problem with him. He wasn't that way with me. His wife was usually there on set. When she wasn't, he didn't act any differently, but was just a decent man and a strong director."

The question remains: Why did Hitchcock's interactions with actresses in the forties and fifties, like Grace Kelly, Kim Novak, or Ingrid Bergman, distinctly differ from his conduct in the early sixties when working with emerging talents like Tippi Hedren and Diane Baker? With Grace, there had been some off-color jokes here and there, but Hitchcock had kept his desire under wraps and behaved professionally. As time passed, though, he couldn't do the same with Tippi.

By age sixty-two, it was evident the director's long-repressed sexuality could no longer be held down and was rearing its head in both his professional and personal life. With *Psycho*, *The Birds*, and *Marnie*, Hitchcock would also play on the new allowance handed to filmmakers to deal with previously forbidden subject matter. In her study of *The Birds*, Camille Paglia referred to the early sixties era as Hitchcock's time of "existential crisis." Self-conscious of his weight, the auteur had spent his entire youth shy of women and clueless as to any sort of approach.

His social awkwardness had always made it difficult for him to connect with others in general. In a 1964 interview with Canadian screenwriter and journalist Fletcher Markle, Hitchcock admitted, "I don't think I'm very good in the company of a lot of men and I don't know what it would be like among a lot of women." Additionally, according to biographer John Russell Taylor, Hitchcock had confirmed during an interview that his sexual relations with Alma were minimal at best. His confident leading men like Cary Grant or Jimmy Stewart, who'd never had any problem getting a date, were his way of vicariously living out a romantically and sexually fulfilled life.

The auteur was now getting older and, as health issues arose, was examining his mortality against the backdrop of a changing American culture. "It's partly the aging, repressed male and then the whole sexual revolution," explained Joseph McBride, who co-produced the documentary *Obsessed with Vertigo: New Life for Hitchcock's Masterpiece*. "When you think about a guy like him and the revolution is erupting around him and he's an old man, he's never had the sexual freedom that he wished he had, but it came out in unpleasant ways with Tippi."

If *Rear Window* represented a cheerful and harmonious set for Hitchcock, *Marnie* embodied its complete antithesis with a tense and stormy atmosphere. Things between Hitchcock and Tippi escalated to a point where she could no longer bring herself to speak to him, let alone work with him after filming ended. Even though she was currently locked into an iron-clad contract, she decided to walk away, even if that meant not working for several years.

Tippi would complete her obligations to *Marnie*, but immediately after, would close the chapter with Hitchcock as she put an end to their toxic dynamic. To top it off, the film was misunderstood and panned by most critics. Though, similar to *Vertigo*, in later decades cinephiles and art house experts would appreciate it anew. Even so, Hitchcock was never the same after *Marnie*.

CHAPTER TEN

A Brave New Wave

CHANGING THE GAME

IN MID-FIFTIES PARIS, WITHIN THE CONFINES OF A CRAMPED OFFICE LO-
cated at 146 Avenue des Champs-Élysées, a group of young, opinionated film critics congregated around a table. They smoked cigarette
after cigarette as they debated the latest films—European and American—that were making an impact. They talked about what was blow-
ing up the box office, what deserved more exposure, and what moved
them emotionally or intellectually. They had no time for avant-garde
snobbery. These movers and shakers were only interested in what was
authentically good, no matter what country it came from, or how commercially viable the director.

The magazine they worked for, *Cahiers du Cinéma*, read by the
Continental it-crowd, was fast becoming a top reference for European
film. It was originally co-founded by renowned critics André Bazin,
Jacques Doniol-Valcroze, and Joseph-Marie Lo Duca in 1951. But
there was a hidden caveat for aspiring writers who joined their prestigious staff. They were required to share Bazin's traditional vision of
French cinema and idol worship of its filmmakers. In the early fifties,
he brought in some youthful protégés, like François Truffaut and Jean-
Luc Godard. But these young writers refused to conceal their perspective when praising commercially successful American filmmakers like

Hitchcock, John Ford, and Howard Hawks on *Cahiers du Cinéma*'s pages.

This act of rebellion was a godsend for Hitchcock. A new generation looked up to him and appreciated what he was doing. While his American audience remained faithful, Hollywood sometimes took Hitchcock for granted, a view clearly echoed by the Academy. On initial release, his film's intent occasionally went over the heads of American critics, but these French theorists savored every morsel of a movie and dug until they understood its inner layers.

The young critics separated from André Bazin in 1954 after an article in the January issue by François Truffaut challenged what he called "La qualité française" ("the French quality") and panned several French directors like Claude Autant-Lara and Jean Delannoy for adapting ordinary, oversimplified, and even unethical versions of literary works to film. Though they eventually gained control of the magazine, François, Jean-Luc, and others like Jacques Rivette and Claude Chabrol would eventually tire of just talking about cinema and become directors themselves. This creative movement in the Parisian community would be known to the rest of the world as the French New Wave.

More than a movement, these films were an explosion of unique cinematic style, which colored outside the lines of convention. They played with nonlinear storytelling, antihero characters, jump-cut editing, and a documentary feel that made one sense that they were actually taking part in the scene. The films held a type of cool factor Hollywood simply couldn't replicate. Reminiscent of *Rear Window*, they were experimental journeys of the theoretical aspects of film and its boundaries.

The year 1959 was significant for François Truffaut. He made his first semi-autobiographical film, *The 400 Blows*, about a young troublemaker with negligent parents experiencing the hard knocks of life in postwar France. He won over the Cannes Film Festival by securing the honor of Best Director. (Conversely, Hitchcock had a fear of authority and the law as a child, while François defied it and even served time in a juvenile facility as a youth.)

This would mark the official beginning of the New Wave. At twenty-seven years old, François was the toast of Paris and would become a prolific director with films like *Jules et Jim* (1962) and *Fahrenheit 451* (1966). But he would still make time for a crucial project close to his heart. François first met Hitchcock in 1955 when he interviewed him for a piece about *To Catch a Thief* for *Cahiers du Cinéma*. Soon after, in his efforts as a filmmaker, he came to fully comprehend the significance of Hitchcock's contribution. His calling was clear.

In 1962, when Hitchcock agreed to a fifty-hour-long interview with him, François wrote what would be considered the ultimate film theory book and examination of pure cinema using Hitchcock's full filmography as a reference tool. In *Hitchcock/Truffaut*, the two filmmakers objectively dissected Hitchcock's experiences in his forty-year career, which consequently showed a more relaxed side to Hitchcock's persona. In the past, he had deliberately derided many journalists' questions, which had exacerbated some critics' view that he was merely an "entertainer" and not an "artist." But this conversation demonstrated a less inhibited side to the auteur. Though by this time, François was already an esteemed director, he took on the position of "student" during the interview and designated the role of "master" to Hitchcock.

As Truffaut struggled with English and Hitchcock spoke no French, Helen Scott from the French Film Office in New York was flown to Hollywood to facilitate the interview, translating between the directors as they conversed in both languages. Beginning August 13—Hitchcock's birthday—the trio kept their conversation running from nine to six each day. The product was part master class, and part autobiography, and remains an eternal staple of every cinephile's library.

The mindful approach Truffaut and his counterparts took with Hitchcock's films began to hush some of the jaded criticism surrounding his popularity. In an updated 1972 introduction to his book, Truffaut wrote, "American and European critics made him pay for his commercial success by reviewing his work with condescension, and by belittling each new film." Referring to *Rear Window*, Truffaut recalled an interview where he "praised it to the skies" and a cynical American critic commented, "You love *Rear Window* as a stranger to New York, you know nothing about Greenwich Village." Truffaut was compelled to respond, "*Rear Window* is not about Greenwich Village, it is a film about cinema, and I *do* know cinema."

While discussing *Rear Window* in 1962 (*Rear Window* was Truffaut's favorite Hitchcock film, along with *Notorious*), Hitchcock still experienced a swell of pride surrounding his masterpiece in experimentation. "It shows every kind of human behavior—a real index of individual behavior," he elaborated. "The picture would have been very dull if we hadn't done that. What you see across the way is a group of little stories that mirror a small universe."

In surprising hindsight, Hitchcock admitted he'd been dissatisfied with the way *Rear Window*'s theme song "Lisa" unfolded from a storytelling aspect. In his mind, one hour and fifty-two minutes didn't provide adequate time for the ballad to be believably written. "I wanted to show how a popular song is composed by gradually developing it throughout the film until, in the final scene, it is played on a recording with a full orchestral accompaniment. Well, it didn't work out the way I wanted it to, and I was quite disappointed." Additionally, when Truffaut hailed *Rear Window* as Hitchcock's "very best screenplay in all respects," Hitchcock predictably brushed past the subject of John Michael Hayes, referring to him as a "radio writer" without commenting further on his role.

According to Truffaut, after the release of the book, "American critics began to take Hitchcock's work more seriously." *Hitchcock/ Truffaut* was the beginning of a friendship of respect between the British auteur and French filmmaker. Their mutual trust was so great that in the seventies when Hitchcock prepared and revised the screenplays for *Frenzy* (1972) and *Family Plot* (1976), he sent them to Truffaut for feedback, something he generally didn't do with fellow filmmakers.

Truffaut was mutually influenced by Hitchcock's choices of material and would adapt Cornell Woolrich's noir novel *The Bride Wore Black* to film in 1968. It was a connection Hitchcock hadn't shared with any other filmmaker in the past. The two remained friends until Hitchcock died in 1980. Truffaut died just four years later at age fifty-two of a brain tumor.

The influence of Truffaut and his peers in the French New Wave demonstrated to Hollywood that films could thrive without adhering strictly to a single niche. And directors could have the autonomy to tell human stories that everyday people could relate to. In conjunction with studio financial struggles, changing public tastes, and the power of television, the New Wave contributed to the end of the Hollywood Golden Era forever.

HOLLYWOOD CIRCLES

AFTER BEING FORCED TO TURN DOWN *MARNIE*, GRACE OFTEN HAD PERIODS of melancholy and nostalgia for her old life. She didn't pine for Hollywood, per se, but she longed for the company of her old friends and a chance to be creative again. She missed clowning around on set with Jimmy Stewart and having the challenge of a new script to sink her teeth into. Nevertheless, she understood the need to embrace current circumstances. Grace was an avid letter writer and treasured her bonds with industry friends like Rita Gam and Edith Head. In June of 1957, she wrote to Edith in hopes that they would meet that summer.

> *Dear Edith,*
>> *We are off to Switzerland tomorrow, where our address is:*
>> *Comte et Comtesse de Rosemont*
>> *Chalet Saarehus*
>> *Schonried/Gstaad*
>> *If you find yourself nearby, please come to see us. Car-*

*oline is sweeter each day and I am longing for you to meet
her. The best place to send something would be here at the
Palace, as all of our things will be forwarded from here.*
Much love,
Grace

Although Edith regretfully couldn't make it to Switzerland that
year, Grace hosted numerous family members and Hollywood friends
at the palace, providing them a calm refuge from the realities of work
and life. As a student, Grace's cousin John Lehman often hitchhiked
from Cambridge University to Heathrow Airport and hopped on a
cheap flight to Nice. Once his plane touched down, a limo and footman
were waiting to whisk him off to the palace for summer vacation or a
holiday season abroad.

Some of the highlights included Christmas Eve dinner with navy
submarine officers, drinking pints in the replica of an East Falls Philly
Irish pub that Grace had constructed in the palace, and entertaining
movie stars who frequently visited. "One of my proudest accomplishments was teaching Elizabeth Taylor how to do the funky chicken,"
remembered John. "Liz and Richard Burton were making a film close
by and were often at the palace."

But Grace was just as generous with strangers in need as she was
with her famous friends. "She really didn't have a mean bone in her
body as they sometimes said," said John. "She always cared about people, even the ones that didn't care about her; she was a wonderful human being."

On one of John's visits, there had been an accident on the highway near the palace involving a man who was tragically killed. He left
behind a wife and eight children, which included an infant. Grace,
hearing about this, immediately sprang to action and went to the widow's home. She consoled the woman, who was in shock, then brought
the children back to the palace to be cared for while the man's widow
found her bearings. "She was absolutely obsessed with no one finding

out that she was doing these things," remembered John. "She told me several times the worst fear she had was to be portrayed as a person dispensing favors or a lady bountiful; what she did never made the press."

At the Red Cross Ball in 1974, years before he became a celebrity in his own right as U.S. secretary of the navy, John was seated at the royal table next to one of Europe's biggest stars, Josephine Baker. It was the night she would make her big comeback performance after tremendous hardship. Grace had recently taken Josephine and her twenty-four adopted "Rainbow children" in when Josephine fell into substance abuse and bankruptcy. When things escalated and the children were placed in orphanages, Grace hadn't wasted any time stepping in. "Grace took her by the hand and got Josephine to recognize that it was time to change direction in her life," said John. "Grace and Rainier supported the twenty-four children while she was drying out, got them to move to Monaco, and provided a home for them."

The two women had met over two decades before in 1951 when Josephine took a few friends to dinner at Manhattan's Stork Club, where they were denied a table. Grace was at the club that evening, and was so outraged by the obvious display of racism that she walked over to Josephine—whom she had never met before—took her by the arm, and stormed out with their entourage of friends. Grace swore to the press she would never return to the Stork Club and always stayed true to that promise. That evening, a lifelong friendship was solidified.

Josephine's comeback performance blew the roof off the Sporting Monte-Carlo complex the night of the Red Cross Ball. From the moment she bowed to a standing ovation, she'd always remember what her friend had done for her. Yet there was no media publicity surrounding Grace's efforts to restore Josephine to her rightful place as a star. The truth was she'd made Josephine swear she wouldn't talk to the press or anyone else about it. John recalled, "The only way I know about it is because I sat next to Josephine at the ball and she told me the whole story!"

THE BOY NEXT DOOR MEETS THE GRADUATE

IN THE LATE SIXTIES, JIMMY STEWART WAS LIVING IN A HOLLYWOOD HE no longer recognized. With the demise of the studio system, the new up-and-coming trend of independent dealmaking was unfamiliar territory to him. He looked back on his days as an MGM player with sentimentality. He often defended the studio system when asked if the rumors were true about it being an authoritarian factory with control freaks working the strings.

In recent years, he'd transitioned out of romantic lead roles and slid successfully into rugged westerns. Jimmy's first western, Anthony Mann's *Winchester '73,* released in 1950, was a critical and commercial hit, setting the stage for his continued success in the genre in later years. In films like *The Man Who Shot Liberty Valance* (1962) and *How the West Was Won* (1962), John Ford jumped on the same western bandwagon and benefited from Jimmy's intangible quality of likeability. Ford remarked of Jimmy, "He was good in anything. He played himself but he played the character. People just liked him." The western was a niche that suited him to a T and he would make a total of eighteen of them in his career.

The year 1967 transformed the industry and officially put the nail in the coffin of Golden Hollywood. Thirty-year-old Warren Beatty, known for years as Shirley MacLaine's little brother, was now jumping in the producer's seat with *Bonnie and Clyde.* Starring Warren and Faye Dunaway as its unlikable protagonists, it was revolutionary in its bloody violence and depiction of the moody counterculture era.

That same year, Sidney Poitier would also be the first Black man to play a detective in *In the Heat of the Night,* a film about the pain systemic racism causes. Newcomer Dustin Hoffman also starred in an offbeat film about a recent college graduate with deep anxiety about his future and entangled in an affair with a friend of his parents played by Anne Bancroft. Director Mike Nichols was a Hollywood newcomer and the film had a rather ambiguous ending, but *The Graduate* hit a

strong chord with moviegoers. Its profanity and sexual nature were unheard of in mainstream Hollywood cinema until then and the sense of
isolation and anxiety about the future Dustin Hoffman portrayed was
all too relatable in a changing America.

Jimmy Stewart hadn't made a point of seeing many New Hollywood films. They were a bit out of his comfort zone and didn't seem to
reflect the Hollywood he remembered. Instead of going to the movies,
he and Gloria often preferred to relax in front of the TV with *Laugh-In*,
or *The Ed Sullivan Show*, and if they were feeling adventurous, they'd
watch *Bonanza* with Kelly and Judy. "I think if he would have gone to
more of them, he would have had a lot of respect for the films in the
Taxi Driver era," said Kelly. "There was that time when it was Scorsese films and *Easy Rider* when America was making really, really good
films." In the late sixties, Jimmy couldn't name the New Hollywood
films he'd been impressed by, but all that was about to change one Saturday night.

In those days, Connie Wald, widow to prolific Hollywood producer Jerry Wald and best friend to Audrey Hepburn, held legendary
dinner parties in her Beverly Hills home. Jimmy and Gloria, who lived
close by, were often invited to join the festivities. Connie was a fixture
of the Beverly Hills scene and her guest list boasted almost every icon
of the Golden Era, like Fred Astaire, Rosalind Russell, Billy Wilder,
Joan Crawford, and Gene Kelly. She liked to keep things low-key but
lavish with a cuisine spread that was out of this world. An array of cus-
tards, bread puddings, and roast chicken were served for dinner, and
decadent pastries and chocolate rolls came out later for dessert. After
dinner, her favorite activity was screening the latest and greatest Hollywood films for her guests.

It was during one of these parties Jimmy saw *The Graduate* for the
first time and was completely entranced. Kelly joined them that night
and remembered her father's reaction. "I'll never forget it. Dad *loved*
The Graduate. He thought Dustin Hoffman was one of the greatest
actors since I don't know when," she said. "He had great respect for

him, and that's one of the few modern movies I've ever heard him rave about."

Unbeknownst to Jimmy, the feeling was mutual for Dustin Hoffman. Over a decade later, when Dustin addressed the audience at the American Film Institute's tribute to Jimmy in February of 1980 at the Beverly Hilton Hotel, his admiration was clear. "My father worked with you on the lot when you were making films with director Frank Capra. He's your age . . . my mother is *my* age." The twelve hundred guests threw their heads back in raucous laughter. Dustin went on to admit that he'd just seen *It's a Wonderful Life* for the first time a few days prior. "You made me laugh, you made me cry, you made me wish for a country we perhaps haven't seen for a while. You made my parents very happy, you made me very happy, I'm going to see to it that you make my children very happy, and if this world has any kind of Capra luck, you're going to make my children's children very happy."

Though Jimmy wouldn't keep up with every New Hollywood trend, he and Dustin Hoffman now had a solid bond of familiarity that transcended a changing generation. Though at first glance, the actors each had their unique brands, they identified with each other in a shared love of the craft and the need to reveal both the darkness and light in a character's humanity.

Jimmy had always been ahead of his time in his search for more vulnerable roles during the studio era. It differentiated him from more "macho" actors like Clark Gable or John Wayne. Even in prewar Hollywood as an MGM player, Jimmy was much more in tune with his emotional side than most actors of the day. While he viewed himself as a craftsman, his use of emotion and feelings set him apart, leading to his strong kinship and fascination with Dustin Hoffman.

As the sixties came to a close, political unrest was beginning to shake up the whole country. America had already been in a divided state over its involvement in the Vietnam War. But soon after, Middle America would join the antiestablishment in its feelings of disappointment over being let down by its leader. When the world discovered President Richard Nixon's attempts to cover up his involvement in the June 1972 break-in of the Democratic National Committee headquarters at the Watergate Office Building in Washington, D.C., the American dream would finally reach its tipping point. The fantasy of a worry-free land of prosperity dissolved before everyone's eyes. A tense rebellion filled with protests escalating in violence and casualties raged on until the Vietnam War ended on April 30, 1975.

Tragically, Jimmy suffered one of the saddest days of his life on June 8, 1969, when he received the devastating news that his stepson Ronald had been killed in combat in Vietnam. During a patrol, eleven miles northwest of the Vandegrift Combat Base in Quang Tri Province, Ronald, known to his troops as Lieutenant McLean, saw one of his men fall wounded. Without hesitation, he rendered first aid to the injured man just as a hostile soldier began to appear in his peripheral vision. The soldier aimed. Ronald immediately pushed his companion down to protect him and was killed by the enemy fire. He was just twenty-four years of age and had been proud to follow in the footsteps of his stepfather and step-grandfather. He was posthumously awarded a Purple Heart and a Silver Star for his bravery. Ronald's death cut so deeply, that there would never be true healing in a cathartic sense. It was a wound Jimmy would somehow have to learn to live with.

In a 1982 interview with *Good Morning America*, Jimmy became emotional when his stepson's death was brought up. "I don't think there's a day that goes by that I don't think of Ron," he said. "He wanted to serve his country . . . I don't think it's a tragedy. It's a loss . . . I don't know . . . it's a terrible, terrible loss, but tragic, no. He died for his country." Once the words came out of his mouth, Jimmy was overcome with grief. He could no longer continue with the interview.

CHAPTER ELEVEN

Seventies Hollywood through the Rearview Lens

LIGHTS, CAMERA, LITIGATION

DURING THE SEVENTIES, THE GRADUAL INFLUENCE OF AMERICAN COUN-terculture simultaneously manifested in mainstream society and film theaters. Sixties Hollywood had given the restless moviegoing public a taste of real life in their entertainment and now they wanted more. Escapism was now officially a thing of the past. Michael Cimino's *The Deer Hunter* (1978) and Francis Ford Coppola's *Apocalypse Now* (1979) confronted the realistic horrors of the Vietnam War without holding back. And though it was technically set in the sixties, *One Flew Over the Cuckoo's Nest* (1975) directed by Milos Forman was a powerful critique of institutional authority and conformity, and captured the spirit of the counterculture movement in America.

Actors like Robert De Niro, Elliott Gould, Woody Allen, and Jack Nicholson were the new leading men of the day. They lacked the macho quality of Steve McQueen or the boy-next-door likeability of Jimmy Stewart. Neither did they possess the traditionally handsome looks of a young Marlon Brando or Paul Newman. But they were compelling, charming, neurotic, and most importantly, they commanded everyone's attention.

Simultaneously, a new batch of directors, just as young and hungry as the actors, blew into Hollywood like an indestructible whirlwind. Names like Roman Polanski, Martin Scorsese, John Cassavetes, and Steven Spielberg were now running the show in a less rigid freelance atmosphere. It was a situation that could potentially leave legends of the studio system out in the cold if they didn't find a way to fit in with the changing times. What was a traditionalist like Hitchcock to do?

As it turned out, fitting into New Hollywood wasn't the only problem Hitchcock had to contend with throughout the seventies. When Cornell Woolrich suffered an infection from a too-tight shoe left untreated, which consequently caused his leg to be amputated, he lived the rest of his days in a wheelchair at the Sheraton-Russell Hotel on Park Avenue. Staff members often took turns wheeling him to the lobby where he could peer out the window and watch New Yorkers pass by. With his immobility and voyeuristic tendencies, by the end of his life, Cornell Woolrich had truly become *Rear Window*'s original L. B. Jefferies. He passed away in September of 1968. As a complete recluse who had cut his ties with many, he only had five attendees to his funeral.

But there was one individual who took great interest in Cornell's death; a businessman named Sheldon Abend. Cornell had died just two years before the original copyright term for the "It Had to Be Murder" short story expired, and two years before he could file for a renewal copyright. In December of 1969, the Chase Manhattan Bank, acting as agent for Cornell's estate, renewed the copyright to the story. But in early 1972, Sheldon, who owned Authors Research Co. and American Play Co., bought the rights to the short story from Chase Bank for $650, plus ten percent of all proceeds from its exploitation. And so, the trouble began.

A New Yorker by birth, Sheldon was full of grit. He became a boxer, then a coal stoker on tugboats at a young age. He then went on to work for American Play Co. in 1957 and became a rights negotiator for David O. Selznick, RKO General, and Warners. He didn't have a formal education, but he knew his way around a courtroom. The problem was he seemed to know the law a little too well for everyone's liking.

In 1971 and 1974, ABC broadcast *Rear Window* on television through a licensing agreement with Hitchcock, Jimmy Stewart, and MCA Inc. Cornell's original agreement was to renew the copyright once it expired and assign it to the owner of the movie rights. As the new owner, Sheldon refused to play nice and comply as *Rear Window* had been broadcast "without his permission." He filed a lawsuit against Hitchcock, Jimmy, and MCA in a United States district court in New York for infringement of his copyright. The lawsuit was settled out of court when Sheldon agreed to withdraw his complaint in return for $25,000.

Jimmy had always seen it as a lucrative move for an actor to participate in the gross of a film. After World War II, Lew Wasserman, who was Jimmy's and Hitchcock's agent and later head of MCA Universal, made a deal on Jimmy's behalf. When he starred in Anthony Mann's *Winchester '73* in 1950, Jimmy was to receive part of the gross. Some of the actors in the thirties, like Fred Astaire and Greta Garbo, also had gross percentages in their films. "That was not publicized because the studios hated to give gross percentages to people," explained film historian Joseph McBride. "But Jimmy Stewart actually co-owned some of the films that he made with Hitchcock and Ford." When some of Hitchcock's most beloved films, including *Rear Window*, went out of circulation for the remainder of the seventies, Hitchcock kept them in storage vaults and they began to slowly deteriorate with time. It wouldn't be until the early eighties that they would be available to the public again.

After Hitchcock's passing, like a dog with a bone, Sheldon took MCA and Jimmy to court a second time in the late 1980s. It was a landmark case that ended up in the Supreme Court after MCA re-released the *Rear Window* in theatrical form, on cable television, and video-cassette. The lawsuit again resulted in a settlement between Sheldon and MCA over continuing rights to use the story in the film. This time Sheldon ended up with a settlement that, together with the potential earnings due heirs, reached the double-digit millions. It resulted in a

1990 Supreme Court decision that established the so-called Abend Rule, which deals with the continued distribution of a derivative work during a copyright renewal period. Moving forward, studios would have to examine all movies that were based on literary works. To their horror, they discovered that in many cases they had to renegotiate the underlying rights if they ever wanted to show those films again.

The opportunistic pattern of purchasing literary properties at the convenient time of an author's death wasn't limited to *Rear Window*. Sheldon also represented the estates of authors including George Bernard Shaw, Tennessee Williams, and Damon Runyon. After Runyon died of cancer in 1946, Sheldon acquired the copyrights to Runyon properties that had been sold to the movies in the sixties. Then, after Runyon's son died in a car crash in Washington, the rights to all other Runyon works went straight into Sheldon's pocket.

FRENZY

AS 1971 PRESSED ON, HITCHCOCK DID HIS BEST TO PUT THE FIRST COURT proceeding behind him. Honestly, he didn't need this nonsensical drama. Alma's health was currently on the brink of deterioration. In July, the Hitchcocks returned to their hometown of London to begin production on *Frenzy*. As they attended casting meetings, they stayed in their favorite hotel, Claridge's in Mayfair. Alma had provided several script and continuity issues to be addressed in the screenplay when suddenly, she suffered a debilitating stroke.

Hitchcock's physician, Dr. Walter Flieg, was on hand to tend to her. She insisted on staying with her husband and being treated at Claridge's instead of a hospital. Hitchcock was deeply worried about his wife. How would he go on without her? She was the only person in the world who really understood him. Miraculously, within a month, Alma made an almost full recovery, though her speech remained affected and she permanently lost movement in three of her fingers. Hitchcock rescheduled all his *Frenzy* cast and crew meetings to be held at Claridge's so he could be close to Alma as production continued.

Frenzy was a bona fide serial-killer film, more graphic and disturbing than anything Hitchcock had attempted in the past. It made *Rear Window* and even *Psycho* seem almost quaint in comparison. If *Marnie* had opened the door to the auteur's sexual repression, *Frenzy* tore it right off its hinges. In contrast to his entire past filmography, *Frenzy*'s blatant violence and lack of subtlety made it seem more like an *anti*-Hitchcockian film in a sense. With the Hays Code now a simplistic notion of the past, Hitchcock discarded all innuendo and took full advantage of his new autonomy.

The late sixties hadn't been easy on Hitchcock, as audiences seemed less responsive to his new ideas. Throughout the fifties and early sixties, he was able to work effortlessly with Grace Kelly, Jimmy Stewart, Janet Leigh, and Cary Grant, who instinctively understood his directions, but things were rapidly changing to fit a modern culture. He had struggled with Paul Newman daily on the set of *Torn Curtain* (1966).

The first time he'd invited Paul over to his Bel Air home, as was customary with those he worked with for the first time, the young actor had taken off his jacket and draped it on his chair at the table, then declined Hitchcock's vintage wine. When he got up to grab a beer from the refrigerator himself, Hitchcock had a feeling they wouldn't get along on set. When Paul asked several times about the character's underlying motivations, the auteur was ready to blow his top. To make matters worse, the unfavorable critical reception to *Torn Curtain* and *Topaz* (1969) suggested that the auteur was falling behind and unable to keep up with a changing audience. He'd need something edgier to get attention.

For the London shoot of *Frenzy*, he cast lesser-known British actors like Barry Foster, Barbara Leigh-Hunt, and Jon Finch. Going back to his roots, Hitchcock worked with playwright Anthony Shaffer to create a modern-day *Psycho* meets *The Wrong Man*. The caveat was this time, there would be graphic nudity and a rapist who commits necktie murders on his female victims. It was the first English film Hitchcock had made in over twenty years and it wasn't unreasonable to assume a change of scenery might result in a winner. But there was one thing he overlooked in the brave, new non-Hays Code world: the women's movement.

Upon release in 1972, *Frenzy*'s treatment of women was heavily criticized. A July 1972 article in the *New York Times* by Professor Victoria Sullivan blatantly asked, "Does *Frenzy* Degrade Women?" Sullivan wrote, "I suspect that films like *Frenzy* may be sicker and more pernicious than your cheapie humdrum porno flick, because they are slicker, more artistically compelling versions of sadomasochistic fantasies." That same year, America's National Organization for Women also granted *Frenzy* their annual "Keep Her in Her Place" award for male chauvinism.

Even *Rear Window* was viewed under a more evolved lens at the height of the women's movement. In 1975, feminist film theorist Laura Mulvey published the groundbreaking essay "Visual Pleasure and Narrative Cinema" in *Screen*, which would be dissected by professors and filmmakers from every angle for years to come. In her radical critique of contemporary cinema, she states that with a "so-called voyeur's film—like *Rear Window*—in its most extreme form, the pleasure of looking becomes a perversion, producing obsessive voyeurs and Peeping Toms whose only sexual satisfaction can come from watching, in an active controlling sense, an objectified other."

New Hollywood was a rough town if you weren't used to the way the new game was played. It seemed now that the Hays Code that Hitchcock cleverly crept his way around during the production of *Rear Window* had actually worked in his favor. If you weren't a particularly inventive director or didn't have the imagination that Hitchcock had, the Code could have been stifling, but, Hitchcock understood that titillating the audience and forcing them to use their imaginations had a stronger impact than anything that could be shown to them. Fully removing the Code's boundaries had somehow left Hitchcock in the dark with mainstream audiences.

REAR WINDOW RIPPLE EFFECT

NO MATTER HIS CURRENT STRUGGLES IN AN UNFAMILIAR NEW HOLLY-wood, everyone and their mother regarded Hitchcock as the ultimate pioneer of suspense, especially the young up-and-comers. The new seventies directors considered films like *Rear Window* and *Vertigo* to be the Holy Grail of cinema. They wanted to learn from the master however they could.

Before New Hollywood filmmaker Peter Bogdanovich became a runaway success with *The Last Picture Show* (1971), *What's Up, Doc?* (1972), and *Paper Moon* (1973), he was a twenty-four-year-old film journalist in New York in 1963. He had recently landed a project that put him in charge of organizing a series of films at the Museum of Modern Art devoted to Hitchcock, Orson Welles, and Howard Hawks, and gave him the opportunity to meet and interview each director.

As a precursor to *Hitchcock/Truffaut*, Hitchcock's interview with Peter was more succinct than the later more elaborate one with François Truffaut. But it was a trailblazing discussion, which initiated the shutting down of naysayers by showcasing Hitchcock's theoretical explanations of his select filmography. This initiated a more serious view of America's imported "showman."

"There are two primary uses of cutting or montage in film: montage to create ideas—and montage to create violence and emotions," Hitchcock told Peter. "In *Rear Window*, where Jimmy Stewart is thrown out of the window in the end, I just photographed that with feet, legs, arms, heads—complete montage. I also photographed it from a distance, the complete action. There was no comparison between the two. There never is." There was no question that Peter Bogdanovich was in awe of his hero who presented a master class of tools the fledgling director would later apply to his work.

The influence *Rear Window* had on young filmmakers couldn't be calculated, but all one had to do was look around New Hollywood, and the denseness of its themes and ideas were everywhere. The Scorseses and De Palmas of the new scene were raised on *Rear Window* and *Vertigo* (though for much of the sixties and seventies, these films were out of circulation, which added further to the urban legend of their untouchability). Whether the new filmmakers were conscious of it or not, Hitchcock found his way into their work.

Taxi Driver (1976), directed by newcomer Martin Scorsese, depicted a post-Vietnam Manhattan where a military veteran portrayed by Robert De Niro seemingly suffered from PTSD and psychosis while trying to navigate his loneliness. The moodiness and urban alienation of *Rear Window* infiltrated the film, whose central theme was the claustrophobia of New York life.

It was evident again in Brian De Palma's *Dressed to Kill* (1980) with the same technique used to manipulate the audience to the brink of madness. In a very *Rear Window* move, De Palma limits the viewer to shots of Michael Caine dressed in drag and convinces the audience there is a blond female slaying other women all over New York City. He simultaneously uses a split screen and split diopter lens to toy with the viewer and their sense of what they're actually seeing on the screen. "When you think about the technique of just showing the audience what you want them to see and nothing else," said film historian Sloan De Forest, "that kind of magic of controlled filmmaking—it's a great example of Hitchcockian cinema."

De Palma's 1984 film *Body Double* is another love letter to *Rear Window* in its plot about a struggling and lonely actor who spies on a beautiful, scantily clad woman from a telescope (the film also ironically features a career-making performance from Tippi Hedren's daughter, Melanie Griffith, as an adult film star). This inevitably pulls him into a murder mystery he's compelled to solve, just like L. B. Jefferies thirty years before him. De Palma even gives a nod to *Vertigo* with the main character Jake (portrayed by Craig Wasson) having a debilitating fear of confined spaces, as opposed to heights. When he appeared on *The Dick Cavett Show* in 1978, Brian De Palma explained his love of the master of suspense. "Hitchcock pioneered a whole type of film grammar. He taught us how to express things as clearly, visually, I think as they can be expressed."

Curtis Hanson's classic, *The Bedroom Window* (1987), is like *Rear Window* set in the eighties. Terry Lambert, portrayed by Steve Guttenberg, finds himself in trouble when he takes credit for reporting a man assaulting a woman from his bedroom window, which he didn't actually see, to protect his married lover, who was the one who saw it. Hanson re-creates voyeuristic Hitchcock, yet he molds that style into something fit for 1987. In a crowded nightclub, as Terry enters, there's big hair, neon lights, and synthesized pop music. Though *The Bedroom Window* oozes a sensual appeal that Hitchcock was restricted from by the Hays Code, it has all the nods to *Rear Window*. The extreme close-ups and point-of-view shots. The same experimentation with the Kuleshov effect. And the glamorous, feisty female partner in crime, portrayed by Elizabeth McGovern.

Young directors would stop at nothing to absorb what they could from the master of suspense, even if he was unwilling to demonstrate his secrets in the flesh. In 1965, an unknown nineteen-year-old filmmaker named Steven Spielberg tried his luck at entering the set of *Torn Curtain* to see if he could watch his role model at work. He grew up idolizing Alfred Hitchcock and this would be his only chance to learn from the master firsthand.

Gathering all of his courage, young Steven passed through the doors onto the set, doing his best to behave as if he belonged there. For the next ten minutes, he observed the man at work, but just as soon as he'd arrived, he was asked to leave. Hitchcock's film sets were formal and notoriously difficult to enter. With their airtight security, there was a dark cloak of secrecy surrounding them. It proved to be highly effective, as spoilers for Hitchcock films rarely escaped.

A decade later, in the summer of 1975, Steven, now a celebrated filmmaker, had literally just blown everyone out of the water with *Jaws*. No one imagined money like this could be made from a single movie. With a meager $9 million budget, it outperformed all other films in its opening weekend and made $476 million in its lifetime. Well-received by critics and moviegoers, it took home three Academy Awards in 1976. *Jaws* was the definitive symbol of the future of Hollywood filmmaking.

But similar to *Rear Window*, *Jaws* didn't come to be without near insurmountable technical problems and feverish moments of questioning whether the whole thing should just be scratched. On multiple occasions, the mechanical shark almost ended production. At one point, it sank to the bottom of the ocean where they filmed in Martha's Vineyard, and just days later, they discovered the salt water had eroded the shark's motor. To top it off, cast member and screenwriter Carl Gottlieb narrowly escaped decapitation by the boat's propellers when he fell overboard.

Steven Spielberg knew he'd have to find a way to show the predator without *showing* the predator. He later said, "I had no choice but to figure out a way to tell the story without the shark. So I just went back to Alfred Hitchcock. 'What would Hitchcock do in a situation like this?' . . . It's what we don't see which is truly frightening." Taking a line from *Rear Window* and the bloody crime that is never shown, Steven borrowed this tool as his guide to save *Jaws*. Hitchcock might have secretly been kicking himself about the success of *Jaws* since he'd been offered the film first and turned it down. And this twenty-nine-year-old prodigy had come out of nowhere and turned it into a phenomenon.

That same year, Steven made a second attempt to enter a set of Hitchcock's. This time, it was the auteur's final film, *Family Plot*. He was determined to meet the master of suspense if it was the last thing he did. And now, Steven was no longer an unknown kid trespassing on a film set—he was the toast of Hollywood. There was no way he'd be turned away.

But, shockingly, he was denied entry a second time. Hitchcock wouldn't meet Steven or allow him to watch him shoot. Some have pointed out that he was likely insecure about the young director's meteoric rise in the box office. "You'd hope the old master would embrace the young master," said *Star Tribune* film critic Chris Hewitt. "But maybe he was just too jealous of the opportunities he knew this guy was going to have, and that the public was buying it."

There's also the possibility that Hitchcock was greatly misunderstood in his self-consciousness and lack of social etiquette. In 1964, Hitchcock's longtime assistant and producer of the *Alfred Hitchcock Presents* series Joan Harrison pointed out, "He'll never come on the stage when one of the television directors is directing the show. He feels it's embarrassing for them, and he's perfectly right."

Then again, *Family Plot* star Bruce Dern later recalled additional details of that day in his autobiography. When Steven was turned away, Bruce claimed he'd told Hitchcock to reconsider meeting him. "You're his [Steven's] idol," he said to Hitchcock. "He just wants to sit at your feet for five minutes and chat with you." To that, Hitchcock reportedly responded, "Isn't that the boy who made the *fish* movie? I could never sit down and talk to him because I look at him and feel like such a whore." Bruce was perplexed by this bizarre response, but it was later revealed that Hitchcock had recently become the new voice of the *Jaws* ride at Universal Studios. They had paid him one million dollars for it, which had supposedly made him feel like somewhat of a "sellout." Only Hitchcock truly knew if denying Steven's entry to the *Family Plot* set was meant as a slight or if deep down, he deeply feared the judgment of such a gifted new director.

Another young observer having just as much trouble getting onto the *Family Plot* set was journalist Joseph McBride, who had been assigned to write a piece for *Variety* on the film. "I made a request and they turned me down," he remembered. But help was on the way. "I asked my editor, who knew Hitchcock from way back, and he called him up, and they finally let me on, but it wasn't easy."

The atmosphere on the set was formal and restrained, with Hitchcock and his assistants dressed in typical black suits and ties. Joseph spent three days observing Hitchcock at work and conducting interviews in his trailer when time permitted. As to be expected in a Hitchcock production, everything was planned down to the last detail and the scheduling ran like clockwork.

But Joseph made a discovery about the director's working style that was astounding to him. Hitchcock sometimes improvised entire sequences. It had become Hollywood folklore that Hitchcock storyboarded absolutely everything in his films, especially after the release of the *Hitchcock/Truffaut* book where some of his sound bites gave that implication. Though it's widely known and recorded in Hitchcock's papers and production documents that he storyboarded action and special effects scenes, now his reputation for strict austerity of every scene revealed itself as a myth. "The scenes with dialogue, he did not storyboard for *Family Plot*," confirmed Joseph. "He directed them just like any other director did where you rehearse the scene and you watch people shooting."

By that stage, Hitchcock's health was declining, and he had just undergone pacemaker surgery, which delayed production. Despite this, he appeared to be in a better headspace than he had been during the *Marnie* years. The seventy-six-year-old director was sharp and just as full of progressive ideas as he had been in the Golden era.

In the pivotal scene where the kidnapped Bishop Wood, played by William Prince, is given a hypodermic needle by the antagonist couple, played by Karen Black and William Devane, Hitchcock experimented with different shots with the enthusiasm of a playful child. "Hitchcock and the cinematographer, Leonard South, got excited as they figured out how to do the scene with the needle and he improvised seven shots," remembered Joseph.

Though Hitchcock often felt cold and uncomfortable during location shooting in San Francisco, he pushed through and remained present for his cast. On the set, he formed bonds with New Hollywood stars like Bruce Dern and Barbara Harris, who played a dishonest cab driver and con artist psychic who get involved in a dangerous scheme in order to find an heir.

"He was a very good director of actors and people don't give him credit for that," said Joseph. "The key to this is the small parts are always just as wonderfully acted in Hitchcock's films. With *Rear Window*, you got Thelma Ritter and Raymond Burr and Wendell Corey, and of course, he had two good leads; he was just a good director of actors."

As they got to know each other between scenes on the *Family Plot* set, Hitchcock and Bruce Dern discovered they shared the same outlandish sense of humor, which sometimes left others feeling they'd missed the punch line. While sitting on location in San Francisco and waiting for the setup of the scene where Bruce's character, George Lumley, is lurking around a city back alley, the crew set up a wind machine to simulate the turbulent effect of leaves and debris on a windy day. Hitchcock and Bruce joked about spraying graffiti on the wall of the garage for a grungy feel. It was common knowledge that *Jaws* had recently made an obscene amount of money at the box office. Bruce playfully suggested that they draw the logo of the shark's head on the wall with chalk, but Hitchcock took it a step further. "No, Bruce, I know what we should write. 'Fuck MCA.'" The two men threw their heads back in laughter over a bonding moment.

"It was interesting because Hitchcock was the third biggest stockholder in MCA at the time," said Joseph, who observed the whole scene. "He was making a lot of money because the stock was going through the roof because of *Jaws*. So every day I saw somebody bring him the box office reports on *Jaws* and he was very excited." This makes it all the more confusing why Hitchcock refused to meet Steven Spielberg. No one would ever fully understand the deep-rooted reason for his reluctance to play mentor to someone he should have seen his reflection in. He may not have consciously known himself.

Family Plot was well received by critics, but the public was less enthusiastic in its response. Moviegoers wanted the classic Wrong Men, Cool Blondes, and MacGuffins Hitchcock was known for, not this quirky "comedy-melodrama" as he referred to it. Hitchcock felt trapped in a suffocating box that he couldn't break out of. There was still so much more he wanted to say as an artist. He envied the new directors of Hollywood and Europe, free to express their changing experiences of life. In the summer of 1970, when he wrote to François Truffaut, he vented his frustrations. "How lucky you are not to be categorized and stamped as I am, for this is the root of my difficulties in acquiring a good subject, especially in respect to acceptance by the audience."

ALFRED & ALMA: A LOVE STORY

ON MARCH 7, 1979, THE AMERICAN FILM INSTITUTE HELD A TELEVISED Lifetime Achievement Award ceremony on CBS as a tribute to Alfred Hitchcock's fifty-five-year career. Ingrid Bergman hosted the show before an all-star Hollywood audience that included Jimmy Stewart, Cary Grant, Janet Leigh, Anthony Perkins, Teresa Wright, Robin Williams, Gene Wilder, Diana Ross, Tippi Hedren (curiously), and Christopher Reeve (who would star in a loose remake of *Rear Window* almost twenty years later).

The guests and presenters seemed overjoyed to be there, but an aura of sadness orbited Hitchcock as he took his seat at the table of honor alongside Alma. He sat and gazed at a montage of his accomplishments crossing the screen, which now seemed like apparitions from a time that no longer existed. He often looked down at his plate as presenters directly addressed him. But he mustered a grin when Jimmy

Stewart got up to speak. "When you work with Hitch, you don't try doing a scene two ways. You do it one way—his," he joked. Everyone in the room laughed out loud except Hitchcock.

Though Sir Alfred Hitchcock had achieved more than any artist could hope to in his lifetime, the frailties and limitations of the human body had now come between him and filmmaking. His crippling arthritis and weak heart made it impossible to work at the standard he was used to. CBS used editing tricks to distract from his obvious melancholy, but it was clear to everyone that the life was draining from his eyes the way it had from Janet Leigh's after the infamous *Psycho* shower scene when she is left to make her final peace.

"I too was forced to deliver a cheerful tribute," François Truffaut wrote about the evening in his final 1983 edition of *Hitchcock/Truffaut*. As he waited backstage for his cue, he overheard Ingrid Bergman whisper, "Why do they always organize this kind of ceremony when it's too late?" On the podium, he spoke eloquently. "In America, you call this man Hitch. In France, we call him Monsieur Hitchcock. . . ." But his words fell on deaf ears. "In front of an all-star Hollywood audience," he wrote, "which eulogized them with anecdotes, film excerpts, and toasts, Alfred and Alma Hitchcock appeared to be present, but their souls were missing."

When it was Hitchcock's turn to give his thanks for the award, he initially struggled to stand and regain his balance, but as soon as he spoke, he transformed back into the master of suspense everyone knew, full of exuberance once again. His words focused on the one person who had been the most important in his life, his wife. "Had the beautiful Miss Reville not objected to a lifetime contract without options as Mrs. Alfred Hitchcock some fifty-three years ago, Mr. Alfred Hitchcock might be in this room tonight," said Hitchcock. "Not at this table, but as one of the slower waiters on the floor. I share my award as I have my life with her."

Just one day younger than Hitchcock, Alma Reville was his senior professionally when they first met in London. She worked as an editor

and continuity supervisor and usually knew more about a film's prog-
ress than anyone else on the crew. She had gone into the film industry at age sixteen at Twickenham Studios, just around the corner from
where she was born.

It wasn't until Hitchcock earned the assistant director title in *Woman
to Woman* (1923) that he dared telephone her to ask her to work with
him. "Since it is unthinkable for a British male to admit that a woman
has a more important job than his, Hitch had waited to speak to me until
he was in a higher position," Alma once said wryly. The two began a
working relationship and quickly bonded. When plagued by a lack of
self-confidence, he turned to Alma for constant reassurance that he was
doing marvelously. She also handled delicate situations with the cast and
crew that Hitchcock couldn't bring himself to face. "Like a man, I left
Miss Reville to do all the dirty work," he admitted. Alma Reville and
Alfred Hitchcock eventually became more than creative partners in life.

On December 2, 1926, he married Alma, who converted to Roman Catholicism when they became man and wife. She became his
biggest cheerleader, though she wasn't afraid to correct his blunders
either. The more films Hitchcock had under his belt, the more he ex-
plored women's hopes and fears: the fantasy of love and romance and
the terror of rape and murder. Alma's opinions on the workings of the
feminine mind controlled the behind-the-scenes narrative.

Alma's career took a back seat to Hitchcock's as he began to have
success in England and then Hollywood. Though the 2012 film *Hitchcock* exaggerated her on-set involvement by showing Helen Mirren, who
portrayed her, directing imperative scenes of *Psycho* when her husband
fell ill, Alma worked tirelessly on the backend and received continuity
credits on *The 39 Steps* (1935) and *Sabotage* (1936), and screenwriting
credits on *Suspicion* (1941) and *Shadow of a Doubt* (1943). "Although
she took credit on very few, she worked with him on every picture,"
said Hitchcock's only child, Patricia Hitchcock-O'Connell. "She was
the one person he relied on to tell him the truth."

In his wife, Hitchcock found someone who shared his sense of humor and ambition. In the past, there have been psychoanalytical theories written about the auteur in an attempt to understand his paradoxical behavior during certain points of his life. But Alma was the only person who would ever comprehend his inner emotional life.

It's been strongly suggested that Alma was deliberately presented as a subservient wife to the public eye. After observing the *Family Plot* set, Joseph McBride was curious to know more about the woman behind the man and approached Alma at a book party at Chasen's restaurant in Los Angeles in 1976. The two hit it off and after a sufficient amount of small talk, he requested an interview with her for a *Sight and Sound* piece he was writing (Hitchcock's office had already turned him down). Even though she gave relatively few interviews, she happily obliged.

They arranged for Joseph to visit the Hitchcock's Bel-Air home on a weekday afternoon at 2 p.m. As they sat in the living room and began the interview, she was warm and eager to talk about her early career. She also made a point of mentioning she had begun in the business before Hitchcock. Naturally, Joseph decided to save hardball questions about their marriage and how much she contributed to Hitchcock's work until the conversation had warmed up.

Suddenly, at 2:30 p.m., Joseph spotted a black limousine pull up outside the window in Hitchcock's driveway. Hitchcock got out and headed toward the front door. "He left work early because I was interviewing Alma and he was nervous about it," said Joseph. "He came in and sat down next to her and took over the interview; it was interesting because she kind of clammed up and deferred to him. It became rather disappointing in a sense, although I got some good comments from him and a few from her," remembered Joseph. "But I didn't get the interview that I wanted from Mrs. Hitchcock." These were the public personas the Hitchcocks had invented for themselves.

Alfred and Alma's relationship was not the stuff fairy tales are made of. With the auteur's ups and downs through the years, the marriage was unconventional and even depicted as bizarre at times. But it was their version of love and a partnership that birthed the gift of genius to the film world.

Around the time of the interview when Hitchcock once appeared on a television press junket, a journalist asked a rather bland question, which revealed a telling response. "When one is seventy-six years old, and one wakes up in the morning and one is Alfred Hitchcock, what does it feel like?" Hitchcock didn't need to ponder his reply. "When the film is a success, one feels very good, but if it isn't, one feels miserable!" The answer reflected a man who had trouble distinguishing Hitchcock, the person, from Hitchcock, the master of suspense. He lived for his work, and life without it was unfulfilled and empty.

Two weeks after the American Film Institute ceremony that honored his life achievements, Hitchcock finally accepted the fact that his diminishing health wouldn't allow him to make another film that met the Hitchcockian level. He broke the news to his staff, closed up his office, and went home.

On April 29, 1980, Sir Alfred Hitchcock passed away. A few days later, a mass was held in a small church on Santa Monica Boulevard. There would be no coffin present. Similar to the nature of his film sets, it had been sent to a top-secret destination. The guests were checked in at the door by Universal's security men and the police kept the crowds under control outside the church. Alma Reville would die just two years later, bound to her husband in spirit forever on July 6, 1982.

CHAPTER TWELVE

The Resurrection of *Rear Window*

FINAL ACT

BY 1980, GRACE KELLY'S DUTIES AS HER SERENE HIGHNESS PRINCESS OF Monaco afforded her little time to catch her breath between ribbon-cutting ceremonies and charity benefits. She had now resigned herself to the fact that she couldn't be a princess *and* an actress. Not that she didn't receive tempting offers. Her former agent, Jay Kanter, tried to entice her back to work with Hollywood scripts, most notably for *The Turning Point* (1977). "He told me I could have either of the two parts," Grace said in 1982. The roles eventually went to Anne Bancroft and Shirley MacLaine, who portrayed lifelong friends and former ballerinas with lingering conflicts. "He hoped I would return to the screen, but my answer was 'no.' In America, performers can have public and private lives and keep them apart. But as the wife of Prince Rainier, I can have but one public life—that of being a princess."

Grace couldn't attend a dinner party without a director or producer from her past life inquiring as to when she'd be back in Hollywood. Her cousin John Lehman recalled the time he'd accompanied her to a small party when Rainier was away in Paris and they'd had a chance encounter with the legendary studio head and producer Sam Goldwyn. "He really put the pressure on her there at the cocktail party and took her aside," said John. "He did his best to talk her into coming back." But it was futile. Though she still ached to be part of a film or theater production, too much time had elapsed. Grace resigned herself to the fact that she had chosen her path for the second chapter of her life and she had to honor it.

On February 28, 1980, it was Jimmy Stewart's turn to be honored by the American Film Institute. Hollywood's elite once again gathered at the Beverly Hilton Hotel to pay tribute to the seventy-one-year-old legend. However, the spotlight would be on Princess Grace, who stunned and seduced Hollywood all over again that evening. Tonight she would make an exception to her overflowing philanthropic schedule and appeared onstage to honor her favorite costar.

Joseph McBride, who produced the event for broadcast, wrote the speech she delivered to Jimmy at the ceremony that night. Earlier that day, during rehearsals, he met with Grace and showed her around the ballroom, which was being set up for the night. As they entered the grand room filled with a crew in the throes of chaotic preparation, Grace noticed the chairs at the tables. Each one had a sign on the back with each star's name so the cameramen were able to locate them for close-ups during filming. "I remember she looked at one of the chairs and said, 'Who is Tom Bosley?'" Joseph recalled. "He was starring in *Happy Days*, and she had no idea who he was!"

Likely feeling out of her element in this new culture of rising stars she'd never heard of, Grace changed the subject and kept discussing her speech with Joseph. Suddenly, she spotted a name she *did* recognize. "She saw Henry Hathaway's son's chair and said, 'Oh! *Fourteen Hours!*'" Hathaway had directed Grace in her first-ever film, *Fourteen Hours*, in 1951. She began to relax and suddenly, she was back in the Golden era that she recognized.

To add an element of surprise, things had been kept under wraps about Grace's appearance leading up to the ceremony. That night, Jimmy was stunned to see his *Rear Window* leading lady in the flesh after twenty-five years. The two former costars sat next to one another and laughed and reminisced throughout the ceremony. Hollywood was just as surprised to see Grace as she received an overwhelming standing ovation when she first took to the stage.

As she walked toward the podium to deliver her speech, a fitting backdrop of a *Rear Window* film still featuring her and Jimmy appeared behind her. Grace looked as breathtaking as ever in a gown with royal purple puffed sleeves and her hair swept back in a regal chignon. Time had been kind to the princess, who became more elegant with the passing years. "In *Rear Window* we had a little love scene that Hitchcock made us repeat *over* and *over* again to get it perfect, and you know, Jimmy *never* complained," she joked. "He didn't mind at all!" The camera zoomed in on Jimmy's sheepish grin as the crowd howled in appreciation. After so many years away from the big screen, Grace still had the audience in the palm of her hand. Hollywood finally had their fire and ice princess back, if only for the night.

Two years later on the morning of September 13, 1982, Princess Grace departed from Roc Agel, the family's summer refuge in La Turbie, with her seventeen-year-old daughter, Stéphanie, in her 1972 Rover 3500. They were heading back to the Prince's Palace and Grace needed to pick up a dress that was ready for her to wear to yet another royal function. The Rover had very few miles on it, as driving was an activity she generally detested. Grace's chauffeur had offered to drive them in the prince's Rolls, but she insisted she could make the twenty-five-minute drive herself.

As they drove along the cliffs overlooking the Mediterranean Sea, spirits were high. The warmth of summer still lingered, with temperatures reaching eighty-two degrees Fahrenheit. They followed the Moyenne Corniche, the same road she had sped along with Cary Grant in *To Catch a Thief* almost thirty years earlier. Nearby, the memorable picnic scene where she had famously offered him "a leg or a breast" of chicken, in classic Hitchcock double entendre, had been filmed. As the car turned onto the road, the sun glistened on the water.

But suddenly, seemingly out of nowhere, the car swerved and

missed a hairpin turn, sending it over a 120-foot mountainside. It tumbled down the steep embankment until it stopped near the sea. Immediately, they were rushed to the Monaco hospital for their injuries. Grace suffered a brain hemorrhage and multiple fractures, while Stéphanie had a neck fracture and concussion. Stéphanie survived the crash, but her mother did not. In a split second turn of events, everything Grace thought and felt vanished forever. At 10:35 p.m. on September 14, 1982, Grace Kelly Grimaldi, Her Serene Highness the Princess of Monaco, was pronounced dead at the age of fifty-two.

It was later found that Grace had experienced a piercing pain in her head and had momentarily lost consciousness just before the turn on the road. Dr. Jean Chatelain, chief surgeon at the hospital where she was treated, told the *New York Times* she was suffering from a "cerebral vascular incident" at the moment before the car lost control. Stéphanie's sister, Caroline, explained to the *Chicago Tribune*, "Stéphanie told me, 'Mommy kept saying, "I can't stop. The brakes don't work. I can't stop."' She said that Mommy was in a complete panic. She told me right after the accident, 'I pulled on the hand brake but it wouldn't stop. I tried but I just couldn't stop the car.'"

Four days later, Princess Grace of Monaco's body lay in the Ardent Chapel in the palace that had been her home for the past twenty-six years. She was dressed in an elegant high-necked white lace dress and laid on a quilt of orchids. Afterward, she was transported by a funeral cortege led by Prince Rainier, and her children, Prince Albert and Princess Caroline, through the streets of Monaco-Ville from the palace to the cathedral. It was the same church where Grace and Rainier had been married in 1956. Still recovering from a broken vertebra, Princess Stéphanie was unable to attend the procession.

Draped in the Monégasque flag, the coffin was carried into the cathedral. The air was heavy with sorrow as a devastated Prince Rainier walked behind the coffin. He couldn't contain his emotions and wept for his wife with every step. It all felt surreal—how could his beloved princess suddenly be gone?

Grace's cousin John Lehman, now the United States secretary of the navy, and First Lady Nancy Reagan were chosen by President Ronald Reagan as official representatives for the funeral. Grace and Nancy, friends since their Hollywood acting days, had shared a common connection as former actresses and wives of political leaders. She stood solemnly, her face partially veiled, and struggled to conceal her heartbreak. John, his voice filled with emotion, remembered, "The grief was just so intense, and it was a terrible tragedy." He received the call that she had died on his birthday, and immediately brought one of Grace's sisters and her brother, Jack, to Monaco on his plane.

After the overwhelming shock of his wife's death, Rainier struggled to cope with his grief, as his appearance seemed to transform in just a matter of weeks. John and his wife, Barbara, had stayed in Monaco for a long weekend in June before September when she died. John remembered, "In that period, Rainier's hair turned white. It was a salt-and-pepper color in June and in September it went pure white." Rainier was never the same after his wife's death and he never remarried.

Years later, Grace's nephew JB Kelly was still filled with memories of his aunt and their time together before her death. One of his most treasured recollections was the last holiday season she spent with the whole Kelly family in the palace. "It was the year before she passed away," he remembered. "I spent Christmas and New Year's with her and the whole family. It was a precious time." Then, in early September of 1982, something arrived in the mail from his aunt Grace. "When I got engaged, I received a letter from her. Unfortunately, I got it a week before she died, but I'm glad to have gotten it," he said. "She gave me advice about my marriage and wished me well as I launched this new part of my life. Not many aunts do that with their nieces and nephews."

Even after Grace's death, the relentless tabloid press refused to allow her peace. Persistent stories that Stéphanie had actually been the one driving began to circulate. This was due to a claim provided by Sesto Lipio, the commercial truck driver who first discovered the scene of the crash. He'd told the police that he'd pulled Stéphanie out of the driver's side first. "I was not driving, that's clear," Stéphanie said twenty years later in an interview with *Paris Match* magazine. "I was thrown around inside the car like my mother, who was catapulted onto the back seat. . . . The passenger door was completely smashed in; I got out on the only accessible side, the driver's."

Stéphanie had finally decided to speak up after two decades because the rumor continued to darken her life like a looming shadow. She had grown tired of it, the unfounded details cashing in on Grace's death and the inaccurate headlines that wouldn't go away. "I can't take it anymore," said Stéphanie. "I just want to say, 'Stop! Let me raise my children in tranquility and go forward with my own life in serenity.'"

On the day of Grace's funeral, Cary Grant, Princess Diana, race car driver Jackie Stewart, Eddie Fisher, Danielle Mitterrand, wife of the president of France, François Mitterrand, and Barbara Sinatra, wife of Frank Sinatra, were all in attendance. Cary wept openly throughout the ceremony. Because the funeral had taken place immediately after her death, Jimmy Stewart had not been able to attend. But on September 29, 1982, he joined an intimate group of Hollywood friends for a noontime memorial service in Grace's honor at the Church of the Good Shepherd, where she had often attended Sunday masses with her uncle George. Grace's publicist, Rupert Allen, organized the mass to allow her Californian friends who hadn't been able to go to Monaco to pay tribute to the princess.

Jimmy stood before the group of fifty-five and delivered a moving eulogy. "I really loved Grace Kelly," he said with tears in his eyes. "Not because she was a princess or an actress or a friend, but because she was just about the nicest lady I ever met. We will all miss her and now we must keep in touch with her through prayers. I would like to start today: God bless you, Princess. And God bless all of you for being here."

The making of *Rear Window* had a lasting effect on Jimmy, not just because it was his favorite of the four films he worked on with Hitchcock, but also because it had been a bonding experience with his costar.

Sadly, just like the immaculate face of Grace Kelly, *Rear Window* had vanished into the vaults of a Golden Hollywood that no longer existed. Besides the odd time it had been broadcast on television, *Rear Window* was out of circulation and almost impossible to locate. Beginning in 1961, five of Hitchcock's films including *Rear Window* were never seen by the general public. In an unusual deal for a director, Hitchcock took on full ownership of the films. But rather than attempting to profit from their distribution, he banned them from being exhibited. In London, fans took to "secret" underground screenings, but other than that, *Rear Window* had become a lost piece of art.

It wasn't until 1983 after Hitchcock's death that audiences redis-covered (and many discovered for the first time) this important chapter of his filmography. It would take one man at Universal Studios with a big idea that would resurrect Golden Hollywood in the eighties. If he could make *Rear Window* accessible again, it would bring Grace Kel-ly's image to the forefront of culture and cinema, allowing her memory to transcend time and become embedded in the consciousness of the public again.

THE FORBIDDEN FIVE

IN THE EARLY EIGHTIES, THE LAST REMNANTS OF THE STUDIO SYSTEM were no longer visible in Hollywood's rearview mirror. A new tidal wave trend dominated the decade of excess: the blockbuster. This would prove to be too much for some Golden Age veterans to stomach. It began with a small movie called *Star Wars* made for $11 million in 1977, which spawned a trilogy during the eighties. It was directed by a thirty-three-year-old protégé of Francis Ford Coppola named George Lucas. The craze continued with *Indiana Jones and the Temple of Doom* (1984), which followed up *Raiders of the Lost Ark* (1981), and film sagas like *Ghostbusters* (1984), *The Karate Kid* (1984), *Back to the Future* (1985), and three *Jaws* sequels.

With film after film that led to a continuation of plot and character development, audiences developed intimate relationships with their franchises. Soon, there was a whole corporation attached to these movies—action figures, Saturday morning cartoons, sugary cereals, and fashion merchandise to promote them (or was it the film promoting the merchandise?). Some films were very good and some sequels barely watchable.

Up until this point, studios hadn't fathomed that they could make so much money from one film property, but now a new formula was set in stone. "The studios realized they could make fewer films than prior years, but market the hell out of those few and make money like they'd never made before," said Columbia film professor Richard Peña. "By 1980, a film like *Taxi Driver* couldn't have been made. That was really when Hollywood changed into the direction it's still going in."

At the time, Jim Katz was president of the Universal Classics division. Universal had become factory-like in its ability to pump out the most commercially successful franchises in Hollywood. Jim's job required him to do the opposite by digging into the past and re-polishing antique gems or films off the beaten path, then making them appealing to modern audiences. He knew if he wanted to succeed with classics, he'd have to maximize Hitchcock's filmography and repackage it in a new way for the modern public.

"Initially, the library consisted of the pre-1948 Hitchcock films that Paramount had sold to Universal, which they used for television fodder and such," Jim remembered. But he wanted the five key films that the Hitchcock family had inherited, which no one could get to. In total, they owned *Rear Window, Vertigo, The Man Who Knew Too Much, The Trouble with Harry,* and *Rope.* And they were determined to hold on to them. "They didn't have a lot of money, not as much money as you think Hitchcock's family would have, because the studios owned all of his other films," Jim said. These films were the Hitchcocks' bread and butter and they wouldn't be parting with them without a fight.

It was difficult to fathom that one of the highest-profile titles in this collection—*Rear Window*—had now remained off-limits for almost a quarter century. It was never apparent that Hitchcock had concocted any master plan to keep the movies off the screen. Theaters and organizations only figured it out when they approached him and received the cold shoulder. Herman Citron, Lew Wasserman's successor, fielded dozens of offers each year—from film festivals, television networks, colleges, and art houses hoping to bring Hitchcock's most popular films back to life for a new generation. But whether they received a flat "no" or an unrealistic financial offer, Citron had generally found the proposals unworthy. Commercially speaking, this was Hitchcock's finest work, after all.

Just before Hitchcock died in 1980, he was said to be reconsidering the prohibition on his "Forbidden Five" pictures. Investigating the rumor, the *New York Times* asked Hitchcock's agent, Herman Citron, why the director had been so adamant about keeping them from view. "Private reasons" is all Citron would reveal. But three years later, while scanning through the entire Hitchcock filmography, Jim had a flash of genius. He saw an opportunity with these films that everyone could benefit from. He'd get the backing to make an offer no one could refuse and release the five films as a dazzling theatrical event and screen them in specialty movie theaters all over the world. But in the era of *Indiana Jones* and *Alien*, this would undoubtedly be met with resistance by the suits with the money. The public wanted the next *new* thing. They wanted parasitic space creatures bursting from human chests or archaeology professors racing through ancient tombs. Universal had to obey their audience.

Selling anything in the film industry has always required nerves of steel and perfect synchrony of stars. Before an audience sees a movie, it must essentially be sold five times. First, a producer must convince someone to invest money in it, then persuade an actor with box-office clout to take the lead role. This is usually followed by getting a director on board once a big-name actor is attached. Then comes the process of securing financing from the studio. The final hoop to jump through is convincing a distributor to invest in the film. Only then is it ready to be sold to a public audience. In the unique Hitchcock situation, adding to the mix that these films had been made thirty years prior presented all kinds of complications. How would this work in the decadent eighties and did a strong Hitchcock demographic still exist?

It was a risky venture, but Jim went with his instincts and pitched the idea to a roomful of Universal executives. The good news was they liked the idea. The bad news? They were only interested in the films as a television buy. The decision-makers deemed a theatrical release too pricey. Amplifying the situation, when Universal began negotiations to get the films, things began to stall. "They thought the Hitchcock family were driving too hard a bargain," said Jim. "It was too expensive, and now it was just dragging."

Jim was frustrated. Generations of people were missing out on Hitchcock's most powerful work, and the stuffed shirts just weren't getting it. These movies were bigger than blink-and-you-miss-them television broadcasts. They belonged on the big screen. He knew he'd have to go further out on a limb to make this happen. "I was trying to get the head of TV to buy this and let me take it out," said Jim. "They weren't sure if I could make money on these films because they had no idea of the audience that I was looking for, but I knew they were out there."

But opportunity knocks in strange ways sometimes. In Jim's case, it was in the form of a fire drill at his office. He worked in the famous Black Tower, a dark aluminum and glass structure that stood just a few hundred feet north of the Hollywood Freeway. This was where scripts were approved and careers were made (and sometimes shattered). It was also the home of the corner offices of top-division presidents and executives like Lew Wasserman. "When the drill went off, it was raining outside and I said, 'What the hell, I'm not going outside in this rain. What am I gonna do that for?'" Thinking quickly, he took the elevator to the basement garage before anyone saw him, planning to wait out the alarms so he could get back to work again.

But in his travels, he realized he wasn't alone. On the ground, a little farther down from him was the senior vice president of Universal Television, Tom Wertheimer. It was just the two of them in that garage and Jim knew it was now or never. He sat down next to him and broached the subject of the Hitchcock films. "Listen, let me take them out in my division theatrically," he said. "I can really do something with these." As they sat in the dusty darkness of the garage, Jim pitched his marketing plan for the films and broke out the potential audiences who would appreciate them. Suddenly, Tom was a believer. Jim's sheer drive and belief in the films won him over and soon after, a theatrical deal was negotiated with the Hitchcock family.

Once Jim received the official green light, he located the film reels in a large L.A. storage vault filled to the brim with Golden Age Hollywood. But this experience would be a rude awakening about the way these films had deteriorated over the years. Throughout the seventies and eighties, Hollywood film reels were typically stored in units, specialized facilities designed to preserve and protect the physical film prints. These vaults were supposedly constructed with controlled temperature and humidity levels to prevent deterioration of the film stock, which is sensitive to environmental conditions.

But that wasn't what Jim discovered when he unearthed the original *Rear Window* film reel. "It was a place that was one hundred degrees during the day and fifty degrees at night—about the worst conditions for storing films." Some of the movies had begun to suffer from "vinegar syndrome" where the chemicals on the film were beginning to decompose. "I took them out theatrically, but I didn't have any idea that these problems existed," he said. "That was my first reality check on the way films were being taken care of after their release." Years later, he would take action helping to preserve some of the most important films in Hollywood history, which included *Rear Window*, but for the time being, his mission was to get Hitchcock's most iconic work back in theaters.

REAR WINDOW HITS THE ROAD

THE SHREWD BUSINESSMAN THAT HE WAS, JIMMY STEWART HAD A PIECE in some of the Forbidden Five Hitchcock property because of his Patron deal with Hitchcock thirty years prior, and he still received a percentage in any deal connected to *Rear Window*. Jim Katz decided to get in touch with him on the off chance that he might star in a trailer for the theatrical re-releases of *Rear Window*, *The Man Who Knew Too Much*, *Vertigo*, and *Rope* if his schedule allowed. To Jim's delight, Jimmy jumped at the chance to revisit and promote some of his Hitchcock favorites, making himself fully available to Universal.

Jimmy was so enthusiastic and proud of the films that in addition to starring in the trailer, he made multiple press appearances, even while there were still doubts among Universal executives as to whether the films would bring a return on their investment. But they needn't have worried about that. "We started to get interest from the U.K. and France," Jim recalled. "Then there was Germany, Australia, Canada, and all over the world; they all wanted to see these films!"

A European press tour was organized for Jimmy and Jim to spread the word about the films. Jimmy had been suffering from a variety of health issues and his wife, Gloria, thought it would be too risky for him to go, but Jim had an idea. His wife, Marjorie, was an operating room nurse and he convinced her to join them on the tour as well. Now Gloria would have peace of mind knowing that Jimmy would be traveling with a registered health professional throughout the trip.

One of their first stops would be London. On a cool evening in 1983, they departed from New York's Kennedy Airport on a Concorde jet. "An hour out of New York, we could see the lights of London because we were flying so high around the curvature of the earth," said Jim. "I was thinking it was all too good to be true." With Jimmy's status as an air force general, the pilots aboard were starstruck and full of questions, not just about Golden Hollywood, but about his war piloting days too. Even at his advanced age, Jimmy was as patient and professional as ever, fielding every question that came his way.

As soon as they landed, word spread among London's celebrity circles that Jimmy Stewart was in town. By the time they checked into their hotel, there was a waiting list of calls and requests to meet the Hollywood legend face-to-face. English A-listers stopped by Jimmy's suite daily for the chance to meet their idol. The demand became so overwhelming, that eventually, a table was set up in the hotel dining room by Universal London publicists who screened and set up appointments. Their visitors included Vanessa Redgrave, John Hurt, and opera singer Plácido Domingo. "They would come and have dinner with Jimmy Stewart and he would answer their questions, but then, all he would do was go right back and talk about how excited he was about the five Hitchcock films," said Jim. "He didn't stop selling."

After London, it was on to press promotion in Madrid, Paris, Berlin, and Munich, with each hotel more lavish than the last. It was an experience they'd never forget. "It also broke the ice and gave me a parameter on how much we could sell these films abroad," remembered Jim. "Jimmy was unbelievably all in, and to have someone like that at your disposal, it was a pretty amazing situation."

Rear Window was the first of the five films to make its premiere in the United States. It was the hit of the twenty-first annual New York Film Festival after two retrospective showings in October 1983. As Jimmy Stewart sat at the screening, he and the audience were seeing *Rear Window* for the first time in twenty years. The next morning at his hotel, he told the *New York Times*, "The audience was really with it, and I thought that was just amazing. It just bears out the feeling that so many of us had about Hitch and his way of doing things." Seeing *Rear Window* after so many years also stirred up sadness for the still-fresh loss of his friend Grace Kelly. "The wonderful thing about Grace was that she was just completely at ease with her lines," he said. "I remembered that very vividly, and it was really brought back last night. Absolutely fascinating woman."

Critics all over the country were now examining *Rear Window* in a different light and retrieving deeper meaning from it. Against the backdrop of 1983, it was a brand-new film. After the New York Film Festival screening, Vincent Canby, a prominent film critic of eighties cinema, wrote for the *New York Times*, "Ever since I saw *Rear Window* when it was initially released, I've had fond memories of it, but, as rarely happens, those memories turned out not to do full justice to the film I went back to see last Sunday morning at the Cinema Studio. It effortlessly demonstrates all that we now understand to be the splendor of the Hitchcockian cinema of the absurdly logical. Yet *Rear Window* enchants us immediately, and need not be analyzed to death to achieve its place in the pantheon."

Richard Peña, who served as director of the New York Film Festival from 1988 to 2012, observed Hitchcock's gift for timelessness. "He's so tapped into human nature. It's almost like he was able to predict the future," he said. "He's a great artist and great artists often do that. They have certain ideas that eventually become embraced by culture as sort of dominant."

After the New York premiere, *Rear Window* began playing simultaneously in Manhattan's specialty cinemas, like the Plaza Theatre and the Paris Theatre, before it gravitated to other parts of the country. In just a few short weeks it earned more than $1 million at fewer than two dozen theaters. Hitchcock's daughter, Patricia, observed that *Rear Window* made more money on its re-release than most of the new pictures that came out at the same time, adding: "Its success shows, I think, that audiences are starved of good, classy films."

The next step for the previously forbidden five was a VHS release. In a design Hitchcock would have approved of, the box set featured a picture of the director standing in profile with his trademark belly protruding out. *Rear Window* alone grossed $9.1 million on re-release. *Vertigo* also made an impressive $4.5 million. Jim Katz had put his neck (and his job) on the line for his vision of a new generation enjoying Hitchcock's best work, and it had surpassed his wildest expectations.

"We got them out there and they just went gangbusters," he recalled. "They were breaking all sorts of clearance records in New York. When the films were released all over the world to theaters, VHS, and cable, they grossed over fifty-five million dollars, which was unheard of, I mean, nobody expected numbers like that."

The monstrous success of the films was also bolstered by the sudden resurgence of nostalgia for the fifties. Reminiscent of the nostalgic revival culture of the twenty-first century, with hits like *Stranger Things, The Americans,* and *GLOW*, the eighties embraced a rose-colored view of the Golden Age. Retro-themed films like *Back to the Future* (1985) and *Peggy Sue Got Married* (1986) were released, as well as remakes of *Little Shop of Horrors* (1986) and *The Blob* (1988). Even the MTV generation caught the fifties wave as Madonna vamped toward the camera as Marilyn Monroe in the "Material Girl" video. In hindsight, there couldn't have been a better time to remove *Rear Window* from the vault, along with Hitchcock's other career highlights.

Inspired by the success of *Rear Window*'s re-release in 1983, classic divisions of other studios began to investigate how they could fiscally benefit in the same way from Golden Hollywood. But with the expenses of advertising and making prints, it was always a gamble. Not all films of the studio era were embraced the same way by moviegoers of the eighties. In 1982, the Goldwyn Company failed to bring in revenue with the 1955 version of Rodgers and Hammerstein's *Oklahoma!* Warner Brothers barely broke even the following year when they re-released the 1954 Judy Garland musical *A Star Is Born* in Toronto, New York, Los Angeles, and San Francisco (though, the two remakes in later years, which starred Barbra Streisand in 1976 and Lady Gaga in 2018, were both commercial successes).

A crucial reason Hitchcock's re-release of *Rear Window* succeeded where others failed was that it was simply ahead of its time. Audiences of the eighties and beyond could watch and relate to the humanity of Hitchcock's storytelling. With each fresh viewing of a Hitchcock film, a new plot device or subtle symbolism that had been missed the last time reveals itself to the moviegoer. Another major factor was that films like *Rear Window* and *Vertigo* were rarely on television throughout the years, adding to their mystique. Keeping them out of circulation tremendously increased their value with an audience. "You're not going to fool the film buffs," Jim Katz told the *New York Times* in 1983. "*Rear Window* had an aura—out of circulation, not on television. It's a detriment if a film has been on television."

CHAPTER THIRTEEN

A Race of Peeping Toms

THE NICE GUY MAKES A COMEBACK

BY THE MID-EIGHTIES, HOLLYWOOD HAD IN CERTAIN RESPECTS COME FULL circle. By now, the ideal leading man wasn't all that different from the Golden era. Macho was back in a big way, and tanned, brawny action stars like Sylvester Stallone, Arnold Schwarzenegger, and Kurt Russell were the new heroes filling theaters and driving up box office revenue. But a new star on the horizon contradicted Hollywood's musclemen in every way, and he was becoming harder to ignore. Tom Hanks was different from all the other guys. He had an honest face, he was relatable, and most of all, people liked him. He also reminded *everyone* of Jimmy Stewart. "Tom Hanks always comes to mind when people say, 'Who's the closest actor to your dad?'" said Kelly Stewart Harcourt. "Dad played more types of roles than he does, but I think Tom Hanks has that same talent."

In 1984, when Tom appeared in *Splash* at age twenty-seven as a New Yorker in love with a mermaid, he gained positive reviews, but by 1988, when he starred in *Big* as a child mysteriously stuck in a grown man's body, his face was suddenly everywhere. Similar to *It's a Wonderful Life*, *Big* possessed the same ethereal fantasy element that appealed to moviegoers who were tired of seventies grit and wanted to dream again. And Tom brought the timeless brand of vulnerability and boy-next-door presence Jimmy had displayed over forty years before.

Tom would have appeared just as at home as an MGM contract player in the studio system as he was in an eighties rom-com.

The comparison was even more pronounced in the nineties when Tom pushed himself to embrace the darker side of real-life issues in *Saving Private Ryan* (1998) and *The Green Mile* (1999) while remaining beloved by the American public. Jimmy and Tom followed a similar trajectory throughout their careers—from the lanky man-child to the serious craftsman with somber material, and finally to the elder statesman who everyone looks to as a moral compass.

In *Cast Away* (2000), just like Jimmy in *Rear Window*, Tom battles the overwhelming loneliness of human isolation after finding himself marooned after a plane crash. His character Chuck Noland shares similar workaholic traits before solitude forces him to pause and reassess his life, as with Jefferies's broken leg. But instead of peering at neighbors across a courtyard to pass the time, he relies on his only friend, a volleyball he names Wilson.

The loose remake of *Rear Window* in 1998 starred Christopher Reeve as a quadriplegic voyeur, though it didn't stay faithful to the original version, and led some to wonder why Tom Hanks hadn't been cast in the role. If there were to be an exact remake of *Rear Window* as it was in 1954, Chris Knight, chief film critic of the *National Post* agrees Tom Hanks would be the only man for the job. "He's probably the only one in the history of Hollywood at any period who would be able to pull that off because he has to walk a fine line," explained Chris. "Jimmy Stewart's character—if he's wrong at the end of the movie, he's a horrible person." It's possible a modern audience could only trust Tom to lead them down *Rear Window*'s dark, winding path of no return.

Here's something else to consider: Would Tom Hanks have been as successful in cinema without the foundation laid by Jimmy Stewart? He certainly paved the way for a relatable brand of likeability in a star that couldn't be manufactured. And Jimmy and Tom never appear to be "acting" in their films. It's an authenticity that's hard to define and that one simply has to be born with. Not a larger-than-life figure or an alien-like matinee idol, but a person who feels like a familiar chum you greet whenever you catch them on-screen. Someone you'd want to grab a beer with in real life. The public has also quickly forgiven them of their career missteps like *The Magic of Lassie* (1978) in Jimmy's case or *The Bonfire of the Vanities* (1990) in Tom's (as opposed to their contemporaries, like Henry Fonda or Michael Keaton, both cursed with "box office poison" phases in their careers).

When Tom had the opportunity to meet Jimmy face-to-face in 1989, it was for a cover piece with *Life* magazine where modern stars teamed up and talked with Golden era legends. At the height of fifties nostalgia fever, matching Jimmy and Tom was a no-brainer. The cover photo of the two together suggested that Jimmy was handing the "Hollywood everyman" baton over to Tom. But during the *Life* piece, the two men also got to know each other outside of their personas.

When Tom visited Jimmy at home on Roxbury Drive, the two forged a connection and exchanged stories as they sat in the sprawling back garden. Then Jimmy gave Tom a tour of the house. "He's showing me around his living room," Tom reminisced to Stephen Colbert in 2020, "and there is no sign of Jimmy Stewart, the movie star, anywhere!" There were family photos of Jimmy without his hairpiece (usually worn just for public appearances) and a painting on the wall of a horse named Pie, which had been painted by Henry Fonda. The library—the most used space in their home—was the only room that suggested his line of work. It was the location of his Oscar statue for *The Philadelphia Story* (1940). Tom was genuinely stunned by the unassuming demeanor of such a legend and the proof echoed in his surroundings. Jimmy Stewart would lead a modest, decidedly un-Hollywood life until the very end.

NAVY SEAL OF APPROVAL

IN THE YEARS FOLLOWING GRACE KELLY'S PASSING, HER SPIRIT LIVED ON, not only within Monaco but through the enduring Hollywood connection of the Kelly family. Grace's cousin, John Lehman, while serving as secretary of the navy during the Reagan administration from 1981 to 1987, left an indelible mark on American politics and on a particular Hollywood film. During his tenure, Lehman advocated for the six-hundred-ship navy and led one of the most significant naval buildups in American history. As a result, Paramount approached him for permission to use a legitimate navy facility and for quality control on their upcoming film *Top Gun*, set for a 1986 release.

Producing partners Jerry Bruckheimer and Don Simpson approached John cautiously, as the navy hadn't worked with Hollywood in years. *An Officer and a Gentleman* (1982) had been a significant boost for the navy, even though Paramount didn't have permission to film on a navy facility, leading them to use an abandoned army post in Washington state. However, Paramount aimed for excellence with *Top Gun*. Knowing they were going the distance with the film, they needed authenticity. Bruckheimer and Simpson went straight to the source and reached out to John, explaining their plans. The goal was to accurately depict fighter jets and facilities while solidifying Tom Cruise's career as a superstar. Intrigued by the proposition, John, a navy pilot with Hollywood in his blood, was immediately open to the idea.

Admittedly, John liked what he read in the *Top Gun* script when the studio had sent it over. But he decided to play it cool with executives and producers in case it got into the wrong hands and someone made a mess of it during production. He couldn't bear to see another inaccurate depiction of fighter pilots like *The Right Stuff* (1983) on the big screen again. "Jerry Bruckheimer had a dinner party with just the principals—about eight of us," remembered John. "Of course, I lost a lot of my leverage when they seated Barbara, my wife, next to Tom Cruise!"

But the meeting went better than expected. Bruckheimer and Simpson gave John a privilege very rarely bestowed in Hollywood— the right to have his opinion heard, but most importantly, the power of script approval. Paramount would also be required to show him the rough cuts for top-level approval as they filmed various action sequences. Once John had been out twice to the studio to meticulously go through the footage, the navy finally granted Paramount the green light and arranged for them to film on two of the original aircraft carriers and to modify two F-14 planes to carry the crew's cameras. It would have been a very different (translation: much less successful) movie without them.

When John finally watched the film in its entirety, he was elated. "I jumped out of my seat and I lost all my leverage because I said, 'You really have got it!'" he recalled. "I ended up not changing a word in the script. They just really got what naval aviation was all about."

And so, John, like his cousin Grace Kelly thirty years earlier, continued to carry the Hollywood torch to help make movie history. *Top Gun* was one of the biggest films of the decade, and just like Hanks, another Tom (Cruise) consequently became one of its biggest stars. As a tribute to Grace, the Kelly family lineage continued to leave its mark on Hollywood.

REAR WINDOW IN THE DOT-COM DECADE

AS THE EXCESSIVE EIGHTIES GAVE WAY TO THE MINIMALISTIC NINETIES, the filmmaking formula of *Rear Window* maintained its momentum. Voyeurism, isolation, and loneliness were themes that had the everlasting potential to continue building on themselves over and over in Hollywood cinema. It appeared *Rear Window* had now infiltrated itself into the landscape of modern thrillers.

The new erotic thriller genre, triggered by the success of 1987's *Fatal Attraction*, took a serious line from *Rear Window* in what it concealed from the audience. In *Basic Instinct* (1992), Michael Douglas's Detective Nick Curran is in the same position as L. B. Jefferies, as the viewer is limited to seeing only what he sees, which isn't the full picture. Is Sharon Stone's Catherine Tramell the real deal or is she a cold-blooded killer playing him for a fool? *Basic Instinct's* limited viewpoint technique with a subjective camera was a hallmark of the Hitchcockian technique.

This trick also made its way into modern horror and mystery. In *The Sixth Sense* (1999), similar to Brian De Palma's *Dressed to Kill* (1976), director M. Night Shyamalan exerted visual control over the audience to hide a crucial plot point about Bruce Willis's Malcolm Crowe in the controlled way that *Rear Window* pioneered. This type of withholding of information has become the norm in the sense that it no longer registers to an audience as Hitchcockian, though the auteur was the first to popularize it. "Any movie where the director is manipulating you that much to keep information from you is somehow influenced by *Rear Window* because that wasn't a thing until *Rear Window*," said film historian Sloan De Forest. "It started there with that kind of refined, controlled, perfect manipulation of every shot to give the desired effect."

In the ultimate tale of suburban midlife crisis, *American Beauty* (1999) places teenage Ricky Fitts (Wes Bentley) as the voyeur of the piece. The audience again has the opportunity to gaze through his camcorder as the observer of others' activities. By the millennium, *Panic Room* (2002) borrowed the Hitchcockian idea of confined space to portray fear and isolation as Meg Altman (Jodie Foster) and her daughter, Sarah (Kristen Stewart), are confined to their panic room and fighting for their lives during a terrifying home invasion.

In the mid-nineties, when *Rear Window* made its way into the biggest modern pop culture reference of all, *The Simpsons*, it was obvious this film would never be retired to the category of "forgotten favorite" like the Golden Hollywood films that had won all the Oscars in their day. *Rear Window's* modern appeal had created a league of its own. In the 1994 episode "Bart of Darkness," in a parody of *Rear Window*, Bart, after breaking his leg in a swimming pool, sits in a wheelchair spying on his neighbors through a telescope, convinced that Ned Flanders has committed a murder.

In 2001, director Curtis Hanson remarked of *Rear Window*, "If one were to ask, 'What are the movies of Alfred Hitchcock like?' you could show them *Rear Window*, and in a sense, touch on everything in Hitchcock. You would immediately see his technical brilliance. You would see his ability to tell a story in a uniquely captivating way."

Rear Window has continually been an inspiration to filmmakers throughout the decades because it's a movie that quite literally focuses on the mechanical and psychological apparatus that makes film possible. Transporting the audience to a meta-film universe, Hitchcock uses the narrative to capture the atmosphere and the future he sees for America. "We can see that this is a film where Hitchcock is clearly using this story by Cornell Woolrich to explore the context of an America that has become obsessed with images and the whole idea of surveillance and closed circuit television," observed Columbia film professor Richard Peña. In hindsight, Hitchcock was already exploring issues in *Rear Window* that would become viable in the decades to come.

Studying Hitchcock's methods, filmmaker Laurent Bouzereau gleaned practical insights that influenced his own work. "He was so meticulously prepared that he knew where the camera was going to travel to, meaning that if the camera was going to go from one place and didn't need to be going another place, then they would not build that part of the set because it's never going to go there," he explained. "I really admire that, because it's something that forces you to think out your visual story before you get to the set. And then if you have to improvise because of performance or because of a new idea, you can do it freely because you are so well prepared."

When Laurent spoke with Janet Leigh about her experience making *Psycho*, she spoke of the freedom she felt while filming scenes, which imparted further evidence of the autonomy Hitchcock offered actors. "He would say to her, 'The film is the pie, and I'm giving you a slice and within that slice of pie, you can do whatever you want with it.'"

"I talked to Bruce Dern and he said Hitchcock's style was very liberating for an actor," Joseph McBride said, echoing Janet Leigh's sentiment. "Hitchcock knew exactly what was in the frame and yet he gave the actor freedom within that frame. As long as you did the movement he wanted, you had a lot of freedom to act the way you felt it should be acted."

IT WAS A WONDERFUL LIFE

WITH ALL THE ATTENTION *REAR WINDOW* CONTINUED TO RECEIVE WELL into the nineties after its 1983 re-release, its loss at the 1955 Oscars seemed all the more poignant. But by the end of the decade, the Library of Congress and the American Film Institute would finally recognize *Rear Window*'s legacy with the honors it deserved. The film was selected for preservation in the United States National Film Registry by the Library of Congress in 1997. Then, in 1998, the American Film Institute unveiled its list of the 100 Greatest Films of All Time. *Rear Window* was included on the list as number forty-two. It was also included on the AFI's additional lists, AFI's 100 Years . . . 100 Thrills at number fourteen, and number three in AFI's 10 Top 10 Mysteries list.

But 1997 was also a year of heartache and loss for *Rear Window* fans. On July 2, at the age of eighty-nine, American film legend and military hero James Maitland "Jimmy" Stewart passed away from cardiac arrest at his home on Roxbury Drive—just three years after the death of his beloved wife, Gloria. A memorial service was held on July 7 at the Beverly Hills Presbyterian Church. More than three thousand people attended his funeral, including Nancy Reagan, Bob Hope, Lew Wasserman, June Allyson, and Esther Williams. He was laid to rest next to Gloria at Forest Lawn Memorial Park in Glendale, California, to a twenty-one-gun salute in honor of his military service. His gravestone was inscribed with the fitting words, "For he shall give his angels charge over thee to keep thee in all thy ways."

"He was my favorite friend," Lew Wasserman told *Variety*. "It's very sad for me but I also know that he will live on forever in the films he made." Throughout his career spanning from 1934 until 1991, Jimmy appeared in more than ninety-two films, television shows, and short subjects. He was the tirelessly hard worker who valued his solitude above all. There was no method to his magic. He simply stood on his mark and allowed the moment to take its course. When he spoke, it set off a chain reaction of impressions of his distinctive "Waaaaal," a stammering speech that became an endearing trademark.

"Dad truly brought himself to his roles and that's the way he talked; he didn't put a lot of mannerisms into acting," said Kelly Stewart Harcourt. "That's actually what he was like. I think people's perception of him as an actor was affected by his public persona. So, they respected him for his war effort, and he never let his public down." Jimmy was always comfortable with himself and that translated to his on-screen presence. Regardless of the typical drama that trailed his Hollywood peers, he navigated life his way. Until the day he died, Jimmy Stewart would remain the eternal boy next door.

THE "REMAKE"

SHELDON ABEND WAS BACK AT IT AGAIN, GRINDING THE GEARS OF THE *Rear Window* moneymaking machine. In the late eighties, after the runaway success of the *Rear Window* theatrical and VHS re-release, he had taken MCA, Jimmy Stewart, and Hitchcock's estate back to the Supreme Court aiming to see how much juice he could squeeze out of the deal as current owner of the literary property. After the case concluded in a monumental 1990 Supreme Court decision that established the Abend Rule, Sheldon took his millions and planned his next move.

By the late nineties, after much back and forth, he had now appointed himself to the role of film producer. A remake of *Rear Window* starring Christopher Reeve and Daryl Hannah was finally in the works. It was a made-for-TV film that broadcast during prime time on ABC on November 22, 1998. Though Christopher Reeve was hailed as excellent in the lead role (his first role since the 1995 equestrian accident that left him a quadriplegic), anyone looking for a film that resembled the original *Rear Window* would be sorely disappointed.

Christopher played Jason Kemp, an architect left paralyzed after a head-on traffic collision, who watches neighbors in the same voyeuristic way L. B. Jefferies had over forty years earlier. There's the same game of cat and mouse with an antagonist who may have murdered his wife, but that's where the similarities end. From then on, it's less about a man confined to his apartment, and more a thriller focused on a man's disability and the medical devices and machines in his large home used as a form of protection.

In fairness, the remake weaves in aspects of the original *Rear Window*, like a murderous neighbor, Peeping Tom syndrome, and a glamorous blond sidekick in Daryl Hannah. But where critics unanimously agreed it objectively failed was the lack of any dynamic interaction between neighbors, as well as a lack of setting. Greenwich Village was a crucial feature of the original 1954 production. Though the new version was filmed on location in New York, there are no visual clues as to what city the film is based in. The interplay and location elements were such vibrant aspects that made the original so enticing that once taken away, it was difficult for the audience to engage with the characters or scenery.

While Christopher Reeve was left with all the emotional heavy lifting and heroically took on the burden of carrying the film himself, there's a dark cloud of disorientation that surrounds him. On *Rear Window* 2.0's release, *Entertainment Weekly* conceded, "The problem here isn't Reeve's performance so much as it is the slack, awkwardly updated, and frequently confusing teleplay."

If 1998's *Rear Window* was meant to be an homage to the original, it missed the mark by lacking any form of Hitchcockian tribute. Though matching an original like *Rear Window* would be a tall order under any circumstance, it was difficult for critics or viewers to find any glimmering moments the easily forgotten new version could offer in its own right. But Hitchcock fans needn't have worried. Thanks to modern technology, the original *Rear Window* was about to make such a mighty comeback that its technical and creative brilliance would now shine like never before.

THE RESTORATION

ON APRIL 29, 1974, TWENTY-EIGHT-YEAR-OLD FLEDGLING FILM ARCHIVIST Robert Harris attended the Film Society of Lincoln Center Annual Gala Tribute to Alfred Hitchcock. The event drew the biggest and brightest stars of Hollywood and New York society. Legends like Joan Fontaine, Teresa Wright, and Janet Leigh graced the stage to honor their beloved director. Robert's trip to Manhattan was a mix of pleasure and business, as he sought information for a film book he was working on. He bought a ticket to the event, in hopes that it might spark some creative inspiration or lead to some introductions.

As the screen filled with a montage of flashbacks from *Rear Window*, *Vertigo*, and *Shadow of a Doubt*, Robert was mesmerized. He had always idolized Hitchcock's work, owning every film he could find that was in circulation and studying each one of them frame by frame. But the true magic of the evening happened as the event concluded. While rising from his seat to leave, Robert found himself mere inches away from one of the most glamorous women on earth. Her Serene Highness Princess Grace of Monaco, regally chic in a white gown and matching satin cape, slipped past him on her way out. "She was gliding, and I had a feeling afterward that maybe she was on roller skates," he chuckled. "Probably not. I mean, she was just so beautiful. She was luminous."

He didn't realize it at the time, but his brush with Grace Kelly was critical to his future. It became an inspirational moment that propelled his career in film restoration, where he would save some of Hitchcock's films of the Golden Era from extinction over a decade later.

However, Robert began his restoration journey in 1981 with Abel

Gance's *Napoleon* (1927), which he reconstructed with Francis Ford Coppola's Zoetrope Studios. Next, he would piece together a three-hour and thirty-six-minute cut of *Lawrence of Arabia* (1962) in 1989. It would be one of the most difficult things he'd ever done professionally. The print was in rough shape and looked battered and pale from the passing years.

Simply preserving or enhancing an image in a film often just involved a quick purchase order to a lab. But to fully restore a film and reverse the ravages of time required at least one year, sometimes two, of dedicated hard work. "*Lawrence of Arabia* took me twenty-seven months to do," said Robert. "The director, David Lean, used to say, 'It took Robert twenty-seven months to put the film back together again. I made it in just sixteen!'"

After the re-release of the new and improved *Lawrence of Arabia*, Robert realized his work was making an impact on Hollywood and he was gaining somewhat of a celebrity status. This became clear during the *Lawrence* restoration party in Los Angeles, which Roger Ebert and Gene Siskel attended. "They were following us around during all the openings," remembered Robert. "I was having a chat with Gregory Peck because he had produced and starred in a picture called *The Big Country* (1958) and was looking for some technical information. Suddenly, I feel a tug on my arm and it's Roger Ebert and he's standing there with Gene Siskel, who's pulling on my sleeve. He simply said, 'Introduce us.' It's great to get two of the top film critics in the world who are fans."

Soon after, he called on his friend Jim Katz at Universal Classics for help. They had met on the *Napoleon* (1927) project almost a decade prior and stayed in touch. Jim had been intrigued by Robert's extensive knowledge of how to save Golden Age films from destruction and make them look better than before. He also hadn't forgotten the serious wake-up call he received when he witnessed the state of the films and the ill-suited environments they were stored in during the *Rear Window* 1983 theatrical release.

Jim and Robert teamed up to raise money through the studios that owned the films and work on a series of restorations together. As they were choosing the films, studio politics often came into play. "We got a million dollars out of Universal chairman Tom Pollock to save *Spartacus*," Jim remembered. "It was mainly because his wife was a *Spartacus* fan and it was relevant to Universal, because who was now the head of Universal—but Kirk Douglas's agent, Lew Wasserman!"

But, with the time it took, they couldn't save every movie in Hollywood. They would have to be discerning. *Lawrence of Arabia* was a 1961–62 production originally photographed in Eastman color and processed by Technicolor London. Although the negative was cracked and falling to pieces by the late eighties, there was still hope for the film, and new color protection materials could be created. Not every film they came across would be so lucky.

As Robert and Jim did further preparation for *Spartacus* (1960), they realized it would come with a whole new set of issues. After searching through almost two thousand cans of the film's footage from Universal's vaults, they found that the original negative was completely faded. "We had to spend months looking for cut bits of the camera negative," remembered Robert of the tedious process. When adding the significant "snails and oysters" scene between Tony Curtis and Sir Laurence Olivier that had been left on the cutting room floor, they discovered its soundtrack was now nonexistent. Curtis was on hand to redub his lines, but at this point, Olivier had passed away.

Robert and Jim decided to approach his widow, Joan Plowright, and get her take on who might best mimic her husband's voice. To their surprise, she immediately responded, "Anthony Hopkins." In fact, it had been a running joke while Olivier was alive. "Tony used to do impressions to Laurence's face at cocktail parties all the time," said Robert. Anthony was up to the task and happy to lend his voice to the scene.

After they followed up *Spartacus* with the Audrey Hepburn vehicle *My Fair Lady* in 1994, they finally moved into Hitchcock territory with *Vertigo* in 1996. The faded picture and sound of Hitchcock's weathered masterpiece were now in dire need of preservation. "You don't just start a restoration," explained Jim. "You have to do a lot of research. We brought elements from all over the world to one place where we could look at them and access the picture quality and sound and decide at a certain point: Can we do this at all? Many films aren't possible to restore."

Luckily, that wasn't the case with their next project, *Rear Window* in 1999. But they soon realized it would be their most ambitious. Upon investigation, they discovered the original negative had been stored incorrectly and was overprinted. This time, they'd be doing things differently, though. *Rear Window* would be the first restoration to use Technicolor's recently revived dye transfer printing process, phased out in 1974, but brought back to assure permanent retention of a film's exact color scheme. And thanks to updated modern technology of specialized computers that correct color fading, a new negative could be reconstructed.

To stay completely true to Hitchcock's vision, they would need all the help they could get from anyone who could provide it, especially considering that Hitchcock, Jimmy Stewart, and Grace Kelly were no longer there to provide answers. Surviving members of the cast and crew, like Herbert Coleman, Georgine Darcy, and Doc Erickson, came into their Los Angeles studio and advised them with recollections of film production and helped explain why certain scenes looked the way they did. They even helped locate any missing paperwork from 1953.

Jim picked through the Universal costume vault and eventually located some original costumes, including the pink hot pants Georgine Darcy wore in the opening scene as Miss Torso. This would help immensely with color matching. Georgine, the youngest surviving cast member, spent much time with them in the cutting room and regaled them with stories of the production. As Robert and Jim pieced the puzzle of *Rear Window* back together, no detail was spared and everyone banded together to help. "Even Hitchcock's daughter, Pat, came in to help," said Robert. "We got to know her pretty well, and her daughters and their husbands—they're a nice family."

The new color process produced sharper, less grainy prints than ever before, which was imperative to *Rear Window*, where the most suspenseful scenes often occurred in the darkness of the night. Once the process was applied, an animated vibrancy emerged that had never been present before. The bricks on the courtyard buildings, the faces of the neighbors Jefferies spies on, and even the patterns on the costumes were more vivid. This was the first time the world would witness *Rear Window*'s full-color spectrum the way it was meant to be seen. It was a unique project close to the hearts of Robert and Jim. "For my personality and my interest in film, Hitchcock's specific type of filmmaking was very special and that's what led me to it," said Robert. "I don't restore films that I don't like."

Even the tiniest details were given a new lease on life. In the scene where the grieving neighbor's dog has been killed, everyone immediately turns their lights on and goes to their window as she publicly laments the lack of human connection within the apartment community. Everyone except Thorwald, whose apartment remains noticeably pitch black. "Originally, in his apartment, you saw a tiny bit of a cigar glowing in the distance, but in the 1983 re-release, that disappeared," said Robert.

This detail affected the plot, as there was no longer a clue as to whether Thorwald was home or if he was the culprit who'd murdered the dog. For the restoration, they were able to bring this clue back into focus. "That was very important to the story. The creation of our restoration negative of the dye transfer printing through Technicolor was to make that cigarette stand out. To make it glow," explained Robert. "Unless you saw either an original print or the restoration, you wouldn't know that he's in there."

When taking on a project like this, there is an invisible delicate line restorers need to walk. There's always the nagging question of whether one should restore a film to what it's fully capable of being in the present day or whether one should stay completely faithful to the original and restore it to what it was the year of its release. "That's always an argument among archivists and film historians," said Columbia University film professor Richard Peña. "But Bob's restoration of *Rear Window* and *Vertigo* were first rate."

The original ending, in which Jefferies's closing bamboo blind yielded to a view of the Paramount logo, cut in the previous Universal reissue, fortunately had been restored as well. Another huge difference that blew the audience away? Now when they watched *Rear Window*, they could see vivid details through the windows from across the courtyard. When Ross Bagdasarian Jr. first saw the restoration, he felt he was watching his composer father for the first time all over again. "When I saw the new version, it was fun to see shots that I didn't know he was actually in, where I got to see more of him," he said.

The *Rear Window* restoration premiered for the first time on January 21, 2000, at the Film Forum in New York before spreading out to major markets in subsequent weeks. Promotion of the restoration appeared everywhere from Siskel and Ebert's *At the Movies* to CBS's *The Early Show* and NBC's *Today*. Similar to its first release in 1954, and its re-release in 1983, a new twenty-first-century buzz was beginning to surround one of Hitchcock's most contemporary films.

Film historian Sloan De Forest recalled moviegoers' responses when she went to see the *Rear Window* restoration premiere in Dallas. "The theater was packed and people loved it," she said. "Everybody was cracking up, laughing, and the one-liners were just so sharp. The jokes were really landing almost forty-five years after the film was released."

Robert and Jim stood at the back of the theater at the premiere and sized up their work. "Not bad, not bad at all," Robert said to himself. On *Rear Window* and other projects, Robert and Jim always worked for the love of the art. They typically broke even on restoration endeavors, rarely making a large profit themselves and balancing their passion with other film industry jobs. They teamed up again to restore other classics like *The Godfather Part I* and *II* in 2008 and *It's a Mad, Mad, Mad, Mad World* in 2013. Though film restoration may not have been the most financially lucrative game in show business, it was worth it to see the looks on people's faces, especially those discovering the films for the first time.

To further promote the restoration, Jim Katz hosted screenings and discussions on *Rear Window* at Californian post-secondary institutions like the University of California in Santa Barbara and Berkeley. Whenever he was about to show the film, he often asked the packed room of students if there was anyone who had not seen the film on the big screen before. A significant number of hands often went up, but Jim noticed hesitancy in others. Suddenly, he realized, ". . . Wait a minute . . . How many people have never seen *Rear Window* period?" An even larger sea of arms immediately shot up in the crowd.

A huge number of students were seeing it for the first time on a big screen with a good projection and a marvelous print. "It was fascinating for me to see the reaction of people who had never seen it before," said Jim. "Young students, including my kids at the time of the restoration, were born during the dead period of *Rear Window*, so they were never exposed to it until then."

Rear Window would now become a twenty-first-century story, not a forgotten vintage favorite that once had its time in the sun. The ambitious leap Hitchcock's imagination had taken all those years ago was now as relevant to the world as on that release day, August 4, 1954, when he blew Hollywood away.

CHAPTER FOURTEEN

Hitchcock's Legacy on Trial

REAR WINDOW VERSUS *DISTURBIA*

SHELDON ABEND DIED AT THE AGE OF SEVENTY-FOUR IN MANHATTAN'S Mount Sinai Hospital on August 24, 2003. Though he earned acknowledgment for his role as an executive producer, particularly for *Original Sin* (2001) (based on Cornell Woolrich's 1947 novel *Waltz into Darkness*), he remained most infamous for the pit bull tenacity he displayed while pursuing *Rear Window* in court. By the end of his life, his relentless ability to stick out the longest of legal battles ultimately created what became known as the U.S. Supreme Court's *"Rear Window* decision."

When *Disturbia* hit movie theaters in April 2007, without missing a beat, the Sheldon Abend Revocable Trust picked up where he left off in 1990 and filed a new lawsuit against Dreamworks, Universal Pictures, and their distributor, Paramount. This time, in place of Alfred Hitchcock, their main target was *Disturbia* producer Steven Spielberg. Decades after Sheldon's two cases against Hitchcock, Jimmy Stewart, and MCA, the legal battle was resuscitated, and Sheldon's estate followed in his brazen footsteps.

Within the first week of its release, film critics immediately observed *Disturbia*'s resemblance to *Rear Window*, if sometimes unflatteringly so. (David Denby of the *New Yorker* wrote, "As an adolescent, suburban version of Hitchcock's extraordinarily sophisticated 1954 urban thriller *Rear Window*, this movie, written by Christopher B. Landon and Carl Ellsworth and directed by D. J. Caruso, can rightly be called a travesty.")

Sure, *Disturbia* starred Shia LaBeouf as a teenager under house arrest, not as a thirty-something photographer with a broken leg. But the elements of his voyeurism and his belief that one of his neighbors is a killer cut a little too close to home. Sheldon's team was confident that a third court settlement was in the bag. Adopting Sheldon's pure chutzpah, the trust accused the studios and Steven Spielberg of "'infringing'" the copyright of the Cornell Woolrich short story. But what they didn't take into account was the many distinctions between the two films. Unlucky for them, a federal judge in New York did. The court immediately dismissed the lawsuit, ruling that "no reasonable trier of fact could find the works substantially similar within the meaning of copyright law."

Naturally, in the spirit of the Abend Rule, the trust wasn't going down without proving they were as litigious as Sheldon had been if not more. Retaliating with a sixty-eight-page complaint, they claimed that Universal breached its covenant by not removing portions of the *Rear Window* story from *Disturbia* and by using *Rear Window*'s resemblance to the film to market *Disturbia*. It also stated that the parties had multiple conversations before the release of *Disturbia* and that Universal ignored their legal warnings by releasing the film.

But this time, without Sheldon Abend as lead navigator, their argument was flimsy and revealed distinct holes. *Disturbia* follows a disgruntled teen confined to his home under house arrest due to his trouble with the police, whereas L. B. Jefferies is a man whose best friend is a police detective. Secondly, in *Rear Window*, Lars Thorwald is a married man who becomes fed up with his wife and murders her, yet the antagonist of *Disturbia* is a seemingly single serial killer. Lastly, *Disturbia* is set in a suburban California neighborhood, while *Rear Window* takes place entirely in Greenwich Village, Manhattan. The evidence spoke for itself.

In contrast with the past two *Rear Window* court cases, the court was squarely on Universal's side by the time a verdict was reached in September 2010. U.S. District Judge Laura Taylor Swain granted Steven Spielberg and other producers of *Disturbia* summary judgment in the suit, determining that the common elements between the two works were not protectable. "There is no substantial similarity between the total concept and feel of the short story ["It Had to Be Murder"] and that of *Disturbia*." Judge Swain wrote in conclusion, "Where *Disturbia* is rife with subplots, the short story has none. The setting and mood of the short story are static and tense, whereas the setting and mood of *Disturbia* are more dynamic and peppered with humor and teen romance." The court ruling was final. "Similarity at this level of generality is not probative of the question of infringement."

The *Rear Window* versus *Disturbia* showdown was like the grand finale of a legal thriller that had everyone in show business taking notice. The ripple effect of Sheldon Abend's *Rear Window* legal trilogy would extend far beyond the courtroom, leaving a lasting mark on the film industry. Though entertainment laws evolved and changed in the years following Sheldon Abend's time on the stand, copyright cases of the twenty-first century are still the subject of ongoing debates on the search for the sweet spot between artistic expression and creative protection. The copyright legal drama was a prime example of the filmmaker's sometimes impossible task of distinguishing between a nod to a classic and actual plagiarism. However, in Hitchcock's case, this logic would lead one to question whether he could have sued almost every filmmaker who utilized his voyeuristic camera style.

Though the *Disturbia/Rear Window* ruling emphasized that similarity should be more than just a shared theme, a creative slippery slope of paranoia had now been established. It became a warning to filmmakers, screenwriters, and producers to do a thorough test of projects before a release, especially with content that played on pioneering classics. *Disturbia* luckily passed that test, and in September 2010, Sheldon Abend's *Rear Window* court saga was finally put to bed for good.

AN ELEGANT BID

CHRISTIE'S AUCTION HOUSE, LOCATED ON THE AFFLUENT KING STREET IN London's St. James's district, hummed with excitement on November 25, 2010. Christie's pop culture specialist Katherine Schofield was busy overseeing one of their most prestigious auctions of the year. Original watercolor and pencil sketches of Grace Kelly's *Rear Window* wardrobe were about to be introduced to the bidding market for the first time. Each portrait featured a drawing of Grace in one of the timeless *Rear Window* costumes and the handwritten signature of Edith Head. Katherine's hopes soared as she anticipated the collectibles fetching top dollar at the Popular Culture Film & Entertainment auction that day.

Auction bidders have always gravitated to the storybook narrative surrounding Grace Kelly. Each marketplace sale has illustrated their willingness to pay whatever it takes to feel like a part of her world. Case in point, the original Mark Cross overnight handbag Lisa Fremont opens to reveal her nightgown and slippers when she plans to spend the night with Jefferies had been auctioned off eight years prior for $5,019. Inevitably, expectations and nerves were running high today. "When a film like *Rear Window* is such a big success or so widely regarded, the costumes are what stand out," explained Katherine. "They are so desirable to collectors and, of course, everyone wants to see the item that was worn on-screen by their idol."

Historically, in both the fashion and film world, there has always been a strong demand for auction pieces related to Edith Head, but the *Rear Window* sketches were particularly unique. They combined Grace's, Hitchcock's, and Edith's star power. Since this was the first time *Rear Window* sketches would be released in a public sale, buyers and institutions were chomping at the bit to get a look at the new drawings. This came on the tail of the retrospective of Grace's style on display earlier that year at the Victoria & Albert Museum, where people were able to witness *Rear Window* costumes in the flesh. It fed the constant frenzy that eternally surrounded Grace's image and contributed to a revival of interest in Edith.

Once the auction pieces were out of the gate, buyers flocked toward the sketch of the most prominent costume in which Lisa Fremont made her first *Rear Window* entrance. Like the real-life version, the sketch showcased Grace in yards of white chiffon tulle from the waist down and the classic black bodice with a low-cut neckline. After a nail-biting tug of war between bidders, it was the first to go when it was auctioned off at £8,125. Next, the sketch of the floral dress Lisa wears while climbing the fire escape and putting her life in her hands went for £6,250, and the impossibly regal pistachio suit sketch was also sold at £6,250.

It wasn't surprising that the auction had been a hit. Over the years, as *Rear Window* was re-released, rewatched, and appeared constantly in mainstream media, its magic penetrated American and international pop culture. Throughout history, the three biggest Golden Hollywood heavy hitters in the auction world always remain Grace Kelly, Audrey Hepburn, and Marilyn Monroe. Throw in Edith Head and Hitchcock and the bids were bound to astronomically increase.

Reflecting on Grace Kelly's consistent popularity with buyers, Katherine Schofield explained, "I think it's the story, isn't it? It's a fairy tale. It's the actress becoming a princess. There's always fascination around these kinds of celebrities who are only with us for this very small amount of time in the grand scheme of things."

Though she only made eleven films in total, Grace's charisma as a star outweighs that of many screen veterans with dozens of pictures under their belts. Her image still burns brightly among the ebbs and flows of other Hollywood careers. She has been listed as thirteenth among the American Film Institute's Twenty-Five Greatest Female Stars of Classical Hollywood Cinema. And through the passing decades, she has continued to top countless fashion and beauty polls. The concept of "the American Oscar-winning star meets European royalty" creates an ethereal image for an audience who loves a sentimental ending. Add the visual element of classic American style and that fantasy reaches a whole new level.

Throughout the past seventy years, women, exhausted by the revolving door of changing trends, have continually returned to Grace's tailored dresses, structured handbags, and timeless sunglasses. "Her look was so classic that it doesn't age. You can see it in pictures of her both in her regular clothes and her modeling shots, and it still carries today," said Grace's nephew JB Kelly. "When women look at them, they don't think, 'Oh, that's 1955. Why would I be interested in that?' They see a beautiful woman who knew how to carry herself and still someone to emulate."

Though Grace was the global household name of the two, Edith Head was certainly no slouch in the legacy department either. When Gulf and Western Industries purchased Paramount Pictures in 1966, Edith had already sensed big changes on the horizon. She'd known for some time she would eventually need to adapt to an evolving Hollywood and roll with the punches. But that didn't mean it wouldn't hurt.

The once grand salon of long tables where Edith and her assistants dressed in black or neutrals so as not to attract attention from Joan Crawford or Elizabeth Taylor during fittings was now the size of a studio secretary's office. Her full tulle skirts and off-the-shoulder formal gowns were now considered behind the curve in New Hollywood. Shortly after her salon was cleared out, her contract with Paramount expired and wasn't renewed. It marked the official end of the full-time studio designer era.

But Edith Head was a survivor, and she didn't become the most powerful woman in a male-dominated industry by accident. If "costs were cut" as they had told her, and fashion inventory was being cleaned out of the beloved salon she'd spent decades creating, she'd need to reinvent. Being a proactive woman, Edith had known that eventually, studios may not be hiring designers on staff. It's one of the reasons she'd spent years packaging her image with television appearances, fashion show commentating, not to mention writing her *Dress Doctor* book. She was prepared because she'd already created a mobile one-woman industry that she could take outside the walls of Paramount if need be.

However, female film roles were changing too. "Women's pictures" were a thing of the past and impossibly elegant actresses like Grace Kelly and Audrey Hepburn had now been replaced by Jane Fonda and Sharon Tate as the mod beauties of the mid-sixties. These new actresses traded the old glamour aesthetic of white gloves and oversized sunglasses for miniskirts and go-go boots. In Paramount's eyes, the "Head look" was now obsolete. But Edith's long-game strategy of focusing on her own star quality as well as the actress's paid off. Universal was happy to employ her nearly immediately after Paramount let her go.

Edith continued to put her head down and change with the times. Eventually, her fame manifested into her bungalow studio becoming a stop on the Universal Studios tour in the late sixties. She continued to work with the same gusto until she was eighty-three years old. She adapted to the cultural climate and designed for iconic films of the day, like *Sweet Charity* (1969), *Airport* (1970), and *The Sting* (1973).

The real Edith Head behind the public image remains a mystery. When she was diagnosed with myelofibrosis, she was fiercely private about her illness. Even her friends and colleagues wouldn't know how advanced her illness was before her death on October 24, 1981, four days before her eighty-fourth birthday. "She had been in the hospital for a while and one day I called her up," her longtime friend designer David Chierichetti remembered. "Rather abruptly, she said, 'Honey, you've got to get out of this movie business, because you don't know how to lie well enough.' That night, she died." Even while on her deathbed, Edith Head was a no-nonsense straight shooter.

Her funeral at the Church of the Good Shepherd in Beverly Hills was packed from wall to wall with Golden era stars like Elizabeth Taylor, George Peppard, Janet Leigh, and Loretta Young. In perhaps one of her greatest dramatic monologues, Bette Davis got up and delivered a part eulogy, part performance, hailing, "Edith Head, the queen of Hollywood designers" and "the greatest costume designer that there's ever been." Edith Head's Hollywood legacy remains as the schoolteacher who did what she had to do, not just to survive, but to become a powerhouse in one of the most competitive fields on earth.

The little woman in the dark glasses and tweed suit, seen scurrying around studio corridors in a rush, was often underestimated, but she ultimately became an immortal legend. She single-handedly took over the motion picture design industry under everyone's noses and defied conventional norms as she climbed the Hollywood ladder. True to her brand, Edith's will stated that she was to leave her $575,000 estate to Elizabeth Taylor, the Academy of Motion Picture Arts and Sciences, her several cats, and her Dalmatian, Boppo.

PRINCES AND POLITICIANS

EVEN AFTER GRACE KELLY'S DEATH, NUMEROUS MEDIA REPORTS HAVE continued to surface over the years claiming that her marriage to Prince Rainier was an unhappy and even an unfaithful one. But her family insists this was just the rumor mill at work, typical in the life of royal celebrities. Tabloid reports, fueled by jealousy or the desire for a sensational story, frequently exaggerated the life of a film star turned princess who appeared to have won life's lottery in the eyes of the world.

But behind the scenes, in many ways, Grace lived a simple life, juggling the same ups and downs as the typical everyday woman. She made sacrifices for her family, worried about her children, and liked to have a good time when she was away from the public eye. The aristocratic image that Rainier and Grace projected for the cameras sharply contrasted with the unassuming lifestyle they enjoyed in the company of family. The couple often let their hair down during card games of thirty-one at the Kelly family beach house in Ocean City, New Jersey, or kicked back at movie nights in the palace screening room.

"My favorite time was a summer in the early seventies when Grace and Rainier took a lake house up in New Hampshire," remembered her nephew JB Kelly. "My cousin Albert and I were across the lake at summer camp. We spent every Sunday with them and it was nice to see them out of the limelight of Monaco, and kidding around with lots of laughter and fun."

Despite his sternness with palace staff, Rainier had a secret playful side that he was required to keep hidden from the public eye. JB recalled an occasion where he and his wife brought their five-year-old son, Nick, to the palace for the first time. "He was at that age where he just got into things and we told him, '*Don't touch anything*,'" he recalled. "He was behaving himself and we were having a nice time. Uncle Rainier got up and left the room for something, and the next thing we knew, we heard this scuffle and things crashing around. I thought, '*Oh no*, Nick's getting into something.' We whipped around, and Uncle Rainier was on the floor wrestling with Nick! He was about eighty at the time, and that's how playful he was." Behind the stoic persona was a human being, like Princess Anne in *Roman Holiday*, who sometimes needed a day off from the pressures and expectations of royal life.

When Rainier became sovereign prince in 1949 at age twenty-five, he had his work cut out for him in elevating Monaco's prominence to a global scale. Amid the ebbs and flows of Franco-American tensions, Rainier made the courageous choice to open the port to American and British ships, transforming the still waters into a lively harbor of maritime diplomacy. This move not only displayed the prince's independence of thought but also put Monaco on the world map of international collaboration. When he married Grace, her elegant presence brought glamour to Rainier's serious image while driving up tourism in the pint-sized country of Monaco.

Though strict royal traditions remain intact, Monaco wasn't a stuffy principality by any stretch. Grace had made sure of it. The palace was a warm refuge for family, old friends, Hollywood elite, men in uniform, and even those in need. She had the old palace garage converted into a film theater and game room for visitors. During sailors' and commanding officers' weekend stays, it became a cozy retreat for entertaining. Well past midnight, Grace and Rainier talked, drank, and laughed with their guests at frequent palace gatherings.

Grace's beloved Irish pub, displaying her pride in her Celtic roots, is located on the ground floor of the palace, a few steps from the courtyard. It's filled with the memories of official visits when the navy ships came to port. Every wall is adorned with cast bronze plaques, each telling a different tale. Grace and Rainier upheld the tradition of gifting plaques to every captain and crew member, which transformed fleeting visits into moments immortalized forever on the pub walls.

One holiday season at the palace, Grace had invited her cousin John Lehman to visit and join in on the palace festivities. He was a young student at the time, who couldn't afford a ticket back to America from Cambridge University for the holidays, and graciously took her up on the offer. As he looked out at the pier from the palace, eleven submarines, including an American one, had docked in Monaco for Christmas. Being curious, he went down to take a closer look. Suddenly, he spotted someone familiar exiting the American submarine. As he walked closer, he came face-to-face with his high school classmate George Kelly. Upon hearing about their serendipitous encounter, Grace sent Christmas Eve dinner invitations to George and his captain. There was no relation between George and Grace, but the Kelly name didn't hurt.

Grace had also heard through the grapevine that George's captain had been victimizing him with the most punishing chores and shifts of the crew. As she welcomed her guests into the palace dining room, Grace was sure to make her subtle statement on the matter. As dinner commenced, the seating arrangement demonstrated a classic example of her innate sense of fairness, regardless of another person's social standing. In a tongue-in-cheek gesture, Grace placed George at the head of the table next to her, and the captain far down below the salt and pepper shakers. It was clear while rising the ranks of Hollywood and as a royal sovereign, Grace had never forgotten her humanity or her standing on inclusivity.

In 2017, Prince Albert II embraced the same traditions set forth by his mother, when he welcomed U.S. senator John McCain within the storied walls of Grace's Irish pub. McCain, with his military background, stood agog amid the endless array of plaques lining the walls—an homage to marines and officers whose presence had graced the palace over the decades. He pored over each one, studying the details of each inscription. When he finally came to the plaque that his captain had received on his cruise, he was exhilarated.

When McCain sat with his friend John Lehman for a quiet dinner in the palace garden with Princess Caroline, the evening took an unexpected turn. Lehman suggested they go back to the hotel for a nightcap and call it an early night, but McCain had other ideas. "The hell with that, we're not going back to the hotel," declared McCain. "We're going to the casino!" The clock struck midnight, and off they ventured into the glittering world of Monaco's craps tables and gaming rooms. The next few hours were spent absorbing the bright lights and energy that engulfed them. At one point, McCain was inadvertently thrust into the spotlight as the focal point of celebrity attention when swarms of tourists clamored for a selfie with him. By the time they bid adieu to the casino at three a.m., McCain's craps prowess had earned him an impressive nine hundred euros.

If the walls of the Prince's Palace could speak, they would tell a thousand tales of the fascinating people who visited and the larger-than-life history that took place within, but it's Princess Grace's influence that's had the greatest impact on the world's perception of the royal monarchy. In the unusual country of Monaco—the smallest in the world, next to the Vatican City—it's her essence that still lives on, weaving itself through every winding cobblestone street and every coral sunset at Larvotto Beach. Her spirit still reverberates through the palace corridors and lives deep in the minds of those who were fortunate enough to know her.

CHAPTER FIFTEEN

Holding a Mirror to the Twenty-First Century

THE ROAD NOT TAKEN

LONG BEFORE JIM KATZ BECAME PRESIDENT OF THE UNIVERSAL CLASSICS division or one half of the *Rear Window* restoration team, he was a journalism student at Columbus's Ohio State University in the late 1950s. Throughout history, the school's world-renowned English department has seen a myriad of visiting world figures, from James Thurber to Eleanor Roosevelt, who lectured students on the power of the written word.

One morning, when Jim walked into his usual classroom, he had to do a double take when he laid eyes on the white-haired elderly man sitting at the head of the room. Robert Frost, one of the twentieth century's most acclaimed classic poets, was about to stand and lecture the students. Jim was exhilarated. He'd scrutinized the meaning behind "Birches" and "The Road Not Taken" since high school English class, and now here Robert Frost was in the flesh. As his Hollywood life was yet to begin, this was the closest he'd come to sharing a room with a living legend.

When Robert's lecture ended, and he opened the room to the students for questions, someone tentatively asked, "How many meanings does your poetry have?" He paused for a moment before answering.

"There are three," he then said with decisiveness. "The first is literal. When we 'bent birches to and fro' when I was a kid, we literally climbed the tree and they bent over and we let them go and they bent to and fro. Secondly, you could tell a bit about me and my upbringing as a kid in New England from my body of work. The third, fourth, and fifth meanings, I leave to high school English teachers."

Robert's words stayed with Jim throughout his Hollywood career. In times of uncertainty, he referred back to the lesson he'd learned that day from America's greatest poet. It was especially applicable when analyzing the multiple layers and interpretations woven through anything Hitchcockian. In the long run, it was what inspired Jim to take his biggest career risk and introduce *Rear Window*'s timelessness to younger generations with the 1983 re-release. Just like the work of Robert Frost, a triad of meanings is evident within the film. "It's a story of voyeurism, it's a story of relationships, and it's a story of any number of things that are subliminally happening today," Jim said. "It's whatever you want to call it when you're looking at somebody and you're coming to conclusions about them and voicing your opinion about them."

When we adopt this outlook, *Rear Window* can be observed in numerous facets of the twenty-first-century world. The new millennium has seen just as many if not more parallels to these themes than any other era. The difference today is that we no longer have to peer out from our windows; we log on to the digital realm that the modern world lives and breathes. People have invited technology into their homes and phones with the irresistible Big Brother–like temptation to watch and sometimes scrutinize others. In a digital landscape where we coexist with people in the cyber realm, their true lives remain a mystery to us.

WINDOW TO THE PRESENT

DECADES BEFORE THE INTRODUCTION OF SOCIAL MEDIA, AS A SUBSTITUTE for a mobile or tablet screen, L. B. Jefferies blankly stares out at a Greenwich Village courtyard in boredom. His eyes scroll from one apartment to the next with the same idle intent reserved for browsing Reddit or Instagram. He's looking for something, though he can't pinpoint what it is. He spots his neighbors going about their daily lives and is quick to reduce them to typical stereotypes, based on small snippets of information observed through their windows. "In a sense, it's what he does to Lisa too," said film historian Sloan De Forest. "He looks at her and thinks, 'Look at your pearls, your high heels, and your lobster dinners. You're so refined and elegant in your hats and your luncheons. You couldn't possibly adapt to my lifestyle.'"

As Jefferies jumps to conclusion after conclusion, whether aloud to himself or in the presence of Lisa or Stella, it becomes increasingly difficult not to recognize an eerie similarity to the way many people spend their time in modern days. They peruse digital communities with status updates and video uploads of strangers and people they know, forming critiques about them based on momentary snapshots. In a sea of networking platforms, the NextDoor app resembles Jefferies's experience the most closely, with its emphasis on neighborhood awareness and connecting with people on your street with shared interests. Though it's harmless in theory, in the wrong hands, it could be a *Rear Window* scenario in app form.

"I think Alfred Hitchcock would be horrified by social media today," said *Star Tribune* film critic Chris Hewitt. With his no-nonsense attitude toward brazen individuals or those whose opinions conflicted with his, as well as his fiercely private inner life, Hitchcock would likely have shunned X's chaotic landscape. Another perspective on Hitchcock's potential view of social media had he experienced it can be found in a pivotal scene in *Rear Window*, as it explores the absence of human connection in a solitary world. As the scene fades in on Jefferies sipping the last of his brandy, Lisa emerges from the bathroom and models a sleek creamy negligee to his underwhelmed response. Suddenly, a painful scream erupts from the courtyard. Lisa lifts the center bamboo blind on the rear window to reveal the childless neighbor standing on her fire escape in distress. She looks down in helplessness at her small dog lying on the pavement next to the flower bed. Everyone except Thorwald comes to their window to see what the commotion is. As she grieves the dog's death—it's clear this pet was like a child to her—she tries to get through to her fellow neighbors about their lack of direct connection with one another.

> You don't know the meaning of the word "neighbors." Neighbors like each other, speak to each other, care if anybody lives or dies. But none of you do!

It's this part of her monologue that strikes a nerve with her next-door residents, who, instead of comforting her for her loss, immediately turn their backs to block out the truth. "Let's go back in. It's only a dog," someone mutters as everyone returns to their evenings of dinner parties and dates. The people of 125 West Ninth Street continue to either give each other the cold shoulder or spy on one another (with a professional-level zoom camera, in Jefferies's case).

Jefferies's antisocial Peeping Tom syndrome has an obvious silver lining of course. It helps him discover a dangerous murderer. He solves a crime, becomes a hero, and by the end of *Rear Window*, his voyeuristic exploits are fully forgiven. But what if he'd been mistaken? Would his views be considered similar to that of an online conspiracy theorist? "When you focus solely on the Big Brother element, it makes one wonder if *Rear Window* would work just as well if it turned out that Jefferies was wrong about Thorwald," said *Star Tribune* film critic Chris Hewitt. "We would still have the suspense of that nail-biting scene where Grace Kelly goes across the courtyard and he sees her in danger and can't do anything about it. But in the end, if he were wrong, it would become one of Hitchcock's comedies like *To Catch a Thief.* Then the question would be, 'What the heck is wrong with this guy who's trapped in his apartment and refuses to marry Grace Kelly?'"

Even if Jefferies had been completely off base about Lars Thorwald's nocturnal activities, his behavior would still be considered commonplace among the masses. The fascination people have with voyeurism comes with an element of risk and excitement just like a dopamine high. And it's not just social apps that play on this human reflex.

When a reality television show called *Big Brother* debuted in the Netherlands in 1999, it was evident that although people had genuine concerns about surveillance, they were also willing to play the Peeping Tom game if it contributed to their entertainment. Throughout the series, housemates lived under twenty-four-hour surveillance and each had their turn in the "diary room" or "confession room" where they expressed their thoughts about other house guests and reflected on inner challenges. The same show format was brought to the U.S. in 2000 and aired on CBS in prime time.

Big Brother was a bona fide hit in America, making a huge cultural impact, and leading the way for the noughties reality boom. It's now considered one of the most significant reality shows in American history, along with *Survivor* and *The Amazing Race*. The titillating aspect of voyeurism in human nature couldn't be denied, especially once it was utilized to amuse the masses and make billions.

On the dramatic side of the modern screen, *Rear Window*'s themes have seamlessly filtered into the content libraries of the most accessible entertainment platforms worldwide, like Netflix, AppleTV+, and HBO Max. In *The Woman in the Window* (2021) starring Amy Adams, an agoraphobic doctor witnesses something she shouldn't when she begins spying on her neighbors, while in *Kimi* (2022) a tech worker with the same condition played by Zoë Kravitz discovers evidence of a violent crime. But similar to *Rear Window*'s Jefferies, she is met with resistance when she tries to report it. Although the possibility of surveillance, prevalent during the McCarthy era, is a healthy fear Americans experience, it's also a deep-rooted fascination when people are the voyeurs themselves (or on the receiving end of voyeurism with a large cash prize dangled over their heads).

PROPHETS OF POP CULTURE

THEY SAY THE GREATEST ARTISTS IN HISTORY OFTEN POSSESSED A KNACK
for envisioning future events accurately. In 1968, Andy Warhol predicted internet celebrities and social influencers with his quote, "In the
future, everyone will be famous for fifteen minutes." During the Mc-
Carthy era in 1949, George Orwell foresaw Big Brother surveillance in
the world, though he posed it more as a warning than a tool exploited
for entertainment value in his book *1984*. In its most disturbing proph-
ecy of human oppression, O'Brien, the grand inquisitor of the totalitar-
ian regime, states, "If you want a picture of the future, imagine a boot
stamping on a human face—forever."

Hitchcock also conveyed concepts of surveillance and the distant
scrutiny of others through *Rear Window*. By the seventies—twenty
years after the film's release, when the McCarthy era was a thing of the
past—concerns about wiretapping, spying, and covert recordings were
prevalent. During the later stages of the Cold War, citizens of America
and the Soviet Union had reason to feel anxious, as it was now common
knowledge that both their governments engaged in espionage activities. This was a genuine fear of many until the Cold War ended with
the official dissolution of the Soviet Union in December 1991.

Today, in the twenty-first century, people still find themselves
grappling with a myriad of technical and privacy issues related to surveillance anxiety. Exacerbating this, more than ever before, contemporary culture has been marked by a constant influx of information and
misinformation, often making it difficult to distinguish between the
two. For better or for worse, whether it's the instantaneous impact of
social media exposing alleged bad behavior or a debate about the context behind a brief video clip, the power to "cancel" our fellow neighbors is now a possibility.

In alignment with the world's present circumstances, *Rear Window* explores the theme of perpetual uncertainty, highlighting the
challenge of never having a complete grip on a situation. It reflects a

struggle to gather more information, mirroring a modern world currently inundated with data. Yet in the throes of cancel culture, many are still unable to conclusively determine guilt or innocence in others. "It's never enough to be able to say one hundred percent 'yes, this person is guilty or this person is innocent,'" *National Post* chief film critic Chris Knight said. "*Rear Window* plays with the very same idea of the more information that comes at you, the less you're able to know." *Rear Window* was ahead of its time in its demonstration of how quickly public opinion can flip-flop based on tidbits of information.

In the search for the truth, a pervasive theme of propaganda has surrounded the political and economic sphere in the twenty-first century. Whether conveyed through a tweet or in a more formal White House address to the nation, the dissemination of mistruths has become a running theme. Though many argue that statements in media by a spokesperson or politician can often be taken out of context or misrepresented, the fact remains that we live in a time of multiple "truths," where individuals sometimes choose the narrative that aligns with their beliefs. But there aren't ten different truths in politics, world issues, or even our daily lives. In the modern world, there is a responsibility for individuals to engage critically with information, verify sources, and seek out the truth amidst the bustle of fake news.

RED SCARES AND FAKE NEWS

IN A RUN-OF-THE-MILL CASE OF HISTORY LOOPING ITSELF IN THE SAME pattern, today's societal issues don't entirely differ from the McCarthy era of the forties. When people were blacklisted for supposed communist involvement, life was heavily censored, and like the ambiguous details that surface online today, rampant rumors were par for the course. In the Hollywood Golden era, the Hays Code was just the tip of the censorship iceberg for America.

In the early fifties, Julius and Ethel Rosenberg were a married couple infamously convicted and ultimately executed at New York's Sing Sing Correctional Facility for espionage. While Julius provided the Soviets with top-secret information about American radar, jet propulsion engines, and nuclear weapon designs, Ethel's role was less clear—though she was aware of her husband's activities, declassified documents would later suggest she did not directly participate in passing information. Columbia University film professor Richard Peña grew up in Queens, New York, close to the Rosenberg home. As a child, he remembered a potent atmosphere of distrust that permeated the surrounding neighborhoods. "The idea that somebody who lived a couple of miles away could be a Soviet spy," he said. "Those are the kinds of things that I think entered the imaginations of a lot of people at that time, that you really couldn't trust anybody."

Fear of communist infiltration gripped America in the 1950s. The perceived threat wasn't of invading armies, but of supposed subversives living in communities and influencing institutions. *Rear Window* was conceived and produced in 1953, notably the same year as the Rosenbergs' execution. Hitchcock, a Brit who came to the United States as a foreigner, continually maintained a strong antenna for what was going on in America. "Even though he's not often thought of as a political filmmaker, I think there are really interesting political readings of his films, including *Rear Window*," said Richard. "In 1954, its release made perfect sense, because this was the atmosphere that existed."

TIMELESS TABOO

IN ITS PRIME, THE HAYS CODE FIT IN COMFORTABLY WITH THE CENSORED climate of America. However, in the sixties, as the code officially lost control in conjunction with the collapsed studio system, New Hollywood filmmakers weren't entirely free to do as they pleased. A new rating system was introduced that still exists now. To this day, the NC-17 rating, which prohibits anyone under the age of seventeen from view-ing the film, remains a thorn in the side of many directors. The Motion Picture Association rating board has the authority to assign this rating, often triggered by extended or graphic sex scenes. This can prompt filmmakers and distributors to release a film unrated.

The rating system became a hot topic in the 2023 news cycle when the NC-17 rating was applied to Ira Sachs's film *Passages* (2023) for its queer sexuality. "There's no untangling the film from what it is," Ira adamantly told the *Los Angeles Times*. "It is a film that is very open about the place of sexual experience in our lives. And to shift that now would be to create a very different movie." Some asserted that the deci-sion of the rating board, in this case, was homophobic. Others declared that the board was contrary in their thinking of what receives this audi-ence-limiting rating, and that at this rate the film industry might as well revert to the Hays Code system.

Similar to the Code days, sexuality is still the central taboo in mainstream filmmaking. "The NC-17 rating was created to distin-guish serious adult films from pornography, which had been lumped together under the X rating. But this new system hasn't worked," said *Star Tribune* film critic Chris Hewitt. "If filmmakers get an NC-17 rat-ing, some movie theater chains won't show [their movies], so they just go out unrated. So, some of the battles Hitchcock was fighting seventy years ago with the code are still being fought now."

AN EVOLVING ERA

IN 1954, AMERICA—AND SUBSEQUENTLY HOLLYWOOD—PORTRAYED women in a way that sharply contrasts with today's societal norms. This was the year after Elizabeth II was crowned, *I Love Lucy* had gained huge momentum on the small screen, and with the invention of frozen TV dinners, women could fool their husbands into believing they had slaved all day in the kitchen. Women were slowly taking part in the workforce in smaller roles but many maintained a desire for marriage and family.

But with *Rear Window*'s Lisa Fremont in a strong female lead, and dynamic supporting characters like Stella, Miss Lonely Hearts, and Miss Torso, the film offered a refreshing, multifaceted portrayal of a woman's psyche and emotional life on the screen. To suggest *Rear Window* is an altogether feminist film would seem like a bit of a stretch for some, but genuine moments of female empowerment are captured in the reversal of traditional gender roles between Jefferies and Lisa, as well as the evidence that in Hollywood noir screenplays, there could be multiple types of women leading dynamic lives.

"Jeff's got these two women, who are both strong personalities, and that's what makes the film interesting," film historian Sloan De Forest said. "It's a relationship of equals. It's not just this man with a hot girlfriend trying to solve this mystery. Lisa could have been this passive arm candy, but she wasn't at all." And though Lisa certainly wants a committed relationship with Jefferies, which it appears they achieve in the end scene, it's never revealed whether the two ever marry in the traditional sense.

Today, younger generations (many, children of divorced homes) are more hesitant to marry than ever. Some don't believe in the institution of matrimony the way previous generations did. The National Center for Health Statistics reported a huge plummet in the desire for marriage among American women from 1970 to 2022. In 1970, there were 76.5 marriages per 1,000 unmarried women, and by 2022, there were 31.2 marriages per 1,000 unmarried women. *Rear Window* mirrored this trend before it even came to be, and was ahead of the curve in its view of modern relationships.

With the Production Code hanging over its head like a dagger, the fifties Golden Age of Hollywood had the responsibility to enforce wholesome traditional family values, which often meant the end objective of romance in a film was marriage. Yet *Rear Window* doesn't hide its cynical attitude toward tying the knot. Jefferies seems to have developed a phobia of the idea of walking down the aisle with Lisa, or anyone for that matter, and the newlyweds across the courtyard are seen in various snapshots in the doldrums of a gradually tedious marriage. And Thorwald is so fed up with marriage, he's even resorted to murder.

The modernized view portrayed in *Rear Window* that marriage might not be for everyone was revolutionary at the time, but today it reflects a larger shift in societal attitudes toward relationships and gender roles, particularly in the wake of the #MeToo movement. In traditional Hollywood narratives that earned the biggest box office returns, women were often relegated to passive roles or romantic pursuits, an outdated stereotype by current standards. Films today often portray the inner feelings of women who are no longer willing to accept unequal dynamics. In parallel to that, there has finally been a shift in the political landscape of the entertainment world.

On October 15, 2017, the *New York Times* published an initial exposé on one of the most powerful moguls in Hollywood, Harvey Weinstein, who would later be found guilty on multiple accounts of rape. Throughout the eighties and nineties, he was responsible for some of the most lucrative Hollywood films ever made. It was an event that shook the whole industry as people began to reexamine Hollywood's code of ethics on and off set. On the day the *Times* article was published, actress Alyssa Milano tweeted, "If you've been sexually harassed or assaulted write 'me too' as a reply to this tweet." The phrase was retweeted more than 200,000 times by the end of the day. Instantly, the most recognizable term for a shift in the world's approach to sexual misconduct was coined.

#MeToo was a tipping point for Hollywood in the way women and other historically underrepresented groups would be treated moving forward. Soon enough, other prominent men in media and entertainment were publicly held accountable for predatory behavior in and out of the workplace. Though Hollywood has further to go in its journey toward true equality, Weinstein's verdict was an impactful step in the industry's acknowledgment of the toxic elephant in the room.

With the accusations that surfaced in the twenty-first century regarding Alfred Hitchcock's alleged misconduct toward Tippi Hedren, a question arises: Has this tarnished his legacy? When Donald Spoto's book *The Dark Side of Genius* was released in 1983, it was the first time anyone had revealed that Hitchcock may have allegedly harassed Tippi. But it seemed to be swept under the proverbial rug in an era still rife with gender inequality.

Then, almost thirty years later, an HBO/BBC TV film called *The Girl* (2012) blew the lid off the matter. Directed by Julian Jarrold, it starred Toby Jones as Hitchcock and Sienna Miller as Tippi Hedren. It focused on Hitchcock's relationships with women and painted him as a sexual predator. On its release, the film provoked controversy over whether what took place on-screen is a fair depiction of what took place in real life. "I feel bad about all the stuff people are saying about him now," said Kim Novak in 2012. "I never saw him make a pass at or act strange to anybody." *The Girl* certainly diminishes the master of suspense's character throughout its 105 minutes. But, despite his alleged cruelty toward others, movie watchers and historians always return to the big-screen world created by his emotional inner life.

TURNING THE PAGE

IN MODERN DAYS, HOLLYWOOD HAS BECOME REFLECTIVE REGARDING ITS unpredictable creative future in an effort to balance art with commerce. Back in 1981, Robert Redford created the Sundance Institute in Utah to encourage independent film, and from there, American cinema seemed to develop on two separate trajectories. One was the traditional Hollywood way: commercial, safe, and astronomically expensive. The other was the independent way: exploratory, unconventional, and on the cheap. Both types of films continue to be made in the twenty-first century. And both still have their successes and flops.

As of 2024, five of the eight Hollywood Golden Age studios still exist—20th Century Studios, Warner Brothers, Paramount, Universal, and Columbia. In the fifties, with a large studio like Paramount backing his ideas, Hitchcock had the opportunity to deep dive into an exploratory universe in *Rear Window*. By fifties standards, it boasted a much larger budget than any independent filmmaker would receive today, but in a digital era of advancing technology, there's a strong probability that exploratory films will continue to prevail in coming years. "I think independent filmmakers will continue to have fresh ideas and work outside the mainstream and do the kind of interesting stuff that Hitchcock did," said *Star Tribune* film critic Chris Hewitt. "Let's not forget he was working in an extremely restrictive studio system that did not produce a lot of unique movies, but he still managed to do it. People today who are working against the grain may not earn a lot, but we've also learned that you can make a great movie without very much money."

However, the disappearance of movie theaters, combined with surviving venues largely focusing on mainstream action films, has understandably concerned filmmakers and other industry professionals. The genuine concern with the lower purchase rate of big-screen movie tickets is that the communal film theater experience will inevitably become less accessible to the masses. These declining ticket sales have forced many movie theaters to close locations and sell off leases. This trend was dramatically accelerated by the COVID-19 pandemic, which temporarily shut down theaters and led to a significant upswing in streaming subscriptions. At the beginning of film history in 1888, when Thomas Edison made a prototype of his Kinetoscope, a peep-show device where individual viewers could watch privately through an eyepiece, he faced stiff competition from brothers Auguste and Louis Lumière. They had invented the Cinématographe, a motion picture camera and projector that could be viewed simultaneously by communities of audiences. The Lumière brothers' approach quickly gained popularity and contributed significantly to the development of cinema as a communal experience. But by today's standards, one might say that Edison has now won, as many now lean toward private viewing in their homes on their televisions and laptops.

Similar to the television invasion of the postwar forties when box office numbers began to dwindle, people have reverted to the contentment of streaming films with the advancements in home entertainment technology and endless content platforms. Those who can afford it have even installed screening theaters in their homes.

"Movie theater chains had a reprieve in 2023 with *Barbie* and *Oppenheimer*, but I'm not sure it will continue," predicted Columbia film professor Richard Peña. "I hope I'm wrong, but I think most movie theaters will eventually be replaced by extremely high-tech virtual reality cinemas, which is where the Marvel fare will go." While 2024 would go on to see successful releases like *Inside Out 2*, *Deadpool & Wolverine*, and *Wicked*, the long-term challenges facing movie theaters persist.

Though it's been predicted they will eventually be located outside of mainstream film theaters, independent and foreign films will always be accessible on the big screen to those who look for them. Besides streaming platforms, some foresee cinema as an upscale museum experience at venues like the Film Society at Lincoln Center, MoMA, or the Art Institute of Chicago.

Hitchcock provided a wry prediction of how cinematic entertainment may look in the far future when he was interviewed in 1967. "In 3000, if entertainment is still needed then, people go into a big, darkened auditorium," said Hitchcock, "and they are mass hypnotized, and instead of identifying themselves with somebody on the screen, they *are* that person. When they buy their ticket, they choose which character they want to be. Under mass hypnotism, they go through the story and it's injected into them by some kind of telepathy and they suffer the agonies or enjoy the romance, and then, the lights go up and it's all over."

The auteur later joked that maybe this idea was his "new conception on how to dispense with actors," but he was onto something with his off-the-cuff prediction. While in Hollywood, Richard Peña heard rumors similar to the choose-your-own-adventure concept Hitchcock had pitched decades before. "It's been said in the future when you go to see *The Avengers*, they're not going to be fighting on-screen, but they'll be fighting next to you," he said. "There's going to be this immersive environment, but it will be very expensive and difficult to run. I don't think there'll be very many of them, but they would likely be in major cities."

Hitchcock had his finger on the pulse of the future of cinema, whether in his exploration of new filmmaking territory or his reflections on industry trends. Throughout the twenty-first century, his ongoing influence shaped many filmmakers who came after him, while *Rear Window*, along with others, has still consistently earned one accolade after another.

Today, *Rear Window* still tops relevant cultural polls like *Time Out* magazine's, where it was ranked at number 26 on their list of the 100 Best Thriller Films of All Time. It remains timeless because it's the kind of film that reveals something new with each viewing. What one uncovers can depend on their own life experience at the time. One might watch it again in later years and walk away with an entirely different perspective.

Its continuing prominence states that while technology, social conventions, and styles continually evolve, the experience of being alive remains a constant web of anxiety, elation, and fleeting emotions. As decades pass, the new generations of Greenwich Village may install air conditioners and close their window blinds, but the complexities of life endure.

People often find ways to temporarily blot out their lonely feelings (whether it's spying on others through a telescopic lens or getting lost in a social media rabbit hole), because making direct contact with others can be a universal challenge, and the temptation to view others without their knowledge is deliciously seductive. The backbone of *Rear Win-*

dow's narrative silently implies that in the end, regardless of the era we have lived in or have yet to live in, and whether we acknowledge it or not, we are all connected in the human experience.

In Hitchcock's endless filmography of time-tested masterpieces, *Rear Window* holds its own as one of the most beloved because it provided the auteur the opportunity to realize his dream of a pure cinematic experience while presenting truths that people didn't want to acknowledge in themselves. "The critic on *The Observer* called this a horrible film because a man was looking out a window at other people," Hitchcock told Peter Bogdanovich of *Rear Window* in 1963. "I thought that was a crappy remark. Everyone does it, it's a known fact and provided it is not made too vulgar, it is just curiosity. People don't care who you are, they can't resist looking."

Though the Hays Code would have strongly forbade showing it, one image moviegoers generally can't escape in their minds when they see *Rear Window* is the gruesome idea of Anna Thorwald's severed head, first buried in the flower bed, then dug up and concealed in a hatbox in the Thorwalds' apartment. Hitchcock understood a fundamental aspect of mankind's essence; the tendency for people to be unable to look away from a car crash. People's morbid fascination with gore, even if it was just imagined, was his bread and butter. His ability to tell stories without showing their full graphic content was a gift because it kept the audience fully engaged in the story.

The Hays Code in one sense was a dark cloud looming over Hollywood, which sometimes inhibited the realism of storytelling. But with Hitchcock's unique skill set in silent film, he learned to make friends and play with the Code. During the fifties, though they had their differences, the Code and Hitchcock were ultimately cinematic soulmates. *Rear Window* was birthed by the combination of going out on an experimental limb and the boundaries of a soon-to-be crumbling system that presented the unique dance of the power of suggestion.

When Alfred Hitchcock, Jimmy Stewart, and Grace Kelly each entered the peaks of their careers in 1953, the elements of *Rear Win-*

dow converged in a perfect blend that remains without equal, despite the fruitless attempts of those that came after. Many of today's films echo its stylistic choices and technical execution, though matching its profound influence will always be an insurmountable task. In the end, *Rear Window* cast too big of a shadow for that.

EPILOGUE

Closing the Lens

THE LAST REMAINING MINUTES ON THE SET OF *Rear Window* WERE building to a thunderous finale in January of 1954. A slice of cinematic history had just taken place on Stage 18 and everyone knew it. Any onlookers lucky enough to observe it taking place in real time would treasure the memory forever.

Alfred Hitchcock paced back and forth as he contemplated any remaining miscellaneous shots, then plunked down in his director's chair, never breaking his focus. It had been one of the most glorious, energizing experiences of his career, he thought, but all good things must come to an end in life. And as the day concluded, the fun and games, not to mention the tiresome, back-breaking labor of *Rear Window*, came to a crashing halt.

The apartment set, once a bustling hive of controlled chaos, stood in its aloneness, as the actors and crew who'd inhabited it over the months disappeared one by one forever. Back to their real lives they went, away from this cartoonish dream world. The set was a universe created to mirror reality, and it had gone above and beyond to transcend its role from a mere backdrop to a living, breathing character. The lines of fiction and reality merged in ways that took the cast and crew out of themselves and into an alternate realm of romance and murder. It was obvious on the faces of everyone who partook in it. It would be painful to leave it behind.

As the camera rolled earlier that day, Hitchcock savored the last morsel of his beloved experiment, which was finally landing with Paramount executives. They were starting to get it. These remaining nuances of voyeurism and tension would now live in a singular film reel, and for many years, discarded in boxes in a Los Angeles warehouse. It was hard to believe something as cold and clinical as a storage room could contain a thing that appeared ethereal and almost not of this world when revisited later.

Grace Kelly, draped in the silky elegance of Lisa Fremont, moved with ease through her final scenes. She was finally beginning to understand the way Hitchcock thought, as she watched him mentally prepare himself before calling action again. "Grace, let's do another take for safety." Hitchcock's words drifted across the set. She knew by now how to read her director and not to expect a gold star of praise, even on her exceptional scenes. This was as close as it would get, which was fine with her.

Grace felt satisfied with her last takes but was flooded by a sense of longing. She had grown attached to Lisa Fremont and was sad to leave her behind. As the screen would later reflect, her commitment to Lisa added layers of complexity and warmth that reached far beyond the boundaries of the script.

Jimmy Stewart navigated his last scenes with the seasoned skill that only comes with decades of experience. This shoot had been superior to the *Rope* experience on every level. Next on his schedule was *Strategic Air Command* with Anthony Mann, but he was now convinced Hitch was a genius. They'd make another picture together as soon as time permitted. Though Jimmy was a stickler for perfection during scenes, as he spoke his last lines, he felt at peace with his performance.

As filming came to its inevitable conclusion and the studio lights dimmed, Hitchcock stood momentarily, taking a mental snapshot of the silent courtyard, which would be torn down in the following weeks, as if it had never existed. The brick complex would swiftly be replaced by the set for the Robert Parish–directed picture *Lucy Gallant*. How could it be over already? The air was thick with sentimentality as everyone packed up to leave Stage 18 for good.

The weight of the journey—the challenges of finding the right leads and character actors, the breakthrough of using microphone earpieces to direct them, the headache of digging out the basement and transforming it to somehow replicate Christopher Street—it all hung in the air. With a satisfied smile, Hitchcock stepped off the set for the last time, leaving behind the parallel universe that had been *Rear Window*. Hitchcock had crafted something that transcended the boundaries of future eras to come. He wasn't aware at the time that the film's influence would remain alive on the screen for the good part of a century. But for now, all that existed was a brief, melancholy farewell.

As they left the stage, with a hopeful eye on the future, Alfred Hitchcock, Grace Kelly, Jimmy Stewart, and *Rear Window*'s ensemble and crew each moved forward with their lives. Stage 18, devoid of the bright buoyancy that fueled production, now existed with a quiet hum of anticipation for what would come next. In the decades that followed, *Rear Window*'s legacy lived on in Stage 18. During studio tours, executives and producers would ask their guests, "Did you know *Rear Window* was filmed *here*?"

In 1967, a journalist asked Hitchcock what vocation he might have practiced had he not become a filmmaker. This question momentarily showed an altogether different side of the man, alluding to his love of a good murder mystery. "I think with one's touch of hammy-ness, that degrading side of me—the actor," he said with a cryptic grin. "Perhaps it might have been amusing to be a criminal lawyer." Without a doubt, Hitchcock would have attacked every court case with the same maniacal inventiveness as all fifty-three of his pictures. The film world owes Hitchcock more than anyone can comprehend, and in our constant analysis of his work, we only find ourselves lost in new symbolic rabbit holes.

This begs the question: What if Alfred Hitchcock had taken a more "practical" approach to his life and had become a barrister? What if there had been no Hitchcockian style in existence, except for in the courtroom? What would have happened to the thriller and horror film genres we know today? To quote the words of Lisa Fremont, without Hitchcock and *Rear Window*, the outcome of the suspense genre may be "something too frightful to utter."

ACKNOWLEDGMENTS

IF HITCHCOCK TAUGHT US ANYTHING, IT'S THAT THE MOST FASCINATING stories come together piece by piece, with each new perspective adding a new layer of truth. The creation of this book was no different, and I'm indebted to those who helped assemble the pieces. I am deeply grateful to Kelly Stewart Harcourt, whose profound insights into her father Jimmy Stewart's life and career opened a unique window into this story. Similarly, my heartfelt gratitude goes out to Grace Kelly's family and friends: John Lehman, John B. Kelly III, and Nyna Giles. Special thanks also goes out to John Waxman, Ross Bagdasarian Jr., Jim Katz, Robert Harris, Joseph McBride, Sloan De Forest, Richard Peña, Chris Hewitt, Chris Knight, Michael Guinzburg, Katherine Schofield, and Laurent Bouzereau—each of you shared invaluable perspectives that brought depth and authenticity to the reimagining of *Rear Window*'s creation.

Every book needs its guiding shepherds. Mine came in the form of my brilliant agent, Joelle Delbourgo, who recognized this story's potential and helped shape its journey, and Jacqueline Flynn, who helped lay the groundwork that pushed the story to reach its fruition. To my amazing editor, John Scognamiglio, and production editor, Stephen M. Smith—just like the master of suspense, your vision and expertise have elevated these pages immeasurably.

This book wouldn't exist without my family's unwavering support: my father and uncle Tom, two Golden Hollywood film buffs who introduced me to the Hitchcockian world of *The 39 Steps*, *Rear Window*, and *Vertigo*; my mother, who recognized and nurtured my writing ability from the age of nine; my sister, her family, and my friends, whose enthusiasm never wavered; and my partner, Vlad, whose patience and support throughout this book rivaled Lisa Fremont's devotion to Jefferies and his broken leg.

This book would also not have been possible without the dedicated archivists and support of the Margaret Herrick Library and the BYU Library. Special thanks to Janie McKirgan at the Jimmy Stewart Museum and Ann-Marie Albrechtson at the Grace Kelly Foundation, whose assistance provided crucial information that enriched this story immensely.

Like Jeff's neighbors whose stories interweaved to create a greater truth, this book is a constellation mapped from countless conversations, archived facts, and shared memories. To everyone who contributed their piece to the making of *Rear Window*—thank you for helping to bring this moment in cinema history to light.

01 14